EXPOSING TERRORISM

EXPOSING TERRORISM
INDIGENOUS SPIRITUALITY
AND
RELIGIOUS EXTREMISM

ED McGAA, EAGLE MAN, J.D.
OST 15287
OGLALA SIOUX TRIBE ENROLLMENT NUMBER

Exposing Terrorism:
Indigenous Spirituality and Religious Extremism
Ed McGaa, Eagle Man, JD. OST- 15287
(Oglala Sioux Tribal Enrollment #)

Front Cover Artist
Evonne Evans

Back Cover Artist
Justin Vood Good

Editors
Lucy Wilson, Ph.D
Anthony J. Lenzo, M.A.

ISBN-13: 978-1544822549
ISBN-10: 1544822545

The Sioux, the Traditional Lakota at least, refuse to argue as to Who, What or even possibly When, as to attempted description or conception of an obviously immense Creator, Maker, Higher Power, God, Gods or Wakan Tanhka- (Great Mystery, Great Spirit.) They also refuse to argue with those who refuse to believe in any God at all - the Atheistic folk. "They have a 50/50 chance of being right; no less odds than what we religionists/spiritualists can mathematically claim. So why foolishly argue or worse attempt to ban, restrict, make miserable, maim or even kill to insist our Way is the only correct Way?" Therefore, God or Great Spirit was simply, pacifically accepted as an ultimate, indescribable, unfathomable Mystery for the pragmatic, common sense championing Sioux mindset. How far out is Space? When did Time begin? Sheer Mystery! Yes, and no record, at least, of the universal repeated wars evolving constantly as befell the 'civilized claimants' who eventually migrated to our hemisphere. Wars of such terroristic scale, convened and mobilized by cunning, convenient, dictators in league with their religious hierarchy's to control and man their military onslaughts.

Wakan Tanhka (Wah kahn Tanh kah) was therefore considered as:

All Truth

All Knowledge

A Mystery - beyond exact attempting human contemplation.

Harmony - IT so desires if one observes Nature's abundant example.

Creator's designed Flora and Fauna obviously displays a Harmonic Lifestyle! So why would foolish two legged choose to thwart this mysterious Entity that quite possibly also has a Beyond World awaiting Twolegged?

Down through time Human has fought endless wars over his adamant declarations that insist his Creator concept is the only correct concept and hence how exactly Man will become destined in a following Beyond World (A rewarding Heaven, punishing Hell.)

Fortunately, America's 'Founding Fathers' discovered true Democracy from the Iroquois and incorporated such into the Constitution and Bill of Rights. They elaborated with the protective Separation of Church and State Clause (Protective for both believers and non-believers.). The horrid Great Inquisition was fresh in their minds, therefore runaway, fanatic religions had to be held in check in order for a true Democracy to flourish. According to history, Man, however, has come forth with his many man-conceived religions and Terrorism evolved.

ACKNOWLEDGMENTS

To Boston Globe Reporters and Producers/Directors of *Spotlight* for exposing Church Pedophilia Cover-up leading to the expulsion of Cardinal Law of the Boston Diocese.

To Dr. David Nagorney, World's foremost Whipple Maneuver pancreatic surgeon – Mayo Clinic.

To Donna Carey McGaa, Holistic Science-based advisor, prayer and care provider. Both saved my life.

To Dr. Dan Petereit, my non-Veterans Administration physician and encouraging, dedicated Kola -(Ally, friend).

Cousin Casey Craven McGaa Peterson, CPA.

American Legion Baseball Coach, James 'Pev' Evans, DDS, Kola and lifetime influencer.

Dave Strain, Dakota West Publishing.

I began this book the day after the critical-at-my-age pancreatic operation (P. M. Dec. 24th). I finished in less than a year. My oath to All Providing Creator, just prior to Mayo Operation. Dr. David Nagorney's commendable, successful operative determination; I must add: His supreme loyalty to the medical profession's Hippocratic Oath and selfless, participating staff. His prognosis - A growing encapsulation demanded no delay regardless of the holiday season.

An oath is a badge of Honor. Only a fool would dare break one to Ultimate Creator. I vowed one other long ago, prior to my volunteering for combat duty as a Marine F-4 Phantom pilot in Vietnam. "Oh Great Spirit," I spoke out fearfully yet resolute in Chief Fools Crow's powerful Spirit Calling ceremony held on my home Oglala Reservation. "I will dance the Sun Dance if I can come back." My aging mother who spoke excellent Sioux was sitting beside me, translating and encouraging. Four days you are beneath the hot, Badlands August sun without food or water, giving back for what Benevolent Creator may allow you. Our Spirituality allows us to communicate with our Higher Power.

TABLE OF CONTENTS

Who knows what Is? The Teton Lakota Sioux regard a Creator, a Higher Power (Wakan Tanka) as indescribable – a Great Unknown. They consider it rather foolish to fight over what is obviously, sheer Mystery.

Ed Eagle Man McGaa

In most of the world's trouble spots, religious extremism is at the heart of the problem."

Senator John Danforth,
R-MO and an Episcopal priest.

So many of the things that are wrong in the world are actually due to religious conflicts.

Rabbi Herbert Schaalman,
an organizer of the Parliament of the World Religions

PROLOGUE

Until Man admits to what obviously is absolute Mystery, he will forever be cursed with tragic, deadly and maiming Terrorism.

Only through admitting the human mind's limits placed by Creator upon each one of us will Man be free from foolishly attempting to control all of which he surveys. Terrorism feeds on insisting that you alone know who your God is and it is the other who deserves the torture, hatred, war, and whatever else you impose on him and her, especially 'Her' after you dispose of 'Him'. Cunning dictators and now present day manipulating politicians have used this successful ruse in league with a supporting religious hierarchy also adept at manipulating the leadership, to accomplish and maintain power whether or not they believe in God, Creator or use the term- Higher Power. The desire to control overwhelms and rejects practical conceptions employed by independent humans who believe Creator's allowance of free will is to be used to seek freely and therefore project a harmonious, rationalizing attempt to probe sheer, obvious Mystery. This manner results too often in rigid conflict however, a deadly retaliation from the religious extremists. Regardless, all religious/spiritual bent sect's recognition of a Creative Power or a benevolent Maker, liberal or extreme, leads them to a hopeful higher rewarding status, an onward 'life' within a Spirit World beyond. Various claims exist however, from the extremists varying to widely exaggerated decrees and prophecies and most often, not supported by intelligible, probing scientific verification. I readily admit or at least presume that Science is simply applying diligent, focused exploration of Creator's Creation.

Contrariwise, differences aside, a life of disharmony, especially a harmful one that casts despair and suffering upon innocent others is deemed to result in a non-rewarding, negative evolvement for those who thought only of themselves. How so? You can observe those who avoid and reject Creator's True Harmony. Look at how disastrous their lives end and the absence of real contentment their trail of greed, selfishness, economic gluttony, dishonor and guilt steadily builds into abject despair. Age seems to bring on a dimmer view at the end of the tunnel, does it not for those who promoted only themselves? Every 'Dead Beat Dad' I have encountered has reaped a despondent attitude. The self-indulgence of addiction speeds up the process. Those who detoured their life seeking solace in excess alcohol or disastrous drugs leads many to overdose or end with forlorn suicide.

Sioux spiritual tradition had no Hell or Heaven per se nor Devils and Satan before the White Man came. They did adamantly hold to the concept of a life beyond and free from the daily, necessary elementary, physical needs of this present life. Missionaries utilized physical punishment, often brutal in the Boarding Schools to attempt fanatic enforcement of their negative, supernatural creations. To this day, Traditional Sioux just cannot comprehend that an all-powerful, all knowing benevolent Creator that has demonstrated daily and endlessly that it is indeed benevolent yet would allow within its realm such horrible opposite entities to control and viciously harm or torture innocent two-legged within what is under its total control. (Yes, IT, not a She or He.) To us at least, such obvious fantasy is rather insulting, actually blasphemous ungrateful projection regarding the one powerful, life giving entity that allows us to be here according to most Traditionals. We are quite liberal however. The Wahshichu (White Man, Dominant Society) adamantly insists that his Devil or Satan is real. So real, it can even fly around on its own 'magic' propulsion. A bit contrary to Creator's

scientific laws of aerodynamic Physics, can you agree? Imagine! A woman could be accused, tortured and put to death over allegedly wearing a pointed hat while riding a magically propelled broom stick around the skies! Hundreds, more so, no doubt thousands were put to death for centuries over such extreme fantasy and yes, tortured beforehand. These enforcers were the ancestors of those who came to this land. Yes, and their Devils can even seep magically through impervious walls. The European immigrant, along with some others as well, has been adamantly insistent of acceptance of his beliefs despite his sheer lack of scientific proof of numerous, obvious impossibilities. Indian Boarding School students were severely beaten for not accepting such fantasy. A common remark from Traditionals in my tribe is simply, "So let him keep his Devil, but please, do not bring it around us."

The Traditional Sioux have a belief that the Spirit World is reflected in the life that we have here in this world – our everyday living. *"We go with our own kind!"* Yes, do we not choose or at least attempt to pick and choose whom we wish to associate with? In the Spirit World our punishment or hopefully our reward will most likely not be our own choice. It seems to be more practical to consider a consensus of those whom are most like ourselves. Thieves with thieves, dead beat Dads (or Moms) will associate with each other: Honorable two legged- those who strived to cultivate/harvest a respectful harmony with like associates. Complacent, blank, unconcerned, disinterested also most likely shall have their numbed Spirit World existence. Notice how connivers, egoists, manipulators, braggarts, exaggerators, embellishers are right at home together. I highly doubt the Christian myth- "You will be bestowed with all knowledge," once one enters the beyond. That marketing fable holds no substantial support if we look at how the reasoning mind according to Creator's design must be prepared to survive, gradually learn how to exist successfully. The unprepared most often fail to survive. Creator's wild animals illustrate vividly how truthful this supposition is solid fact. Animals actually prepare, perfect and hone themselves to survive. What better example exists that teaches – 'one must prepare?' They definitely care for and prepare their young for life's survival. Honorable and observant humans do the same. Not found in the animal world, only the foolish human avoids off spring preparation. Watch a pair of Ospreys or Eagles care for their young during the long summer. An Osprey nest is fortunately within view from my writing desk. Once they are raised, retardant Enabling is never implemented or condoned. The new adults eventually are chased away from the trout lake below the summers nest. Enabling parents of Two-legged too often find their young ill-prepared. The day will come when parents pass on. The enabled offspring are unprepared for life's demands. If you have numerous relatives, most likely you have witnessed several examples.

Nature's Final Solution

Though ignored, even condemned, by superstition opiated Man, Creator's Nature steadily marches onward. She is apparently designed by the Great Mystery Maker to finish Man with an Ultimate Solution if Man unwisely challenges her (Nature) to the extreme. Climate Change, Planetary Heating, Depleted Resources, and Rising Seas along with potable Water Depletion appear to be these forces. The Four Horses of the Apocalypse could be accredited as such although never spelled out precisely within human's self-made black book which he foolishly holds as above the teachings of Nature.

The accurate researched warnings of modern science make even the most resolute deniers aware. Planetary Heating and Rising Seas research backed up by Nature's reactions becomes more difficult to deny. Direct Observation rather than tailored fantasy is irrefutable. Lack of communication allowed stultifying superstitious ignorance to flourish and control since medieval times. Conversely, modern communication world-wide now allows factual real truth to unfold. The Native American never had a Bible, Koran or related 'Black Book'. Coupled with the mind opening example of a city flattened by atomic weaponry unleashed by fanatic rogue suicide bombers, regretfully it will take such tragedy to awaken the free nations such has misleading dangerous superstition gripped human so rigidly. They will react however, no less visible than Japan's sudden, over-night realization. A startling, abrupt change-over has entirely enveloped that once warfare, Bushido coded nation. Before Hiroshima and Nagasaki, it was unthinkable in Japan that the Samurai mentality could vanish so abruptly. Centuries old Samurai-ism, however, was quickly, speedily abandoned following the second atomic bomb.

While waiting for an F-4 Phantom squadron to take on new Vietnam bound pilots, I was fortunate to be assigned by the Marine Corp's good will protocol to teach a conversational English class at Hiroshima University prior to my Vietnam combat tour. Those peaceful students were a far cry removed away from the brutal Japanese soldiers revealed within Iris Chang's book – *The Rape of Nanking*.[1] The vicious samurai mentality was intensely followed and religiously condoned by a 'Divine Emperor' less than a century ago. Shintoism in Japan, purports that only the emperor

---

[1] Iris Chang, *The Rape of Nanking. The Forgotten Holocaust of World War II* (New York: Penguin Group (USA) Inc. 1997.).

and his family are created in God's image (Divine) which, of course the Emperor Hirohito was not about to deny during the course of the war. Not until General MacArthur forced him to confess via radio broadcast nationwide was his religious backed 'Divineness' rebuked and abruptly ended. Military perpetrators of Japan's vicious, brutal terrorism are yet alive and remain unpunished- at least in this world.[2] One third of a million innocent Chinese suffered severely, most fatally in less than a month span. Will their memories calling for some form of retribution carry on into a Spirit World beyond? Needless to say- like a huge Tsunami or tidal wave even more damaging-, the later atomic retaliation for Pearl Harbor left a lasting impression upon post war Japan. Apparently, awesome destruction can and will make Man find a possible solution for change regardless of religion or cultural tradition. The magnitude of such deadly destruction spurs me to rarely make predictions, but I have to supposition that finally, such will move Man toward pragmatic and practical action to overcome 'My Way Only!' Political platitudes will be meaningless against a backdrop of an atomic flattened metropolis. [3, 4, 5, 6]

'I'm Right. You're Wrong!'

Supposition for the future; Religion's traditional support, especially for those that proselytize, will eventually lose their salvation promised audiences. Monumental disaster has that capability! The Internet is rapid-

---

[2] Ibid., p. 54. Shintoism. "Other experts blame the non-Christian nature of Japanese religion, claiming that while Christianity puts forth the idea that all humans are brothers- indeed, that all things were created in God's image- Shintoism in Japan purports that only the emperor and his descendants were created in God's image." [The 'experts' conveniently over look Nazi Germany, a devoutly Christian country. Author.]

[3] Ibid. p. 56. Japan Advertiser, headline – [Two Japanese soldiers,] Sub –Lieutenants in race to fell 100 Chinese in close race by individual sword-Mukai Toshiaki, 89 [victims] - Noda Takeshi, 78 [victims]. December 7, [1937] issue.

[4] Ibid. p. 170. Both officers were ordered to death by the subsequent wartime's atrocities trials (Nanking War Crimes Trial which lasted until February, 1947.).

[5] Ibid. p. 171. Lt. General Tani Hisao, commander of a Japanese Division in Nanking responsible for a significant number of the Nanking atrocities, was sentenced to death by firing squad. The indictment had been long, listing hundreds of stabbings, burnings, drownings, strangulations, rapes, thefts and destruction committed by Tani's division. His forces helped perpetuate a slaughter that claimed an estimated three hundred thousand lives in Nanking.

[6] Ibid. p. 217. Estimate of Chinese killed by Japanese, 19 million killed, all but 400,000 were civilians if deaths caused by looting, starvation and medical experimentation (germ warfare) is considered.

ly removing the Teflon from foolish mythical based superstition which has too long been held out as fact. While the Internet grooms human's intellect, accurate, Nature based Science is finally allowed to reap its long overdue respect wherein organized religion historically punished and murdered scientists for simple research and experiment thus setting technology back for at least half a millennia. That lost technology would be extremely valuable for this potential disaster looming planetary heating dilemma evolving, would it not?

In Australia and the U K, churches are crumbling. Even Spain and Western Europe, churches, monasteries and convents are closed, weedy and boarded. Simply go there and see for yourself and please do not condemn me for truthfully telling you so, based on my own Direct Observation. Eventually, whether the reading audience accepts or not, sooner or later, proselytization will have to be banned, such is its endangerment of innocent millions. Notice I state that proselytization needs to be banned and not particular religions. Such works quite well in China. One can attend a church of choice but proselytization is wisely banned. Not much religious fomented Terrorism exists there does it? If insistent humans can become religiously opiated to the degree that they will strap on a religious based suicide bomb, far more lethal destruction will eagerly be hosted by future fanatics. How foolish is modern Man to deny such a possibility given what blatant evidence and open threats are constantly issued by organized religious based fanatics and now, carried out. ISIS will torture and kill for conversion. In America, the attempt to control is more subtle. What a pity for future victims while the cowardly choose to wait until extreme disaster before taking responsible and effective action. The agony of severed limbs and suffering death will be upon them for waiting so long to react appropriately. Ask the opinion of the Boston Marathon victims or the Orlando Gay night club massacre. Observe France - the repeated terrorism mayhem there.

I do not condone banning religions as the Christian missionaries employed upon us Sioux. Yes, they were so overly zealous to infringe their way over our innocent and quite successful nature based beliefs. Considering the resultant high suicide ratio among our reservation youth of today, this unconstitutional, illegal religious allowance by our government has ended in disaster and will be elaborated upon in latter text. The victims of their extremist boarding schools, the grandparents, parents, aunts and uncles of today's Indian youth were woefully, ill prepared academically. Instead an extreme diet of proselytization was the major non-academic fodder in those home away from home institutions. Today, thanks to the advancement of Dr. Martin Luther King's Civil Rights, our Sioux tribal solution is to return to what was successful. Therefore, I feel justified to take a stance. Proselytizing and Mockery of God's Nature; what proves to be utter Mystery should be circumvented if such procedure leads toward a safer world. Christianity certainly and rightfully takes grave offense at Jihadism, why can't we Sioux voice our historical based concerns? A Religion that advocates sincere, harmony promoting morals and ethics and can openly mindedly allow others their non-destructive beliefs I can condone. Our 'Religion' is actually Spiritualty as it is mostly Earth based. Creator made the Earth, our view, therefor we can state that we are Creator based since Ultimate Maker created all that Nature displays to us. <u>Creator actually reveals such to us daily if we simply observe and learn from Nature.</u>

The unfortunate fading of those mellow, open minded Christian sects I knew as a child is disappointing. The Presbyterians, Methodists, Congregationalists, Episcopalism, some Lutherans - even Catholicism's pre-Pope John Paul II efforts to dialogue, along with Protestantism and the Catholic Universities respect for much of Darwinian-ism taught to me as a pre-Med student, I commend. I wish well to those elements of non-overly zealous Christianity that managed to hold on to reason and plain common sense. I also wish somehow they could return to those older membership percentage levels. I cannot say the same for the extremist Evangelicals who cannot accept sheer, obvious Mystery regarding the Ultimate Maker. Rather, they flock to and support the million dollar Noah's Ark façade in Kentucky complete with dinosaur models as cargo. Need I mention the likes of Joel Osteen and related millionaire, tax free, disregard-for-the-homeless, amphitheater pulpit, 'God's work' charlatans? With this new Pope Francis, I have renewed hope and am quite pleased with. I so state in the Pope Francis chapter of this work.

Jesus?

What are my views on Jesus? Like many citizens in this land, I believe he was moral and ethical, who preached what Creator hopefully wants from mankind- Harmony; and demonstrates in all that it creates to we Traditional bent Indians at least. Such is so indicated in Creator's creation- Nature. This concept I back up by considering the writings of those that knew him. They all paint the concept of a brave, considerate teacher who displayed as well the kinder, gentler aspects of character yet did not back down from corruption or the various degrees of Un-Truth that man consistently manages to promote. Furthermore, a positive, promoting conspiracy among the descriptive biblical writers would be impossible compared to the electronic salesmanship employed today. Mainly, he brought 'Love'; a kinder, gentler God concept compared to the wrathful, punishing God of the past. Jesus was highly exemplary as a role model but if I choose to believe much like the Jewish faith holds, one God, one Creator only, I should have that right. The Indigenous concept of Creator is recognized as benevolent, all providing and naturally obvious through its creation. However, this Ultimate Great Mystery has its stern side. Is not the long winter clear proof? The Earth must need its rest under a blanket of white to prepare for the bounty of Spring. That 1st Commandment given on Mt. Sinai is not one I would dare to break especially since it is Creator's first and foremost. Many of the Founding Fathers may have had a similar view. One may wonder how and why most Indigenous, at least from the North Eastern tribes could so readily adapt to those particular teachings from the Wahshichu (White Man or Dominant Society). As mentioned, the Jewish people hold to One Creator and only One. Secondly, the Ten or whatever few or many Higher Power commandments believed to be issued simply make understandable sense. The basic, Natural Laws of Creator's Creation which the Animal Kingdom unquestionably follow, are certainly emblematic. Thus, they firmly cement what we spiritually moved Indigenous term as convincing - Direct Observation. Observing and backed up by a fathoming, reasoning mind brings us closer to Harmonic Truth. Human too often lies and exaggerates or embellishes for his own profit or gain. Every Indian treaty agreed upon under the proclamation- "In God We Trust"- has been broken by religious Jesus following Christian based Wahshichu. "The U. S. Government had broken many treaties, with the Indians, one would say they had broken all of them – the writer Alex Shoumatoff recently reckoned the total at 378."[7]

The Dramatic Extreme

Imagine the possible extreme. A flattened city will be a powerful catalyst to educate human to swiftly, employ effective prevention. What would be unthinkable under former historic circumstances can no longer

---

[7] Larry McMurtry, *Crazy Horse*, (New York: Viking, 1999), p. 77.

remain fashion. Reigning terrorists are in command of vast finances to recruit and threaten world-wide. Hate is a powerful ingredient to promote recruitment to carry out their threats. Future terrorists will become more capable. They will no longer be limited to small arms since recently rogue nations have come into atomic possession. When atomic attempts fomented by dangerous religions come into play my warning words will not seem as dramatically extreme. Disaster is an effective teacher.

Hiroshima and Nagasaki are exemplary facts of history. Proof exists that Man can and will bring forth needed change regardless of how barbaric a past they were able to swiftly discard and permanently move away from. Yes, Survival is a potent teacher; hence the survival instinct will create a safer world.

If my common sense, oft repeated, science respecting statements anger you please do not place blame on me. I am simply basing such on what the Sioux term as Direct Observation. I am not telling you what you want to hear. Contrary wise I am telling you what you need to hear! Historically we Indigenous (Northeastern tribes of this continent) relied spiritually on what Creator displayed to us daily and not upon mere human's written and most often errant word. Nature is not errant nor does it allow or harbor Superstition. Creator does not issue soothing, foolishly fantasized advice through its all-truthful Nature. Such observation we based our fruitful lifestyle upon. It provided eons of harmonic living within our portion of the planet before being invaded by the European whose lifestyle was based on non-Nature based greed and acquisition. Therefore he had to leave his portion of the planet and subjugate initially friendly indigenous.

Prophecy within many tribes has been orally passed down predicting that the Nature based Spirituality of the North American indigenous would be reduced to a mere glowing ember. The spark of life would not be extinguished however as what befell the Nature based Spirituality of the European Celtics who had encompassed western Europe for centuries.[8] The prophecy also held: It would come back! The Wahshichu would become so desperate to survive. He would not, could not thwart it as his hierarchal religion did to the ancient Celts.

A Sioux oral tradition prophecy: A powerful force, the Wahshichu

[8] William Willoya, Vinson Brown, *Warriors of the Rainbow,* (Healdsburg, CA, Naturegraph Press, 1962).

(White Man) would come to our land in huge canoes and subjugate the inhabitants. My tribe would have to abandon lush living near the great sea and flee toward where the sun sets. We would fight the Wahshichu and deal him severe blows but eventually the herds upon the Great Plains we depended upon for our existence would disappear. We would face difficult times but somehow we would manage to keep our grasp upon our old Way. Eventually while we struggled the Wahshichu would have his trials and would not respect the Great Mystery's creation – Nature. He would begin to destroy himself from within. He would have to learn to think like the Indian if he were to survive.

Is it possible for modern man to overcome what is approaching, this environmental dilemma that is now upon us? What of Terrorism that is upon us? Brutal atrocities are happening exponentially. What foments a terrorist to step outside the war field, the combat theater and prowl hidden to mutilate, maim and kill innocent beings? It is superstition that catalyzes such acts. Is it Creator's desire for all humans to seek Harmony among each other? How did the American Indian avoid dictatorial spawned Terrorism? At least most tribes in the Northern Hemisphere rejected such unnatural affliction. The North Eastern tribes, whom I believe are the most exemplary, if their gift of dictator rejecting Democracy to world society is considered.

The Red Man totally believed that this life was a preparation for that world beyond which had an eternal life span. He actually had a fear of losing a progressing, divine position in that world Beyond (If there is one.) Regardless, he was convinced there was one. It was about the only concept which he was 'dead sure' of. Everything else he held as a Mystery. Thus, he conducted his life 'Here' in a Harmonic manner for he observed such 'Harmony' in everything made by his/her concept of a Creator. I have to agree with them! My Sioux afflicted Mind also deduces that Harmony is the key ingredient making up this Great Mystery. It is what I observe. I see it, feel it all around me. It keeps me from placing the utterances of mere man before Creator's creations as my main, major guide regarding my Spirituality and not Religion.

The avoidance of superstition is the key element that separates the North American Indian from the Wahshichu. To understand this concept, holding or supposition, if you will- read on. Do we not find many a deceased acquaintance in our dream projections that appears quite alive and active? This is but another mysterious yet supportive clue. Along with powerful ceremony, our culture proves enough for me to supposition a spirit life for all of us beyond. Even our dreams seem to offer a semblance of indicative 'Direct Observation'.

Note: Full articles by noted Expose writers are left intact. Their supportive and lengthy notes, for the avoidance of environmental preventive paper waste, may be found in their original monthly and quarterly articles under provided parent magazine dates. Thus; such are listed. Dr. Bryde's Sioux and Cheyenne Notes taken orally as was our cultural custom are under my possession due to his death and supply the bulk of my Sioux cultural and historical concepts. Sioux Spirituality is mostly gathered from my own participation through mainly six annual Sun Dances and hence onward to intricate association learned from oral tradition while participating with Sioux spiritual leaders. Due to my present medical condition I may not have time to finish this work in greater but less essential detail and simply am endeavoring to post the main content of a definite needed expose: Religion's/Spiritualty's profound effect upon Two-legged's (Human's) Governmental, Social, Defense, Historical and Future aspects for the entire planet.[9]

---

[9] John Bryde, *Modern Indians,* (Vermillion, SD: University of South Dakota Press, 1971).

FOREWORD

Ego and Superstition!

Some century from now, Two-legged (Human) will hopefully discover that the two ingredients, Ego and Superstition, offers a dangerous mix, if Creator is All Truth.

Creator, if such entity exists, displays zero Superstition in Its Creation, does it not? Nature bears no Superstition. You cannot find it. Yet, Man's ego is loaded with it. His writings and errant prophecy are tragic proof. Our God's gifted Memory allowed to us and Human's imagination is too often combined despite the myriad of avenues of real truth modern science's exploration offers through direct observation. Human has to be extremely ignorant to avoid confessing that such also results in a bad mix. He ignores to such a degree in these days of multiple weapons that he can maim and kill thousands of innocents upon city streets and not the battle field through his manipulation of such ignorance and in fact is just beginning to do so. He perpetually lies to himself to misdirect Real Truth, yet, he will never find the adequate solution unless he can sincerely understand the meaning of real Truth.

There once was a northeastern people of our continent who had discovered the supreme 'Real Truth' so deeply that they faithfully depended on its required provision, or attainment into a man's soul, for one to rise on respectfully into a Higher Life beyond in an awaiting Spirit World. They were adamantly too fearful of losing their soul or at least of being omitted from the higher rewards- a less burdened life in the afterlife, if they neglected common ethics and morals. Admittedly, that 'conceive-ance' was imagination for the conceiver and hence qualified for superstition; for it had not happened yet and was unobservable as most superstitions are. It was a course, however, that was convincingly so fruitful that terrorism could gain no foothold and hence a safer world came forth for eons. Brutal dictators could not coerce them into enslaving themselves to utter, sheer make believe. Who among you are willing to deny these innocent inhabitants their truthful Track Record? Convincing, undeniable cordial evidence began immediately with the early Roanoke settlement. Throughout the Caribbean islands and Hawaiian as well, the sea going new comers were met with friendly, welcoming greetings. No superstition spewing dictators ruled the Iroquois before the Pilgrims landed nor our Sioux leaders after we migrated inland to avoid the deadly diseases the

Wahshichu had brought upon us.

The earliest of European immigrants knew nothing about Democracy. A coastal tribe kept them alive through their first winter and taught them how to successfully fertilize and plant the meager sandy soil the following Spring. The Indians had long held annual Thanksgivings to a Higher Power come harvest time. The Pilgrims did not invent such spiritual appreciation but soon learned what it was all about. Earlier, the first Virginia settlement, Roanoke, became a failure but not because of the initially cooperative native inhabitants. European over demanding superiority and typical injustice toward darker skinned people doomed the settlement's attempt, is my guess.

Democracy's Freedoms.

This discovery (Democracy) originally revealed from an encompassing, all surrounding Nature, thence honed by political nations of five tribes, was copied through the foresight of Jefferson, Thomas Paine and Ben Franklin. To put it simply: Spiritual leaning Man believed that directly observing to learn from Creator's pure Nature instead of man's superstition fostering imagination, promoted for the migrating Europeans a new and supreme outlook of social governance. Avoiding the ISM's of superstition tainted Man, Nature guided Man illustrated before these emissaries how to prevent the accumulation of decay, erosion, corrosion of life's victim breeding follies accumulated from a scheming path strewn with denial and lack of Introspection. All things Organic eventually decay and change away from their original mold unless constantly cleansed by the purity of God's so-designed Nature. Thus, just another sign of Nature's guidance. This is observable but all men, most of them- Spiritual or Religious- do have at least a commonality that clings to a strong suspicion or wonderment of a higher or lower life which awaits beyond. The Nature surrounded Man honed this 'After Life concept/belief' to a higher respecting level (and safer), however, if we honestly consider the actual track record of America's former inhabitants, at least the North Eastern tribes, especially the Democracy gifting Iroquois of whom the Sioux were highly influenced by. A high degree of harmonic promoting discipline was considered to be required to attain the Beyond's reward. This concept, a spiritual respect for a rewarding or non-rewarding afterlife, is what can put the human race back together again. Even our present environmental dilemma need not become a hopeless cause. Oh! Eventually such will happen. Human will have no choice.

How could a huge area of another continent employ what was discovered and move forward through evolutionary progress toward wisdom and harmony that the animal world has always held in common? Yes, they moved onward flourishing in such a natural, abundant flow for eons? Simple! The North American Indian followed the Laws of Nature-God's ordained designs for each and all the species. Under ancient Iroquois leaders- Deganawida and Degahawitha and no doubt others- these leaders employed Creator's patterns into their own governing bodies for all the tribal members, justly and equally. At that time, obviously there existed no Superstition to mislead them. I once knew a man who told his surgeon when asked about anxiety or stress. "No, Doc. I don't have any. To tell you the truth. I don't know what the hell it is and don't want to know!" Maybe the World War II veterans are an example. They did not know about or were able to comprehend what PTSD (Post Traumatic Stress Disorder) was. Yes, some were shocked into mental dis-order due to war experience but possibly to a much lesser degree than modern war vets. This of course is but a supposition that I hold.

Pilgrims and Democracy

When the Pilgrims first landed, they discovered a people living a distinct and different way of life. Since these newcomers were involved with a life or death situation, it behooved them to become friends with these people who would later be called Indians. The first observable act from the Indians' point of view was to watch these light-skinned Pilgrims steal one of their caches of corn. The Indians could have thought of these newcomers as thieves but being used to natural observation, they did not react to these takers as thieves. Remember, these east coast Indians did not have a value system that held a high regard for possession or marked geographic boundaries denoting ownership of the land. It is possible that they thought that these Pilgrims were simply hungry or might be starving. The Pilgrims, on the other hand, had their point of view. They wrote down that the "Lord had provided for them." Different people have different reactions, different points of view, obviously. This historical comparison helps us to broaden our understanding. Viewpoint, judgment or value evaluation can have various interpretations. There is a line of resistance however. Cruel, murderous Terrorism is meant to be controlled.

The value system of different societies can come up with completely differing points of view. In this example, one could accuse the other of thievery, and throughout history, people went to war over such matters.

Can you imagine Indians landing in England or up the Rhine River in Germany in those times? What would have been the reaction of the local populace viewing Indians appropriating a silo of oats or rye for food? In these two situations, one actual and one imagined, which value system would arrive at a closer verdict of the truth? "Those people must have been pretty hungry," might have been a fairly honest observation and maybe more accurate than, "those damned thieves are taking our grain." No war was the result. Harmonic friendship took place instead, albeit short lived.

The first Pilgrims remembered Indians saving their lives but when new settlers came to the eastern shores, they were taught how to survive by their own kind. The later arrivals might have heard stories about the friendship of the heathens who were camped close by, but when it came to expansion into new lands, appreciation of past deeds of honor were forgotten. The Pilgrim's European value system was too overpowering to learn differently, because in a short time they marked boundaries of ownership and began to annihilate these new found friends who initially saved European lives. Conceptualized, tailored Religion was used to ease their conscience. After all, these Heathens were not "chosen by God" to remain upon these lands. Actually, the early settlers employed a gruesome reign of 'Terror' but this accusation will never become admitted. The Spirit World, however, may hold contrariwise.

Early indigenous society did not place a high value on materialistic acquisition, therefore, the foregoing historical event of true humanitarianism was made possible. Such a tragedy for humanity that early immigrants were not intelligent enough to recognize such charity. They were too steeped in their belief system that rigidly taught, "Our way is the only way." In light of this example, it is important to note that western material values should be modified or lightened if one is considering the Natural Way as a spiritual path. If we are to consider the meaning of government then it must be recognized that values will determine our judgment as to what is government. We have learned how early native values allowed them a more humanistic perception and conduct towards others. How did Indigenous Spirituality affect their concept of government? Incidentally, Democracy came from Original Pre- America and not Greeks or Romans!

Let us look at some more history. In time, the colonists came to this land in a steady procession. Soon they were at odds with the British government, mainly the King's attempts to control their lives. When the Iroquois were still formidable as a military power, they were wooed by emissaries of both sides in the fight for early America between the British and the colonists. Fortunately for the entire world, perceptive men, the likes of Benjamin Franklin, Thomas Jefferson and Thomas Paine, became familiar with the early eastern coast tribes. Interestingly, these men were not bound up in zealous or eccentric religious beliefs. Maybe this characteristic of independence allowed them to be more observant than the average colonist of the times. As emissaries to the Iroquois Nation, Franklin and Paine were astounded to see Iroquoian Indians individually stand up in public assembly within their tribes. They saw that tribal members could speak freely to influence the social decision process. They also recognized that the native people had elected representatives and their equivalence of a king, their chiefs, were elected and not born into a position of governing power. Divine right to govern according to heredity had no place among nature-influenced people. No tribal member was considered lower or higher, nor were there levels of social or acquisition status. A landed gentry did not exist because the Indians considered the air and the waters as unowned, and the earth was equally immune to ownership. No priesthood existed, nor was there a nobility. Medicine or spiritual seers were not in league with any favored group and were readily accessible by all tribal members. If times of hunger befell a tribe, the medicine representatives received no extra favors to avoid the hunger or inadequate shelter from the elements any different than the rest of the tribal populace. When spring time arrived and new buffalo hides were procured to shore up tattered winter dwellings, it was the old and most poor, those that had no one related to provide for them that received the first available hides along with fresh meat of early Spring by generous unrelated hunters.

Many other examples of democracy were also observed and well noted, except for suffrage. Iroquoian women voted and even had the additional power to recall leaders, but this finding, along with substantial evidence supporting matriarchy was omitted from the Bill of Rights and Constitution which would be drawn up later. The majority of these new observations, however, became the pattern for equality and justice within a free government which was about to evolve. Thomas Paine was so moved by his new knowledge that he lived among the Iroquois to learn the language and then went back to France to instill this new democracy into the French revolution.

Iroquoian Democracy and Siouan Democracy however, utilized Earth Based Spirituality and not a hierarchal Organized Religion. There was no political connection between the two, either. On the other hand, in Europe down through the ages, the Organized Church was always on the side of the leadership, those who governed - usually those who owned the most land or merchandising. In Islam the Mullahs dictate considerably. Saudi Arabia and Iran are examples. The richest man in Iran is the Ayatollah. Even ISIS is ruled by a religious Supreme Council.

Regarding Knowledge. The Iroquois relied upon Creator's portrayal of Nature, Its creation and employed it as the basis of their spiritual knowledge. Democracy became their greatest gift from Man to Mankind when the early colonists later adopted it and it spread worldwide. Truth and Knowledge. It is what Creator is according to Traditional Indigenous. Yes, It is what IT is! This, at least, is the belief of spiritual leaning indigenous. Will man ever advance someday, how long if ever, so far that Superstition will eventually become abolished? How many tragic, horrible lessons will he stubbornly endure before he achieves finally through his own gathered, painful knowledge of repeated failure? Or will his failure result in a doomed planet governed by rat hole dwelling warlords supported by religious fanatics as is beginning to happen? Yes, living like ISIS lives now, ignorantly believing that He alone knows what rules the Higher Power has designed for Human to live by and of course how he alone interprets.

It is not difficult for me to believe, at least hope that Ultimate Maker/Designer is All Truth. Simply look/observe what It makes, designs or allows. Why do I conceive that It also is All Knowledge?

Right now there are unnamed, undiscovered electronic energy waves along with the ones we are utilizing and named. Whatever? They are no doubt mysteriously generated from our Sun and certainly not emanating from the Moon is my mere guess.

Let us recall the radio waves, television waves that somehow can emanate/carry/produce/govern sound and pictures across the planet worldwide. Did they not exist before a single vacuum tube was made to accommodate such modern communication? We also have the laser beams, gamma and Wi-Fi to name but a few. What about the mysterious yet unknown, coursing around us now? These we yet know nothing about but I supposition that they are there and will bear fruitful communication eventually for human to discover unless terrorism can become so powerful as in Medieval Ages that scientific research and progress will again be banned. Who has allowed such powerful mystery to be placed here for us to communicate far more efficiently? Whatever! It has to be of extreme knowledge and most importantly, IT evidently wants us to communicate more fruitfully and most obviously is providing us with the tools to do so. Knowledge! It wants us to grasp more Knowledge. My mere opinion. Why? Maybe it wants us to put an end to horrible, tragic, ignorant Terrorism we have errantly, foolishly allowed to flourish over us.

If there is a Creator, it obviously is a Wakan Tanka, a Great Mystery. Wahshichu's overpowering ego will not allow him to admit another's terminology, however. Therefore, God or Creator. Deep down in, however, there seems to be some force, hopefully in many who still clamor for unrestricted true justice. Some Higher Power designed all Physiology; within the Neurology of man; although Man has been gifted with supreme reason, compared to the Wamaskaskan (Animal Kingdom), Creator has obviously placed a limitation regarding the exact fathoming of Ultimate, Benevolent Creator. Who IT exactly is-- we damn well do not know for sure, do we? Hence Foolish Man goes on and creates, tailors his own concepts and most usually for pleasurable, advancing control to the extreme of annihilating others not in league with his self-pleasing fantasy. These he deems as Heretics. Eventually we have Terrorism!

The North American Indians have heard the word 'civilization' all their lives. We in turn now tell it back to the Wahshichu. "Wahshichu! Quit lying and bragging to us that you have brought us to your two favorite words- 'Civilization and Conversion.' You cannot have real civilization unless you eradicate terrorism. Our civilization did not have it! What does that tell you? Who was the most civilized? And as far as your conversion goes, how can you 'convert' when you do not know any more about who Creator is than I do?"

If you want to be truly civilized someday in the future, you must learn these three precepts – All Truth, All Knowledge and acceptance of Mystery. I should also add- Harmony. One should attempt to lead one's life in a harmonic manner with their fellow beings but the rest of the Flora and Fauna as well. Does not Creator, vividly exhibit to us daily in all that it has created? Will this be the guide that will be utilized in the Beyond World, if there is one? Such is not diluted or altered either despite whatever man attained position you think you have arrived at. I hold the Pope, the highest Ayatollah or Buddhist monk as no more knowledgeable about Creator than I am and will die with that belief, such is Creator's Mystery! Learn thoroughly Dear Reader and put observed wisdom along with truthful admittance in your daily practice if you seek to become successful toward a planetary goal which can abolish foolish, destructive terrorism. If you fail to do so – Terrorism will abolish you! Take your place in the long line crossing Europe at the present. Can Man shed his religious Ego in order to do so? Can he become intelligent enough to change? Atomic weapons dictate that he must change. Yes! Atomic weapons exist throughout the planet and are quite capable of being infiltrated to the have-not nations. The worldwide proliferation of lesser weapons adds to the dilemma.

I believe Nature, Creator's creation, has a built in, decisive teaching methodology. She is Mother Earth and has tremendous discipline well demonstrated by the disaster she unleashes periodically upon all habitat. Human is beginning to pay increasingly for breaking her many unalterable rules. Climate Change is an obvious result. Nature is highly patient, however but steadily she is curtailing Human's environmental folly through her own means coupled now with human's non-admittance of dangerous, exponential Over-Population.

In 2015, Organized Religion's most notable leader, Pope Francis toured the United States touting the perils of Climate Change but mentioned nary a word regarding Climate Change's major culprit of causation – Over Population. I admire this pope compared to others, but he needs to be admonished for playing Church Politics with a highly dangerous subject. There is no Hollywood or related Biblical scenario to reverse Nature's wrath which is beginning due to unnatural over population.

The disastrous formula is quite simple. Man's egotistical denial of the powers of Creator which It exhibits through Its Nature has now steadily built up to mass toxins and polluting blockage in our atmosphere. The Earth heats. The human race, so habitually dependent upon religious answers to escape from impending dilemma, become fodder to follow militant soothsayers who prove not to have any appropriate answers. Militant leaders spring up throughout the planet and the people follow. Wars, terrorism begin anew.

CHAPTER 1
SUPERSTITION IS NOT ALLOWED

A tyrant must put on the appearance of uncommon devotion to religion. Subjects are less apprehensive of illegal treatment from a ruler whom they consider god-fearing and pious. On the other hand, they do less easily move against him, believing that he has the gods on his side. — *Aristotle*

If this is not an important book for this day and age of abundant automatic firearms, homemade bombs and worse....atomic weapons, I don't know what is.

Dominant Society Religionists want to tailor their God, which is why they listen to themselves only or others just like them. They immediately go on the defensive if they are criticized. Introspection or the mere mention of their often horrid inhumane Track Record puts them on their immediate offensive. "Don't you believe in God?" is their too often refrain. Introspection is unknown among them.

The original Indigenous living within a concrete-less, minimal polluting environment knew he could not alter Creator's Nature, that entity which remained stable for eons, and which he figured he must learn from in order to live. Therefore he was not hindered from all-true knowledge, preferring to learn from Creator's Creation –Nature and was quite satisfied for eons. Can Man's pronouncements be more accurate, more knowledgeable than Creator's displayed works? Is this what you believe, what you maintain? This is the major dichotomy between the Wahshichu (White Man) and the North American Indian. It takes quite a bit of Ego to choose mere mortal prophets long deceased from a world of little scientific knowledge as your spiritual/religious guides than what Creator can show you directly.

Who, what designed, made, and began this Universe which we live in? Allowing, of course, that a Creative Force exists. Most deem it as a Higher Power, God or Creator and on to a host of many terms. Some two-legged, a minority few termed Atheists, differ from dominant thought and declare that Creator/God does not exist. Compared to the extremists, however, of Organized Religion, they appear to be quite harmless toward society at large other than making an occasional non-terroristic splash upon a newspaper page.

I doubt if many harbor an arsenal of riot weapons in gun cabinets. I have a few fire arms. I hunt with mine, pheasants mostly and not man as a fantasized target. I had enough of 'man targets' in Vietnam. Do they-Atheists, Agnostics have such? (Steel assault rifle/gun cabinets/safes?) If I were to choose a neighbor I would prefer the Atheist rather than the puritanical, 'second coming,' gun fanatic. The Atheist is probably the least likely to commit terroristic carnage. What does that imply regarding religious fanaticism? The Spiritualist is probably a close second. The Religious? Simply observe their historical Track Record down through recorded history. Which would be the first to oppose my conducting a sweat lodge, beseeching to my concept of Creator, some moon lit night? In America an atheist has a constitutional right to believe or not to believe. In some countries one can reap a death sentence or be severely ostracized for not believing in line with the country's dominant religion. Odd, how criminal statistics on Atheists should prove rather scant in comparison to the fanatics regarding taking up arms over religious denial vs religious dogma. I have yet to hear of Atheists calling out threats of Jihadist acts for not believing in their non-beliefs. None have ever attempted to convert me whereas the fanatic religious are the extreme opposite. "Don't you believe in God?" is their ignorant refrain when they attempt to do so and I rebuff them. "Why are you so angry?" they often add.

Am I an Atheist? Absolutely not but I respect our nation's Separation of Church and State clause for allowing them their freedom from persecution and the right to believe or not believe in a Higher Power or Maker. Native Americans have suffered severely from those extremists (and not atheists) that damaged us beginning with their self-serving, non-fulfilling education attempt mixed with extreme child abuse and of course, a heavy content of religion replacing needed academics. That clause makes our country considerably safer to live in versus those that have no related clause. Much safer from Terrorists are the citizens of China which harbors fewer religious sects, cults, churches and or organizations. Besides Japan, I would guess that China is the least affected by the terror agenda taking place worldwide among the larger countries.

Besides seeking economic freedom, religious persecution from the Dominant sects was the other major reason 17th and 18th century immigrants fled to this country. Little has changed for some other countries worldwide however. In this modern era, Sunnis and Shiites have been constantly at each other's throats for centuries along with a host of lesser known religious sects fighting their adversaries. I am at a loss to name a single indigenous tribe espousing some invented jihadist version of their

Spirituality in conflict with another over spiritual/religious belief.

What is Spirituality in contrast to Organized Religion?

Spirituality, in contrast to Organized Religion begins with Nature, it is Earth based. This pronouncement will be often repeated. Presuming God/Creator made Nature, it (Nature) reveals how Creator would like for us to conduct ourselves providing we take the time to observe and contemplate what we are viewing. Scientist do it all the time. Compared to Man, Nature is far more harmonic regarding consideration for the other species and/or for the wellbeing of the planet. What other source could possibly be more fruitful for one's life quest? Spiritual Man does not speculate as to the exactness of who, or what, Creator is. Spiritual Man, however, makes a constant study as to what this Creator, Maker, and Higher Power displays to us free thinking, rationalizing humans. We observe Nature and learn our morals, ethics and values from what Nature reveals to us. Every day, for us at least, Nature will provide for us new, refreshing teachings if we utilize our abilities, sight, sound, communication to look for such.

Why were Spirituality guided Indians absent Dictators and hence far less Terrorism?

Many times I will state, 'Spirituality has no Superstition'. The old time Native Traditionalist was convinced that True Harmony was the reason why we were all placed here or allowed to be here. Simply look at our Creator's Universe outside of human, of course. Everything is in Harmony. Therefore, would IT expect or want us to live our lives accordingly? It is a mystery to me, but yet Benevolent Creator allowed us free choice. If we choose to live a non-harmonic life, obviously we are able to do so, we have that freedom.

Every suicide bomber, every torturer paid for by the CIA or otherwise, every demented truck driver knocking down people like ten pins as happened in France, every Boston style bomber who was bent on sheer superstition based on false causes related to superstition- 72 virgins waiting in an after world or some form of imagined God's blessing and reward for their non-harmonic deadly acts: such are the ingredients of modern day Terrorism. None of these miscreants interpret that their disharmony toward mankind will spell out a negative reaction to their acts in the waiting Spirit World beyond. They obviously refuse to comprehend the reaction of their innocent victims such has fanatic zealotry overcome their reasoning.

Dominant Religion ignores Nature. Rarely, if ever is it trusted for spiritual guidance if one prefers the two books utilized by the leading Organized Religions of the Planet- Islam and Christianity. Such power has the written words of man, much of it extremely erroneous and dangerous if we explore today. Rather blasphemous, would one not think, if merit is not allowed for Creator's intent that mere man should learn directly rather than indirectly? These religious guides, the Koran and the Bible, hold a host of prophets, all males of course back when they were seriously lacking regarding the eye opening communicative and exploratory scientific tools we have today. Those prophets (religious policy makers) thought the world was flat and evolution came from a lone man named Adam. His wife came from his rib once God decided he needed a mate. They lived luxuriously in a fruitful place called the Garden of Eden. Everything - their life style was quite 'Kosher' at first until Eve, Adam's wife was lured by a talking snake to eat a certain forbidden fruit which she was tempted to do. Man was evicted from such luxury and had to go out to face and endure the cruel elements of the planet. Dinosaurs who once roamed freely only 6, 000 years ago, now were suddenly extinct. Somehow, Noah's Ark, complete with all the animals of the then known world were crammed into a man-made ark which eventually floated around for a while until the 'Great Flood' waters subsided (40 days of rain). As mentioned, dinosaur replicas are now depicted aboard the several million dollar, Kentucky tourist ark. Before the carnivore meat eaters aboard decided they had fasted long enough the boat grounded ashore. In the southern states of America you can be shunned/chastised by your neighbors if you believe otherwise. Large Interstate billboards along the Florida bound Interstate ridicule unbelievers and Darwinian Theory.

Christian services, mostly weekly, ignore Creator in their beseeching services. They prefer to use the term 'Worship Services.' Simply attend a few. I must confess I know little about what goes on inside of a mosque in comparison to the other services. How often if ever do they beseech to what I consider as the Nature based Creator or extol outright examples of Its Nature teachings? Maybe Islam attempts to do so but I do not observe such when I attend Christian services occasionally. Every beseechment/worship event is all J.C., (Jesus Christ). Creator, the one that communicated to Moses and issued the Ten Commandments, at least based on my observations, is sorely left out. Again, as I said regarding the falling churches in former bastions of Christendom, take a look for yourself and do not blame me, the bearer of what you do not want to observe, learn or worse (for engrained fanaticism), come to realize!

Thankfully in America, there are still checks and balances primarily to curtail the overly zealous attempts of Dominant Religions to severely impose their beliefs on society at large. The founding fathers were quite aware of the brutal, murderous religious zealotry imposed via the Great Inquisition for centuries in Europe that spilled over into the Salem Witch Hunts. Their commentary is indeed surprising. Therefore the Separation of Church and State protection was written into the Constitution. Many of the new colonies were populated by threatened church groups fleeing toward America's freedoms and looking favorably at such protection. Ironically, the Evangelicals of today have forgotten this fact. The Church/State Clause protected them from persecution by the larger, more influential sects.

Robert Sobel, Orlando Examiner- Posted 20 Quotes of Founding Fathers and Abe Lincoln as to their obvious disdain of extreme Organized Religion. Listed below are my 11 favorites. Odd that the religious fanatics we have today, their religious institution progenitors fled here to our shores to escape from governmental/hierarchal church ordained persecution in Europe. Now established, they want to subdue and enslave with their own man based ideology. No One knows whom or Whatever Creator is so please; 'Leave the rest of us the Hell alone!'

  1. "The hocus-pocus phantasm of a God like another Cerberus, with one body and three heads, had its birth and growth in the blood of thousands and thousands of martyrs." - Thomas Jefferson
  2. "It is too late in the day for men of sincerity to pretend they believe in the Platonic mysticisms that three are one, and one is three; and yet the one is not three, and the three are not one." -Thomas Jefferson
  3. "Lighthouses are more useful than churches."- Ben Franklin
  4. "This would be the best of all possible worlds if there were no religion in it."- John Adams
  5. "I do not believe in the creed professed by the Jewish Church, by the Roman Church, by the Greek Church, by the Turkish Church, by the Protestant Church, nor by any Church that I know of. My own mind is my own Church. Each of those churches accuse the other of unbelief; and for my own part, I disbelieve them all."- Thomas Paine

6. "All national institutions of churches, whether Jewish, Christian or Turkish, appear to me no other than human inventions, set up to terrify and enslave mankind, and monopolize power and profit."- Thomas Paine

7. "It is the fable of Jesus Christ, as told in the New Testament, and the wild and visionary doctrine raised thereon, against which I contend. The story, taking it as it is told, is blasphemously obscene."- Thomas Paine

8. "Religious controversies are always productive of more acrimony and irreconcilable hatreds than those which spring from any other cause. Of all the animosities which have existed among mankind, those which are caused by the difference of sentiments in religion appear to be the most inveterate and distressing, and ought most to be depreciated. I was in hopes that the enlightened and liberal policy, which has marked the present age, would at least have reconciled Christians of every denomination so far that we should never again see the religious disputes carried to such a pitch as to endanger the peace of society."- George Washington

9. "The Bible is not my book, nor Christianity my profession."- Abraham Lincoln

10. "It may not be easy, in every possible case, to trace the line of separation between the rights of religion and the civil authority with such distinctness as to avoid collisions and doubts on unessential points. The tendency to a usurpation on one side or the other or to a corrupting coalition or alliance between them will be best guarded against by entire abstinence of the government from interference in any way whatever, beyond the necessity of preserving public order and protecting each sect against trespasses on its legal rights by others." - James Madison

11. "Religious bondage shackles and debilitates the mind and unfits it for every noble enterprise."- James Madison [10]

As I stated earlier. These men, except for a later era Lincoln were several centuries closer to the effects of runaway unbridled, highly dangerous Religion comparable to ISIS and related affiliates.

North American Indians prior to the arrival of the White Man (Wahshichu) presented a commonality of regard, terming IT (not He or She

---

[10] Robert Sobel, *Orlando Liberal Examiner* (April, 2016)

according to us Sioux) as a Great Mystery or Great Spirit. Yes, my studies have led me to believe this supposition has held true for the vast majority of the Northeastern tribes migrating out of the east to mainly avoid the Wahshichu and especially his devastating diseases. As a former assistant to two prominent Sioux medicine men, Chiefs Fools Crow and Eagle Feather, I earned an appreciable portion of their spiritual knowledge and respect through volunteering as a pledger as mentioned for six of their annual Sun Dances beginning upon my return from Vietnam. This was back when few Indians supported them. A Sun Dance is no mere, com- forted ordeal. Four days, a pledger (participant) endures no food or water (if not a Diabetic) under a hot Badlands August sun to thank/acknowledge Creator for a certain request initiated by the pledger. My request was that I come back from Vietnam combat and not under a flag draped casket or a missing appendage.

Actually, at that time – pre- Martin Luther King Civil Rights Move- ment– the Christian missionaries successfully lobbied Congress in the early 1900s to impose an unconstitutional, illegal Ban upon what they termed – 'Indian Religion and all related ceremonies.' The stubborn Sioux resisted however and blatantly defied the government's missionary insti- gated order. In the old days, the Sun Dance was an annual Sioux celebra- tion to Creator for all that Ultimate Benevolent Power allowed for us through the Four Seasons or Four Directions it obviously provided. Most all Northeastern based tribes and many on into the Southwest have annu- al beseeching ceremonies, usually lasting four days, to Great Mystery All Provider. Among other tribes, Corn Dances, Wild Rice Harvests, related Harvest Gatherings were held to honor and thank Creator for 'all that it provided in order that the tribe may live.' For the Sioux, the Gathering for Buffalo Meat (Buffalo Harvest) to be dried upon drying racks in the hot blowing August/September winds for the long winter was their Sun Dance ceremony. Why this (annually thanking Creator ceremony) should bother the Wahshichu is difficult to fathom. The earliest 'Thanksgiving' by the Pilgrims as mentioned earlier, was initiated by the East Coast Indi- ans and not the Pilgrims. No such annual acknowledgement celebration existed in Europe at that time.

Certain ceremonial celebrants among the Plains tribes would volun- teer and for four days the Sun Dance pledger will endure song and drum under a hot Badlands, August sun without water and no food. These cel- ebrants or pledgers as they are termed have asked Creator for a special request during the preceding year or so if prolonged sickness or healing was an issue which of course must be an ethical/moral request. Being granted, the pledger then endures his pledge. Bound for combat in Vietnam I pledged to Creator that if I came back alive from some rather serious, close air tree top level bombing missions as a Marine F-4 Phantom pilot, I would endure the ceremony. You generally get shot at by the enemy on these Close Air Support missions for your own troops being besieged and are very close to the surface to deliver your ordinance, which not unlike the Spanish toreador, can get 'rather fatal' via too many attempts. There was only one tribal sun dance back then just prior to the Martin L. King era. Likewise, many a Sioux infantryman also pledges the same as a combat pilot would do.

After sun dances I often drove medicine leaders to several meetings with other tribal non-Sioux medicine men. Even some Canadian tribes were present as they are now present at many of my tribe's sun dances. All shared a common belief with regard to the identity of Creator/Great Mystery. No religious arguments ensued. They were of the mindset that it would be quite foolish to attempt religious exactness as to who was the Great Mystery. This is the heart of the problem which exists between Spirituality and Organized Religion. As is the focus of my Prologue, this dangerous, attempted 'exactness' phobia is the heart of the terrorism besieging egotistic man today; at least cunning dictators utilize such in league with religious hierarchy to recruit and keep the public behind them. Coming from a totally differing value system, I conclude it is the major phobia intoxicating the planet by imaginative two-legged and why I had to write this book. "The Pope, the Imam, the Ayatollah and now Abu Bakr al-Baghdadi of ISIS is 'Infallible.' Millions of varied misled believers staunchly follow.

Many a cunning, devious dictator has fed on this ruse to gain control of a nation's mindset whether he believed likewise or not. Adolf Hitler was a perfect example. He spread religious hatred of the Jews based largely on superstition based false accusation coupled with hatred inflaming Aryan Supremacy to gain his way into power. He was aided into Chancellorship by the Roman Catholic Secretariat and soon to be pope- Pius the XII who made a special trip to Berlin to quiet the German bishops who saw through Hitler and were beginning to oppose the Nazi party's inhumanity to the German Jews. ISIS is following a similar course except that they are not centering on the Jews alone.

Suggested readings.

Hitler's Pope, John Cornwell.
Constantine's Sword, James Carroll.

CHAPTER 2
RIGHT OR WRONG

Think!

A two church, one gas station town lies not far from Rapid City, USA. Seven 'Think' Signs, all in a row, border the two way - four lane highway about half way between. The signs are reminders of two pickup trucks which crashed head on, meeting on the median of one of the One Way two lanes. It was not accidental but rather a personal choice for the two drivers nor was it intentional suicide. All of the deceased were friends in high school. Judgement deems they were playing such a dangerous encounter often employed by youthful drivers. Both drivers were betting that the other would veer to safety at the last possible moment. In other words, Human, in this situation, was depending on another person for his safety and ... continuity to live! Each was speculating his life - dependent, trusting upon another. Salvation's last second action for this Earth journey did not happen and thus reckoned the outcome.

Generally, the participants meet somewhere, usually on a lesser trafficked highway either by prior arrangement or just chance passing. One vehicle will turn around and even if an illegal One Way is the tournament field for the moment and if no other traffic is approaching-motors are gunned at each other from an appropriate distance to build up to at least 60 or 70 mph or more, brakes are released and the two vehicles roar toward one another straddling the same median. Nearing the potentially fatal collision point, the driver who first turns out to avoid collision is termed a 'Chicken' but all live to see another day. Of course the "non-Chicken' driver is eulogized, extoled, praised and exclaimed by his admirers. If both drivers are 'non-Chickens' then they become the memory of Highway reminders titled 'Think'!

As the seven signs faded behind me, I thought about my happy-go-lucky gregarious Nephew, a fatal passenger, and how this tragic scenario reminded me of Religion which contrarily is dependent not as much by wordless action but mostly by what other men have to say, their utterances projected through written verse. Men who follow their Koran or Bible are dependent upon other men's religious speculation or suppositions (never women's) for attempting to prepare for their antici-pated life beyond. What about all that Creator shows us through what it has made, designed and we find solidly reliable? Seems there would be more dependable, untainted religious teachings emanating from studious man in comparison. In Spirituality these nature teachings offer a more realistic base. Superstition and molded myth as teach-ability are avoided.

Ancient Values vs Modern

Ancient Indigenous, down through time, painted or carved nothing except for petroglyphs mostly depicting hunting symbolism or winter counts (tribal event history) upon elk or buffalo hides. I have to speculate or supposition that their revealing Nature observation is more of a 'direct line' to the mind, the viewpoints or possible intentions for Man to be guided by God: An 'absence of the middle man' so to speak. Simply immerse yourself in seclusion of yet surrounding, pure Creation - absent wires, concrete and steel and only the songs of birds or a waterfall and a blessed, fulfilling serenity flows throughout one if one has the depth to simply observe. I have yet to view indigenous depictions of nude women sprawled out in sexual pose or two individuals, man on man or man on woman copulating, carved or painted on canyon or cave walls. Obviously the indigenous artist, their entire society actually, had contrary values than the playboy mind of later European stock beset with Kardashian 'sizzling,' 'plunging neckline,' 'blockbuster revealing,' descriptive bust line, ass cheek fascination. My tours in the Orient, noticeably Japan, the same such playboy free artistic values is reflected in their culture as well.

Spiritual human is influenced considerably by what Nature, Creator's creation has to offer. How latter human arrives at the term 'pagan' is disrespectfully odd. The olde ('olde' is intentional) time spiritually influenced Indians, from the northeastern piedmont and coastal tribes, at least, wisely migrated to a temporary safety, the disease free western plains of America; these indigenous primarily observed Nature for their spiritual guidance. I suspect strongly that the 'spiritual intellectualism' of the non-excluded female bardship of the nature based Celtics that once reigned throughout Western Europe would have prevented the terror filled Great Inquisition, had they remained prolific. Terror filled WW II and Hitler might not have happened either.

However, to learn spiritual guidance from how Creator arranges or can influence is considered heretical by those who prefer Man's prophetic utterances and condemn such irreverence for not choosing their own biblical soothsayers. They are stating pompously, "Our Man prophecies are more meaningful than what one can learn spiritually from Direct Observation of Creator's Nature based implementations." Hmmm, I have to wonder what Creator could possibly advise once we reach the Spirit World if there is one. Should be rather interesting. "You mean you preferred to ignore what I put before you!" In a loud, thunder crashing voice. I hope we are not standing over a trap door. One might get a less than pleasant, "Now move on." The hesitant other might hear an angry, "Next," as the trap door is sprung. Anything is possible. Isn't it? Personally, I prefer not to ignore Creator, while on this journey. Something to think about.

Resolve, extreme resolve is the echo I heard as I drove on. I had to contemplate that term 'Resolve' as I drove south for a medical appointment at the Veteran's Administration. I had lived my life but my Nephew was cut short because of that definition – 'Resolve'. Extreme fanatical, dead set Resolve - one could more accurately term such. Yes, Dead Set!

What is it that permeates Man so deeply that despite obvious Superstition and obvious man-made fantasy, Man yet will cling to his religious convictions often bespeaking- "My Way- Right or Wrong. If you do not believe My Way, you will suffer forever (in my concept) of hellfire and brimstone. " Hmmm, I have never been offered the exact location of where this horrid place is physically located somewhere in the Universe. If one is Nature based it is not difficult to term such as foolish Superstition. Oh! I will not deny that we do go someplace – all of us.

I hope I am glaringly in error but my supposition or belief is that most readers of this work will not be able to sit back and introspect their Spiritual or religious convictions to any large degree or become convinced to change considerably their religious view. They will not give up this 'fiery Hell' concept or their Devils, Satan, or Lucifer either. It is quite difficult for most Indigenous, however, those raised close to tribal culture, to imagine an obvious benevolent, all-providing Creator arriving at or allowing such horrid extreme.

Bernard Lewis, his article in *Atlantic Monthly* reveals why the Islamic World is so backward and at a loss technology wise due to too extreme a reliance on Religion, while the rest of the world moved on. Their anger is to blame their situation on the West, instead of themselves. They become ripe for cunning, dangerous Dictators who play into the control seeking Ayatollahs who join in with the Dictator and placate the masses with religion not unlike what the Evangelical movement is attempting in the West. Thus we have Terrorism from Islamic downtrodden countries when those countries social system becomes drastic.

The following excerpts from an article by Bernard Lewis on the Middle East mind set will touch upon such reflections. Such is the power of 'Resolve.' Catastrophe, however, the still not dreaded word at least in this still abundant land, seems to be the only catalyst that has the power to awaken Human (Two Legged is the Sioux term.) to oncoming reality if one recognizes or even dreads Climate Change, Planetary Heating and Overpopulation as the major catalysts. As proof, at least for me, it was the catastrophic confinement and starvation on the reservation that had the power to alter my own people the Sioux away from their highly environmentally successful, centuries providing Nature influencing 'religion'. Granted, the Jewish Tribe did not break religiously in less than a decade of Belsen, Buchenwald and Auschwitz. The Sioux had several generations to endure, however. There was no General Patton or Eisenhower to

come to their rescue; rather, the U. S. Cavalry stood guard over us to allow the missionaries to get settled in and control us, to unconstitutionally lobby Congress and Ban our own religion (Spirituality) and even promote, a federal all Indian Insane Asylum. Elaborating farther, some of the confined were mentally healthy, tribal Medicine leaders, not in accord with missionary religion. Can a reasonable man blame we traditional leaning Sioux for being highly suspicious or at least wary of the fanatic Evangelicals as well as those fanatics in the Mid-east?

While in reservation custody, they (my people) became increasingly in awe of the advanced ways the White Man had developed regarding shelter, mobility, running water, sewage disposal, so many improvements regarding the new comforts of life such that they could not help but to believe Creator indeed had blessed them. The buffalo were being exterminated as well. Other game became scarce. They were always hungry. Along came the Jesuits on my reservation and they were ripe for conversion.

Most 'Traditional Indigenous' do not speculate as to who is either 'Right or Wrong.' A 'Traditional' is one who allows Earth Based or Nature based influence regarding their Spirituality choice. Why speculate such if one doesn't know for sure when it comes to sheer mystery? Seems symptomatic like wasted energy. The once overzealous missionaries we still open mindedly and generously allow on our federal reservations to administer to the converted 'Missionaryized Sioux' who shun or oft bicker about our old Way's return, but they (missionaries) no longer control us administratively, politically or educationally. Yes, that old Sioux resolve from our traditional culture is back indeed!

Increasingly the spiritual return to our Nature base, (Creator based) is by the younger generations who align mostly with our Spiritual leaders and not the White Man's. The large attendance and participation by the younger set at our many summer sun dances is enough proof. Missionaries no longer have the political power to lobby Congress and have our ceremonies Banned as they once did. The missionary lobbied Canton (South Dakota) All Indian Hiawatha Insane Asylum where our medicine men and women were incarcerated beginning early 1900s was torn down brick by brick before WW II and the one hundred and twenty patient/victim graves are deadly proof. They lie hidden along a fairway of the Canton golf course. Such can be the 'Resolve' of fanatic led Man. Man created catastrophe can be very effective as we shall no doubt find out eventually. It can kill a religion or a spirituality quite effectively. Look at how thorough Organized Religion dispatched the Celtic beliefs. The Evangelicals placate the 1% control within our own land and hence the favorable political laws their politicians advance.

*   *   *   *

"I'm Right. You're Wrong. Go to Hell." Bernard Lewis

Atlantic Monthly - May 2003. Bernard Lewis – is a Mid-East scholar who writes for Atlantic Monthly among other periodical articles. I could not think of a more appropriate way to begin this work. The following two articles which he wrote for Atlantic Monthly were written before 9/11 occurred, therefore he should be allowed his optimism for a safer world back then. Otherwise, I believe his dissertation historically, accurately probes into the major instigators of present day conflict not only in the Middle East but erupting worldwide. After a thorough reading, one cannot put down this article and another to follow without a deeper, contemplative insight into the spreading conflict now before us. Terrorism is the dangerous topic of this writing. Yes, not as massively deadly for humankind as exponential Over Population and Planetary Heating for those intellectually aware who believe those two issues also demand our immediate focus. The brilliant Bernard Lewis points directly at the beginning of extreme Terrorism a decade before its worldwide cognitive beginning. His two articles within this work needn't be hidden in a monthly periodical over a decade back for only a few. Bernard Lewis Wikipedia Bio awaits at the end.

> For a long time now it has been our practice in the modern
> Western world to define ourselves primarily by nationality, and
> to see other identities and allegiances—religious, political, and
> the like—as subdivisions of the larger and more important
> whole. The events of September 11 and after have made us
> aware of another perception—of a religion subdivided into na-
> tions rather than a nation subdivided into religions—and this
> has induced some of us to think of ourselves and of our rela-
> tions with others in ways that had become unfamiliar. The
> confrontation with a force that defines itself as Islam has given
> a new relevance—indeed, urgency—to the theme of the "clash
> of civilizations." [11]

Mr. Lewis states that, "At one time the general assumption of mankind was that 'civilization' meant us, and the rest were uncivilized." He mentions the Turkish president, Kemal Ataturk describing civilization as 'modern civilization' and that his newly formed republic had to join such advancement for it was the civilization of the West and the only civilization alive and well…and advancing. The majority of Islam has not followed Turkish Democracy however. Only two civilizations, Christianity and Islam, have been defined by religion according to Lewis. They have much in common, along with some differences.

> To what extent is a religiously defined civilization compatible
> with pluralism—tolerance of others within the same civiliza-
> tion but of different religions? This crucial question points to a

---

[11] Bernard Lewis, "I'm Right, You're Wrong, Go to Hell," *Atlantic Monthly*, May, 2003.

major distinction between two types of religion. For some religions, just as "civilization" means us, and the rest are barbarians, so "religion" means ours, and the rest are infidels. Other
religions, such as Judaism and most of the religions of Asia,
concede that human beings may use different religions to
speak to God, as they use different languages to speak to one
another. God understands them all. I know in my heart that
the English language is the finest instrument the human race
has ever devised to express its thoughts and feelings, but I
recognize in my mind that others may feel exactly the same
way about their languages, and I have no problem with that.
These two approaches to religion may conveniently be denot-
ed by the terms their critics use to condemn them—
"triumphalism" and "relativism." In one of his sermons the fif-
teenth-century Franciscan Saint John of Capistrano, immortal-
ized on the map of California, denounced the Jews for trying
to spread a "deceitful" notion among Christians: "The Jews say
that everyone can be saved in his own faith, which is impossible." For once a charge of his against the Jews was justified.
The Talmud does indeed say that the righteous of all faiths
have a place in paradise. Polytheists and atheists are excluded,
but monotheists of any persuasion who observe the basic
moral laws are eligible. The relativist view was condemned and
rejected by both Christians and Muslims, who shared the conviction that there was only one true faith, theirs, which it was
their duty to bring to all humankind. The triumphalist view is
increasingly under attack in Christendom, and is disavowed by
significant numbers of Christian clerics. There is little sign as
yet of a parallel development in Islam.

Tolerance is, of course, an extremely intolerant idea, because it means "I am the boss: I will allow you some, though
not all, of the rights I enjoy as long as you behave yourself according to standards that I shall determine." That, I think, is a
fair definition of religious tolerance as it is normally understood and applied. In a letter to the Jewish community of
Newport, Rhode Island, that George Washington wrote in
1790, he remarked, perhaps in an allusion to the famous "Pa-
tent of Tolerance" promulgated by the Austrian Emperor Joseph II a few years previously, "It is now no more that toleration is spoken of, as if it was by the indulgence of one class of
people that another enjoyed the exercise of their inherent natural rights." At a meeting of Jews, Christians, and Muslims in
Vienna some years ago the Cardinal Archbishop Franz Koenig
spoke of tolerance, and I couldn't resist quoting Washington

to him. He replied, "You are right. I shall no more speak of tolerance; I shall speak of mutual respect." There are still too few who share the attitude expressed in this truly magnificent response.

For those taking the relativist approach to religion (in effect, "I have my god, you have your god, and others have theirs"), there may be specific political or economic reasons for objecting to someone else's beliefs, but in principle there is no theological problem. For those taking the triumphalist approach (classically summed up in the formula "I'm right, you're wrong, go to hell"), tolerance is a problem. Because the triumphalist's is the only true and complete religion, all other religions are at best incomplete and more probably false and evil; and since he is the privileged recipient of God's final message to humankind, it is surely his duty to bring it to others rather than keep it selfishly for himself.

Now, if one believes that, what does one do about it? And how does one relate to people of another religion? If we look at this question historically, one thing emerges very clearly: whether the other religion is previous or subsequent to one's own is extremely important. From a Christian point of view, for example, Judaism is previous and Islam is subsequent. From a Muslim point of view, both Judaism and Christianity are previous. From a Jewish point of view, both Christianity and Islam are subsequent—but since Judaism is not triumphalist, this is not a problem.

But it is a problem for Christians and Muslims—or perhaps I should say for traditional Christians and Muslims. From their perspective, a previous religion may be regarded as incomplete, as superseded, but it is not necessarily false if it comes in the proper sequence of revelation. So from a Muslim point of view, Judaism and Christianity were both true religions at the time of their revelation, but they were superseded by the final and complete revelation of Islam; although they are out-of-date—last year's model, so to speak—they are not inherently false. Therefore Muslim law, sharia, not only permits but requires that a certain degree of tolerance be accorded them....

It is, of course, a little more complicated: Jews and Christians are accused of falsifying their originally authentic scriptures and religions. Thus, from a Muslim point of view, the Christian doctrine of the Trinity and of the divinity of Jesus Christ are distortions. The point is made in several Koranic verses: "There is no God but God alone, He has no companion," and "He is God, one, eternal. He does not beget, He is not begotten, and He has no peer." These and similar verses appear frequently on early Islamic coins and in inscriptions, and are clearly polemical in intent. They are inscribed, notably, in the Dome of the Rock, in Jerusalem—a challenge to Christianity in its birthplace. Jews are accused of eliminating scriptural passages foretelling the advent of Muhammad. Anything subsequent to Muhammad, "the Seal of the Prophets," is, from the Muslim perspective, necessarily false. This explains the harsh treatment of post-Islamic religions, such as the Bahai faith and the Ahmadiya movement, in Islamic lands.

Muslims did not claim a special relationship to either of the predecessor religions, and if Jews and Christians chose not to accept Muhammad, that was their loss. Muslims were prepared to tolerate them in accordance with sharia, which lays down both the extent and the limits of the latitude to be granted those who follow a recognized religion: they must be monotheists and they must have a revealed scripture, which in practice often limited tolerance to Jews and Christians. On principle, no tolerance was extended to polytheists or idolaters, and this sometimes raised acute problems in Asian and African lands conquered by the Muslims.

Tolerance was a much more difficult question for Christians. For them, Judaism is a precursor of their religion, and Christianity is the fulfillment of the divine promises made to the Jews. The Jewish rejection of that fulfillment is therefore seen as impugning some of the central tenets of the Christian faith. Tolerance between different branches of Christianity would eventually become an even bigger problem. Of course, the outsider is more easily tolerated than the dissident insider. Heretics are a much greater danger than unbelievers. The English philosopher John Locke's famous A Letter Concerning Toleration, written toward the end of the seventeenth century, is a plea for religious tolerance, still a fairly new idea at that time. Locke wrote, "Neither pagan, nor Mahometan, nor Jew, ought to be excluded from the civil rights of the commonwealth, because of his religion." Someone is of course missing from that list: the Catholic. The difference is clear. For Locke and his contemporaries, the pagan, the Muslim, the Jew, were no threat to the Church of England; the Catholic was. The Catholic was trying to subvert Protestantism, to make England Catholic, and, as Protestant polemicists at the time put it, to make England subject to a foreign potentate—namely, the Pope in Rome.

Muslims were in general more tolerant of diversity within their own community, and even cited an early tradition to the effect that such diversity is a divine blessing. The concept of heresy—in the Christian sense of incorrect belief recognized and condemned as such by properly constituted religious authority—was unknown to classical Islam. Deviation and diversity, with rare exceptions, were persecuted only when they offered a serious threat to the existing order. The very notion of an authority empowered to rule on questions of belief was alien to traditional Islamic thought and practice. It has become less alien.

A consequence of the similarity between Christianity and Islam in background and approach is the long conflict between the two civilizations they defined. When two religions met in the Mediterranean area, each claiming to be the recipient of God's final revelation, conflict was inevitable. The conflict, in fact, was almost continuous: the first Arab-Islamic invasions took Islam by conquest to the then Christian lands of Syria, Palestine, Egypt, and North Africa, and, for a while, to Southern Europe; the Tatars took it into Russia and Eastern Europe; and the Turks took it into the Balkans. To each advance came a Christian rejoinder: the Reconquista in Spain, the Crusades in the Levant, the throwing off of what the Russians call the Tatar yoke in the history of their country, and, finally, the great European counterattack into the lands of Islam, which is usually called imperialism.

During this long period of conflict, of jihad and crusade, of conquest and re-conquest, Christianity and Islam nevertheless maintained a level of communication, because the two are basically the same kind of religion. They could argue. They could hold disputations and debates. Even their screams of rage were mutually intelligible. When Christians and Muslims said to each other, "You are an infidel and you will burn in hell," each understood exactly what the other meant, because they both meant the same thing. (Their heavens are differently appointed, but their hells are much the same.) Such assertions and accusations would have conveyed little or no meaning to a Hindu, a Buddhist, or a Confucian.

Christians and Muslims looked at each other and studied each other in strikingly different ways. This is owing in part, at least, to their different circumstances. Christian Europeans from the start had to learn foreign languages in order to read their scriptures and their classics and to communicate with one another. From the seventh century onward they had a further motive to look outward—their holy places, in the land where their faith was born, were under Muslim rule, and could be visited only with Muslim permission. Muslims had no comparable problems. Their holy places were in Arabia, under Arab rule; their scriptures were in Arabic, which across their civilization was the language also of literature, of science and scholarship, of government and commerce, and, increasingly, of everyday communication, as the conquered countries in Southwest Asia and North Africa were Arabized and forgot their ancient languages and scripts. In later times other Islamic languages emerged, notably Persian and Turkish; but in the early, formative centuries Arabic reigned alone....

The Islamic world, with no comparable incentives, displayed a total lack of interest in Christian civilization. An initially understandable, even justifiable, contempt for the barbarians beyond the frontier continued long after that characterization ceased to be accurate, and even into a time when it became preposterously inaccurate....

Today we in the West are engaged in what we see as a war against terrorism, and what the terrorists present as a war against unbelief. Some on both sides see this struggle as one between civilizations or, as others would put it, between religions. If they are right, and there is much to support their view, then the clash between these two religiously defined civilizations results not only from their differences but also from their resemblances—and in these there may even be some hope for better future understanding. [12]

*   *   *   *

Thus, Bernard Lewis offers us a strong, verifiable base to approach the looming destiny before us and our offspring. Let us appreciate the abundance of new knowledge we have gleaned but we must realize that his writing was before 9/11 and well before ISIS. Actions and track record are louder than words.

Bernard Lewis is Jewish and obviously a scholar I highly respect. Although it is not customary to include entire articles in an academic essay, the critical issue of organized world terrorism and the obvious means ongoing to carry out their stated mission of world conquest places this issue right behind the environmental dilemma facing civilized society. The high degree of utmost critical danger, millions of deaths in the Mid-

---

[12] Ibid.

dle East and now spreading worldwide with refugees across Europe supersedes what is 'customary', in my opinion. Why should such a powerful article languish in community libraries while Modern Terrorism bursts modern civilization into flames?

Mayo Clinic and the Burka

I have returned from a brief stay at Mayo Clinic, world famous cancer hospital, Rochester, MN. My childhood friend, Bill Lemley, a doctor's son whose father supported me especially while in law school was also at Mayo. We both viewed our first experience with the 'Burkha'- the entire covering of the Arab woman while at Mayo except for a small rectangular peephole necessary for her to navigate. Worldwide, Mayo draws patients. To put it bluntly, despite a background of world travel myself, I was somewhat shocked to view this poor, inhibited creature under that black garb at the bid and call of her cocky male counterpart dressed oddly in a pair of cowboy boots and western jeans and snap button shirt. We viewed other Arab females so attired. Some had connecting 'pulling or guiding ropes' manned by the male. Both Bill and I were turned off resolutely at such primitive, religious foolishness. Custom or no custom. It is too unnatural a limitation upon half their human population. Granted thankfully, such limitation is not totally rampant throughout the Mid-East. But even one country that subscribes and promotes such 'traditional' cruel laws; we both could not support. Coming from South Dakota where freedom for all is sacred, we were both saddened to have to realize such is practiced in this day and age. Sioux women, all tribes did not require their women to be bound in useless, stifling garments invented by controlling Man. Will world society ever advance to outlawing such ignorance? Hopefully, modern communication can bring about such release.

I have to add a comment regarding historical Sioux women. Each carried a large butcher knife, almost the length of a small sword. They could dexterously handle this tool as well. They were free to emasculate any man that approached them in the least, suspecting fashion. No questions asked. Such then, Rape or violation was a rare happening. A long way from the Arabic Burka, would you not agree?

CHAPTER 3
WHO IS GOD?

I love a people whose religion is all the same, and who are free
from religious animosities.
George Catlin[13]

Humanities II

The suburban Minneapolis high school class (Edina) was titled—
Humanities II. A selected list of 100 questions from students had been
compiled by the teacher over a period of years. These intriguing questions, beginning with 'Who is God?' were given to all speakers who had
agreed to speak on their chosen life style, spirituality and/or religion.

Humanities II was taught in an upper income, Midwestern, metropol-
itan suburban school (Edina, MN). I suspect that this class of young
minds, their curiosity, wonderment, optimism, skepticism, and their set
convictions, are fairly reflective of present day youth in the realm of philosophy, religion and spirituality. Because I am from a culture that suffered severe religious oppression (Native American), I was most apprecia-
tive of the progress which I discerned by such a list from young, questing,
forming minds. My gratitude was also buoyed by the fact that other
speakers aside from the dominant society belief system were actually requested to come into the classrooms to share their views.

These profound questions would never have been submitted when I
was a student in high school. Speakers outside of the dominant mainstream were not invited into our schools. In those days, students held the
same iron clad convictions as their parents. Although unconstitutional,
Indigenous Spirituality was forbidden, via lobbying missionaries, our religion was banned by the federal government which administrated Native
American educational institutions. In these schools, North American native people were processed not to re-examine beneficial indigenous culture and history but instead, were programmed to ridicule, downplay and
degrade their own indigenous culture including our brave and unselfish
leaders, Red Cloud, Sitting Bull, Spotted Tail and Crazy Horse who held
the government forces attempting to subdue us to a standstill for over
two decades mid-1800s.

---

[13] Artist who lived with the Plains tribes, Explorer, Author. 1796-1872.

In my grandparent's time, missionary educators established schools on federal tribal lands and had open access to the government boarding schools in order to promote religious indoctrination. They were even given federal lands to build their schools upon, which was a direct violation of the constitutional protection of church and state separation. Academic education was secondary to their primary goal which was complete eradication of native religion, spirituality and culture. Within both school systems, missionary and federal, the educational curriculum was designed to foster submissive assimilation into the mainstream society. Missionaries went so far as to successfully lobby for the federally constructed all Indian Hiawatha Insane Asylum mentioned earlier. Maybe such a past has influenced me to appreciate these times now that our tribe is allowed a new sense of religious freedom. Thanks to Dr. Martin Luther King's efforts, a new openness came across the land. Congress actually made new law allowing Indians to have their own religion or in reality allowed us to return to our old way of seeing Creator through earth based lenses and which we term as Spirituality rather than the man based religious view of Dominant Society. Maybe that is why I could be moved to such a degree that I undertook the task to respond to their questions which were placed before me. I took the 100 questions and wrote a book on Humanities termed Native Wisdom. They struck deep, deep down in some mysterious way into my psyche, or were they actually reaching into my DNA?

Despite the advent of modern terrorism, its ability to religiously warp human minds into disaster producing suicides among our youth, I tend toward an upbeat attitude in respect to the abundance of knowledge that is coming to two leggeds (humans) as this new millennium which is now here upon us. I do not adopt a gullible attitude that modern Terrorism is not to be ignored however. But it is Knowledge and now coupled with Creator's bounteous allowance of communicative discovery worldwide, which catalyzes my incentive to at least bravely utilize such a God-given tool to conquer and subdue the blinded ogres of civilization. Espionage technology is as important a weapon as communication against the terrorist as we will find out in a later chapter. Around the clock, weapon carrying espionage drones are beginning to subdue them.

The first half of the twentieth century primarily depended on books to extend communication, questioning, reasoning, exploration and storytelling. Radio, movies and then television began to capture increasing audiences through this powerful force called technology and placed among us by an Ultimate All Knowledge Creator. What new electronic waves are out there waiting for our discovery? By mid-century, daily news, world events, the front lines of war or the midst of catastrophe were radio broadcasted. Within a few decades, world events were videoed into the living room. Indeed, the twentieth century was a new world of communication where innovative technology played a strong role towards an exponential understanding based on reams of information available on a daily and changing basis. This twenty first century: what vast discovery will it bring?

The students who wrote these questions signal a harmonic change that is beginning to stir. The colossal information system which is now available is also becoming more accurate. An information access system reaches across the land where millions of like-minded students are not afraid to think, to question science, politics, government; the whole lot of sordid, control entrenched systems and Yes; finally – Organized Religion. Even priests and ministers, a few bishops as well- they are beginning to question Organized Religion. At least Christianity's leadership is challenging old rigidity and dogma, led by a new Pope Francis who out strips any of his predecessors by forbidding cover ups especially regarding church pedophilia and the Vatican Bank.

In classrooms, and more so in colleges, I sense a healthy rejection of that portion of old religious molds which forbade or restricted questioning religious thought. As Christian youth evolve into adulthood, more questions will be asked. I suspect Islamic youth, especially those here in America will also question. A new reference and a respect for the observed truths of Nature is definitely spawning. They are worried about the environment and hence they question Nature's harsh and abnormal patterns it has taken lately to influence this awakening. I think that these questions are quite powerful and could lead us toward a planet saving harmony. We are still in an age when Human is still killing human over religion. So many modern prophets, the crowd fomenters, claim that each is right. At the same time the environment is seriously being weakened. Man is killing man and man is killing the environment. Curative energy is being wasted and diverted from the fields of world peace and the realm of needed environmental healing. It is time to seriously, honestly look at the Track Record of a people and see how it relates to the timely questions these students have projected before us. The following questions were the beginning of the list of 100 and are pertinent to begin this, quite possibly my last literary endeavor. I have said that before, however. My attempt at responding to these questions in their entirety, *Native Wisdom,* is no longer in print.

How does your religion define the Supreme Being?

Share your thoughts on God: Did He create us?

How does your religion explain the unknown, such as creation?

Is this religion based on the existence of an immortal being?

How did the 'higher power' become the 'higher power'?

How does your God manifest itself to humans? Is He always watching?

Does your God have a gender?

Is your religion defined by what one thinks and does?

What is the underlying theme of your religion?

Where do you believe your Supreme Being exists?

I will refrain from responding directly to all of these particular questions above in this present chapter but most will be indirectly responded to in following chapters as well as this writing moves along.

* * * *

Who is God according to Spirituality and not Organized Religion?

Before I can begin to respond to such a question, I must explain that any answer, or attempt to answer, is based on my own background, my personal experiences and that which has influenced me upon my personal journey down the Red Trail of Life or as some may call it, my journey within the Natural Way. Indigenous teachers were major influencers at the beginning of my travels and on into middle age. Serious works from truth seeking authors continue to leave their imprint within my spirit.

I do not speak for my tribe, nor the indigenous tribes. No one can. If someone says that they do, cast a wary eye of suspicion. Another indigenous person will not offer the same answers as mine or of another's. No one speaks for the dominant society so why should members of the dominant society expect that one of us should speak for all indigenous people? Some native peoples may exhibit a commonality, especially if they are of the same tribe. Others will not. The basic commonality of projecting one's beliefs from being Earth based, I believe holds true for most Indigenous who have maintained their beliefs down through tribal eons.

It has been my observance that too many non-Indians elevate every utterance a Native American makes as if it is what all Native Americans will agree with. I have a simple statement in that regard. I have never known two Indians to conduct a sweat lodge in the same way. Even Chief Fools Crow and Chief Eagle Feather used differing procedure in conducting their ceremonies. Most North American ceremonial conductors' descendant from the northeastern tribes and escaping onto the Great Plains to avoid the horrendous epidemics from early Europeans use the same symbolic colors of Black Elk's vision, red, yellow, black and white, but most do not have them in the same arrangement as stated in the book, *Black Elk Speaks*. Red was east, yellow was south, black was west and white was north in Black Elk's vision. They represent the four races of man as well as the four seasons. Each season is an effective

'Power' of Creator as also are Mother Earth and Father Sky – mainly the life ordaining Sun Energy. Most all North American tribes however do utilize as exemplary of Creator's Four Directions the same colors in differing arrangements. Black Elk's vision is the cornerstone of Sioux spirituality and will be thoroughly covered in an ensuing chapter.

Missionary Paranoia

Paranoid missionaries on my reservation, fearing the influence of Black Elk's Four Directions/Six Powers Vision, made an all-out effort to successfully dilute and subdue what we consider his God ordained predictive vision experience. The major, accurate prediction at the end of the Vision portrayed what is happening now, primarily the environmental disaster steadily building and Man's denial due to his greed and selfish corruption. The Vision was received in the latter 1800s and revealed to a White Man interviewer at the beginning of the 1930s.

Our holy men's (spiritual leaders) wisdom, advice, suggestions, conduct, sacrifice and attitude convey a considerable amount of commonality reflected in Black Elk's words. Commonality is an important ingredient when the Indigenous Way, the Natural Way, is being considered.

I was further influenced by Black Elk's son, Ben and also the daughter of John Neihardt, Hilda Neihardt. In regard to these two influencers, I have observed a high degree of similarity with Fools Crow's and Eagle Feather's spiritual philosophies.

Detractors and criticizers love to center in on a color or a mere ceremonial procedure to draw attention away from the magnitude of a knowledgeable person. Detractors often know very little in reference to what they are pretending to know. Therefore, they will attempt to divert attention toward what anyone could recognize as a minor difference. The detractors get their recognition by this method and hence they bloom in the spotlight like a moth before a flame for a few moments. Always ask a detractor or a criticizer, "What is your background or experience? Where is your "knowledge" coming from?" If you are going to allow a detractor to become a "knowledge" source for your trail of life, you are a fool if you do not probe deeply into their background and track record.

Many of my suppositions are strongly influenced by my native teachers, mainly Chiefs Fools Crow and Eagle Feather beginning with Fools Crow's protective Yuwipi Spirit Calling ceremony in which I pledged to Creator that if I would return from combat flying in Vietnam, I would endure the annual Sun Dance. Four Days the Sun Dance pledger endures the hot Badlands August sun without food or water. The ceremony is a promise to Creator to give those four days back in order that I would live and my children would not be orphans or my mate a widow. I only was obligated to participate in one sun dance but I went on to participate for a total of six ceremonies in six hot, consecutive summers mainly to combat the local reservation missionaries, namely the Jesuits who were doing their damnedest to stop our spiritual Way's return.

I was also influenced by a particular pair of books, not only *Black Elk Speaks* but *The Sacred Pipe*. I consider these writings as the words of a great holy man from my tribe and preserved by two honest White Men, John Neihardt and J. Epes Brown. For me, these books are a representation of the spiritual thought of my tribe, back when they were truly traditional and lived freely within created nature upon the Great Plains. (Black Elk's vision will be explored in depth in a subsequent chapter.) As stated many times, I take no issue with the writings of John Neihardt the author of

Black Elk Speaks but I do take issue with the following two versions published under the influence of Anthropologist Raymond DeMallie and several commentators he allowed in as well. DeMallie refers to Black Elk as a 'conjuror'- one who delves into 'the Dark Side'.

Dr. John Bryde, a former Jesuit missionary remains my strongest influencer regarding our Sioux history having interviewed and recorded over 400 Sioux warrior veterans in their own language.[14]

A Christian would not be able to write about Christian belief without mentioning Jesus; a Moslem would surely speak of Muhammad when he or she would write about their Moslem faith. I would have to offer Black Elk's vision as an integral part of my belief system. Other writings, Michael Parenti, James Haught, Bernard Lewis and unsung contributing veterans of three wars, some veterans personally known, have affected me as well.

The works of Jack Weatherford have taught me some important facts regarding what can happen when a people are Earth centered. His book, *Indian Givers*,[15] established that indigenous people were the true cultivators of democracy, saved the Europeans from their endless famines through their agronomy once certain foods were received in Europe, and also they exhibited an exemplary environmental track record which lasted as long as they were this continent's caretakers. His work is a history book and would not be classified as a philosophical or a religious text. Weatherford's *Genghis Khan* will also appear in this work as an exemplary leader who was far advanced humanitarian wise despite the errant vilification by European writers no doubt because they were beaten so soundly by the invading Mongols. Consumptive pride retaliates by diluting, vilifying history writers as long as the conquerors have moved on. Native American history certainly has suffered from its share of vilifying, errant writers who did not move on. At the local library I discovered the Pilgrim's logs which admitted that a generous people kept them alive. I hope this emphasizes that my spiritual influences are not based on pure religious form, nor are they based only on native originated works; far from it.

---

[14] John Bryde, *Modern Indians* (Vermillion, SD: University of South Dakota Press, 1971) and Notes.
[15] Jack Weatherford, Indian Givers (New York: Crown, 1988)

Plato

One of the most penetrating concepts as to my belief 'shaping' comes out of ancient Greece. Plato's 'Allegory of the Cave.' Who among you cannot but allow serious thought once you have discovered such discourse? It certainly influenced me. I have included this powerful 'wonderment' in most of my books which indicates how profound it is. Simply put, Plato's discourse, thousands of years ago, catalyzed serious contemplation regarding the Beyond World, the place where most of us, regardless of which particular beliefs, Spirituality, Religion or somewhere in between, that we may hold.

Plato: "Life is but a mere shadow on the wall compared to the complete reality that lies beyond."[16]

Plato illustrated a cave that had two entrances toward the cave's mouth. A fire blazed toward the front therefore causing a shadow on the caves inner wall of all who travelled on a road between the fire and the high inner wall. Their shadows would reflect upon the wall. As they traversed from one entrance to the other; singles, twos or more, a chariot occasionally, pack animals and no doubt small herds of sheep or goats. Thus the reflections of the travelers would cast differing shadows as the entry fire blazed. Chattering talk would accompany the larger groups while the single travelers would usually be mute. Between the road or pathway and closest to the cave wall, Plato allowed a small number of bound slaves sitting facing the wall only, restricted in such a way that the only visibility for them was the wall itself with its many differing reflections. They would be blindfolded when brought in and allowed only to see forward. This would be the only view upon which they may discern what was behind them and of course what sounds accompanied each passerby.

The restricted concepts of life each slave since birth would derive would be based primarily on the shadows cast and the sounds of each traveler behind them. A rumbling chariot pulled by two horses would contrast with the lone silent traveler as would a cluster of noisy school children going by. Needless to say the slave would have an inaccurate view of reality.

Plato would eventually take the bound slave and show him the situa-

---

[16] Plato, Athenian, B.C. John M. Cooper, (Plato's Complete Works - Plato's Republic (Indianapolis, IN: Hackett Publishing Co. 1997), pp. 1132-1134.

tion. The road would pass on to the cave's mouth where one could look down onto the sprawling city. The slave would be enlightened, suddenly understanding reality; so opposite from what he had imagined.

Plato holds that this life we have today is but a mere shadow on the wall compared to the complete reality that lies beyond. Makes sense to me and cements my concerns regarding Mystery.

My experiences, adventures and observations of Mother Earth (Nature) are my main influencers, especially since my teacher influencers have gone on. This text will emphasize that what one not only learns academically, but personally observes and experiences; these happenings which implant truthful, untainted, reduction free knowledge supports my spiritual beliefs. Direct Observation is certainly more trustworthy. Modern scientists use it all the time. It is highly difficult for the non-Spiritual to believe what Indigenous experience can glean from ceremony. A thought provoking spirit calling ceremony in which all the predictions made therein came true will be offered in a later chapter for those who are at least curious. Mind you, feel free to not accept the reality of which all of us attending the University of South Dakota experienced including learned professors. Unlike too many religious, conversion or proselytization is not practiced by those of Nature's Way.

My trail has not lacked experience or teachers and it has consumed a major portion of the last century. I was influenced by tribal thought, values, culture, art, teachers, history, stories, research, many books and other related information. I have also been fortunate, and appreciate that I live in an age of technology where vast amounts of information are available if one will exercise the initiative to look.

At this point I must confess that I do not offer any answers, really. Rather, my attempt at answers are but mere suppositions. A supposition is an attempt to offer a response with a reserve clause that the supposition could be wrong, or only partially accurate, especially when the subject being discussed lies within the realm of religion and spirituality. Can you imagine reading an author who states he could be wrong? This is indeed a historic publication. "Everything I say is very correct and I am a leading world authority," is what most authors seem to intend or imply, such are the established rules and habits that so-called learned circles have fallen into.

Nature based culture accepts mystery within not only spiritual thought but everyday activity as well. A person who follows or respects the Natural Way could very well answer, "This is my view, my opinion, my belief but the subject is so vast that it is beyond my total purview if I am to be honest or truthful." The entire area or subject of the beyond, the Supreme Being, its creation, is one of profound mystery. I do not believe that any two leggeds know for sure what they are commenting about, regarding these subjects. I will often repeat this view in various form. I abhor repetition, especially in verbal discussion but Supposition has become one of my favorite words along with Introspection. I will not become angry with you if you civilly or respectfully disagree with my viewpoints, my concepts. At best, I can only tell you how or why I arrive at my suppositional conclusions; what facts or evidence lead me toward my views. "I could be wrong! You might be right. I don't know!" Wouldn't the world be a better place if people could just shed their false egos and learn to honestly make these three statements? Another important admission should also become a part of everyone's communication: "Maybe both of us have no idea of what we are talking about but let us explore with open minds and an open heart."

CHAPTER 4
GENGHIS KHAN

Before we look at four Sioux leaders, all of whom were born in the 19th century, let us look at a leader of the 12th and 13th century. This man was Genghis Khan (c.1162 – 1227) who is reviled by European writers as a brutal conquering warrior chief but Author, Jack Weatherford went to Mongolia numerous times and not unlike James Carroll and British Author John Cornwell who dug through Vatican Archives that were briefly made available until the newly elected pope's untimely death, Weatherford discovered entirely contrary information.[17]

Hitler's Pope- Cornwell and *Constantine's Sword* – James Carroll, reveal undeniable Truth regarding the wartime Pope, Pius Pacelli's collaboration with the early Thirties Nazi regime, namely turning a blind eye and a deaf ear to Jewish persecution and resultant death camps. Pius IX, who reigned as pontiff from 1846 to 1878, referred to Jews as "dogs." according to Michael Parenti in a later chapter. On a special trip from Rome to Berlin, Pacelli overruled resistance by the cognizant German bishops themselves attempting to unsuccessfully deny Hitler's rise to Chancellorship and hence – Europe began aflame. One man, could have prevented Hitler's rise but he didn't and now he is beatified by then Pope Ratzinger and awaiting Sanctification. Author Jack Weatherford's research reveals a contrary perspective of Genghis Khan than what the bigoted, racist European writers attempted to reveal. Granted, the 13th century was not a time when nations gathered to promote Ethics, Reason and Humanitarian Conduct. No such slogans like 'Political Correctness' or a United Nations existed back then. It was a harsh world and battles were fought with no quarters asked. Entire cities were often burned to the ground and occupants as well. Slavery or death for the conquered, Caucasian or Asian, was too often inevitable. Genghis Khan, however, was highly unusual, he forbade torture and habitually offered peaceful terms, even offered potential enemies to join his forces to avoid warfare and share with the spoils of war, which many did. Until only recently has he been finally given due credit as the architect for Commerce from India to Western Europe besides initiating early Democratic principles emanating from his

---

17 Genghis Khan and the making of the Modern World. (New York : Crown, 2004).

'Great Law' implementation upon Mongolia and its captured territories. Not formal democracy, admittedly, which is little changed to this day as practiced by the Iroquois but Khan's contribution was more in the order of promulgated laws and conduct demanded from his occupying armies and later administrators. Thus he did progress toward a government unheard of in his time span. [Indeed, I consider this chapter as one of the most important in the book, for it gives we moderns some semblance of hope that somehow a similar leader can rise up from utter 'nothingness' and lead us out of the virtual slavery the '1%' is locking down upon us.] Our children, grandchildren and beyond are mortgaged. Isn't that proof enough? Yes, Dear Reader, the chapters wherein I mention the Iroquois gift of De-

Official court painting of Genghis Khan, now held at National Palace Museum in Taipei, Taiwan. *Unknown artist*

mocracy are as important, as well. That democratic feat lies hidden through sheer Eurocentric prejudice, covered up by egoist, supremacy primarily oriented by southern senators according to Jack Weatherford's *Indian Givers*. Always be thankful to three colonial statesmen who recognized what the Iroquois had and what new America needed. Jefferson, Franklin and Thomas Paine played their role in shaping world history for such a deeply important advancement for government. Realize also Democracy's steady dilution as a result of politicians who cater to the controlling new 'nobility.'

The (European) knights at their tournaments, in their finery, armor and emblems of ancestry, believed they were the foremost warriors in the world, while shabby appearing, un-uniformed Mongol warriors thought and proved otherwise. Mongol horses were small, but their riders were lightly clad and they moved with greater speed. These were hardy men who grew up on horses and hunting, making them better warriors than those who were raised in agricultural societies and cities. Their main weapon was the bow and arrow. And the Mongols of the early 1200s were highly disciplined, superbly coordinated, could endure for days on scant rations and their combat leadership brilliant in tactics. In a span of just 25 years, Genghis Khan's horsemen conquered a larger area and greater population than the Romans did in four centuries.

Fire Power

Like the Sioux, horse riding began at an early age. At 4 to 6 years usually, Mongol youth rode swiftly toward a swinging tethered leather ball target a foot or less in diameter to release child's arrows in rapid succession. The rider rode equestrian style (guiding their ponies with their knees allowing both hands to be free). Their mounts were significantly smaller than the captured U. S. Cavalry horses Sioux warriors would ride centuries later brandishing Winchester repeating rifles but the training was the same. The Mongolian bow, fired rapidly from mounted archers, decimated the foot infantry of the Europeans after the European knights were dispatched, usually taunted out of their ranks for a fatal chase. A common Mongolian tactic was to encourage the heavily armored knights by feinting retreat and fear. This was highly effective bait for the egocentric European. Safely away from the enemy archers and most usually a longer chase, the Mongolian ponies were better conditioned in comparison and able to speed far ahead where fresh mounts would be waiting. Riders would then return to the chase of tiring European war horses carrying a burdening load of European armor on the horse as well. Knights would be tumbling from their mounts before closure of the two forces. The rapid fire from the archers won every battle except one, and that battle was a numerical loss rather than a failure of Mongol combat effectiveness. Likewise the Sioux would have the same success utilizing similar Mongol battle tactics against the U. S. Cavalry.

Spiritual Beliefs

"The Mongols were illiterate, religiously shamanistic and perhaps no more than 700,000 in number." Thus is a description found at Google. (Genghis Khan). A more accurate term is that the Mongols were Religious/Spiritual followers who believed in a Supreme Higher Power, quite indescribable but did rule all things which, of course, was all that IT created. (In reference to their Creator concept, not He or She). Genghis Khan, not unlike the Sioux and especially, Chief Crazy Horse, would go off alone and isolate himself in vast nature and beseech to this Ultimate Mystery which the Sioux would later term similarly; Wakan Tanka, Great Mystery, Great Spirit, Benevolent Maker, Providing Creator of All. Accepting and recognizing one's Higher Power/Ultimate Creator as sheer

Mystery most often prevents disharmony or non-acceptance of other beliefs and faiths quite unlike the intolerant adherents of Organized Religion who too often demand that their Way is the Only Way.

Mongol language today is described as Altaic, a language unrelated to Chinese, derived from inhabitants in the Altay mountain range in western Mongolia. They were herdsmen on the grassy plains north of the Gobi Desert and south of Siberian forests. Before the year 1200, the Mongols were fragmented, moving about in small bands headed by a chief, or *khan,* and living in portable felt dwellings, called by the Mongols ' *ger.*' The Mongols endured frequent deprivations and sparse areas for grazing their animals. They often fought over turf, and during hard times they occasionally raided, interested in goods rather than bloodshed. They did not collect heads or scalps as trophies and did not notch wood to record their kills.

Early Life

Records of the Great Khan's early life are sparse and contradictory. He was likely born in 1162, though some sources give it as 1155 or 1165.

He had a hard childhood losing his father at age 9 and spent several years in slavery. After the death of his Father who had taken him to accept a position of servitude, his mother and siblings had a difficult time subsisting on roots mainly and small game that he and his brother had to hunt down in order to survive. These difficult times did not make him hard and cruel however, but instead made him respect the needy and even pass future laws for their protection as long as they were not enemies. Following a series of raids against his small band, one in which his wife was kidnapped but later rescued, he began to accumulate followers. From his late teens to age thirty-eight in 1200, the Mongol named Temujin (Temüjin) rose as *khan* over various families. He was a good manager, collecting people of talent. He was vassal to Ong Khan, titular head of a confederacy better organized than other Mongol clans. Temujin joined Ong Khan in a military campaign against Tatars to their east, and following the success of this campaign Ong Khan declared Temujin his adoptive son and heir. Temujin delegated authority based on merit and loyalty, rather than family ties. He would even have his mother adopt orphans from a conquered tribe, bringing them into his family. These political innovations inspired great loyalty among the conquered people, making Temujin stronger with each victory.

Ong Khan's natural son, Senggum (Senggüm), known for his cruelty to the conquered - horse dragging captives and boiling them alive - had been expecting to succeed his father and plotted to assassinate Temujin. Temujin learned of this, and those loyal to Temujin defeated those loyal to Senggum. Later Ong Khan's plot to assassinate Temujin failed leading to his defeat. Temujin was now established as the head of what had been Ong Khan's coalition. And in 1206, at the age of 42, Temujin took the title Universal Ruler, which translates to *Genghis Khan*, and he addressed his joyous supporters thanking them for their help and their loyalty. His treatment of those he subdued led to swelling ranks of loyal followers. The united Mongols soon defeated the neighboring Tatars and Jurkins, and Temujin Khan assimilated their people rather than following steppe custom of looting them and leaving. Such was the key to the so-called 'Mongolian Horde' which would eventually sweep into Europe.

Yassa – The Body of Law

Like peoples elsewhere, Genghis Khan's subjects saw themselves at the center of the universe, the greatest of people and favored by the gods. They justified Genghis Khan's success in warfare by claiming that he was the rightful master not only over the "peoples of the felt tent" but the entire world. Genghis Khan continued organizing. He improved his military organization, which was also to serve as a mobile political bureaucracy, and he broke up what was left of old enemy tribes, leaving as ethnically homogeneous only those tribes that had demonstrated loyalty to him. He created a body of law that he was to work on throughout his life. As an incentive for absolute obedience and following his rule of law, the Yassa code, Temujin promised civilians and soldiers wealth from future possible war spoils. As he defeated rival tribes, he did not drive away enemy soldiers and abandon the rest. Instead, he took the conquered tribe under his protection and integrated its members into his own tribe.

The kidnapping of women had caused feuding among the Mongols, and, as a teenager, Temujin had suffered from the kidnapping of his young wife, Borte. After devoting himself to rescuing her, he made it law that there was to be no kidnapping of women.[*] He declared all children legitimate, regardless of the mother's marital status. He made it law that

---

[*]Underlining submitted by author.

no woman would be sold into marriage. The stealing of animals had caused dissension among the Mongols, and Genghis Khan made it a capital offense. A lost animal was to be returned to its owner, and taking lost property as one's own was to be considered thievery and a capital offense. Genghis Khan regulated hunting -- a winter activity -- improving the availability of meat for everyone. He introduced record keeping, taking advantage of his move years before to have his native language put into writing. He created official seals. He created a supreme officer of the law, who was to collect and preserve all judicial decisions, to oversee the trials of all those charged with wrongdoing and to have the power to issue death sentences. He created order in his realm that strengthened it and his ability to expand. As stated earlier, he was far ahead of other realms and certainly far above the numerous materialistic, pleasure seeking addicted Dictators that we are familiar with today.

Conquests in Northern China

In 1210, the Jin dynastry of Jurchen people, who ruled that part of northern China that included Beijing, sent a delegation to Genghis Khan demanding Mongol submission as vassals. The Jin dynasty controlled the flow of goods along the Silk Road, and defying them meant a lack of access to those goods. Genghis Khan and the Mongols discussed the matter and chose war. Genghis, according to the scholar Jack Weatherford, prayed alone on a mountain, bowing down and stating his case to "his supernatural guardians," describing the grievances, the tortures and killings that generations of his people had suffered at the hands of the Jurchen. And he pleaded that he had not sought war against the Jurchen and had not initiated the quarrel.

In 1211, Genghis Khan and his army attacked. The Jurchen (Jin) dynasty had a large and effective army but they were hard pressed by both the Mongols and by a border war with the Tangut. They were also under attack by Chinese from south of the Yangzi River, the Southern Song emperor wishing to take advantage of the Jurchen-Mongol conflict to liberate northern China. But the Jurchen drove the Chinese armies into retreat. The Mongols were benefiting from China having failed during the previous century to make itself a strong military power. They benefited too from the Jurchen (Jin) dynastry ruling conquered people. The Mongols used divide and conquer tactics, using benevolence toward those who sided with them and terror and bloodshed against those who did not. They ravaged the countryside, gathering information and booty and driving populations in front of them, clogging the roads and trapping the Jurchen within their cities, where the Jurchen (Jin) dynasty was subject to revolts. The Mongols used conscripted labor in attacking cities and in operating their newly acquired Chinese siege engines.

Against the Jurchen the Mongols had an advantage in diet, which included a lot of meat, milk and yogurt, and they could miss a day or two of eating better than Jurchen soldiers, who ate grains. Genghis Khan and his army overran Beijing and pushed into the heartland of northern China. Military success helped as people acquired the impression that Genghis Khan had the Mandate of Heaven and that fighting against him was fighting heaven itself. The Jurchen emperor recognized Mongol authority and agreed to pay tribute.

After six years of fighting the Jurchen, Genghis Khan returned to Mongolia, leaving one of his best generals in charge of Mongol positions. Returning with Genghis Khan and his Mongols were engineers who had become a permanent part of their army, and there were captive musicians, translators, doctors and scribes, camels and wagonloads of goods. Among the goods were silk, including silken rope, cushions, blankets, robes, rugs, wall hangings, porcelain, iron kettles, armor, perfumes, jewelry, wine, honey, medicines, bronze, silver and gold, and much else. And goods from China would now come in a steady flow.

The Mongols were happy to be back from China, their homeland higher in elevation, less humid and cooler. As eaters of meat and sparsely populated they felt superior to people in northern China, but they liked what China had to offer, and at home there was change. The continuing flow of goods from China had to be administered and properly distributed, and buildings had to be built to store the goods. Success in war was changing the Mongols - as it had the Romans and the Arabs.

Into Azerbaijan, Armenia and Eastern Europe

While Genghis Khan was consolidating his conquests in Persia and Afghanistan, a force of 40,000 Mongol horsemen pushed through Azerbaijan and Armenia. They defeated Georgian crusaders, captured a Genoese trade-fortress in the Crimea and spent the winter along the coast of the Black Sea. As they were headed back home they met 80,000 warriors led by Prince Mstitslav of Kiev. The battle of Kalka River (1223) commenced. Staying out of range of the crude weapons of peasant infantry, and with better bows than opposing archers, they devastated the prince's standing army. Facing the prince's cavalry, they faked a retreat, drawing the armored cavalry forward, taking advantage of the vanity and over-confidence of the mounted aristocrats. Lighter and more mobile, they strung out and tired the pursuers and then attacked (with fresh horses from a pre-planned staging area); routed and killed them. The Sioux also with superior fire power in America (their Winchesters) would successfully employ similar strategy centuries later.

In 1225, Genghis Khan returned to Mongolia. He now ruled everything between the Caspian Sea and Beijing. He looked forward to the Mongols benefits of caravan trade and drawing tribute from agricultural peoples in the west and east. He created an efficient pony express system. Wanting no divisions rising from religion, he declared freedom of religion throughout his empire. Favoring order and tax producing prosperity, he forbade troops and local officials to abuse people. Soon again, Genghis Khan was at war. He believed that the Tangut were not living up to their obligations to his empire. In 1227, around the age of sixty-five while leading the fighting against the Tangut, Genghis Khan, it is said, fell off his horse and died.

In terms of square miles conquered, Genghis Khan had been the greatest conqueror of all time -- his empire four times larger than the empire of Alexander the Great. The Mongol nation believed that he had been the greatest man of all time and a man sent from heaven. Among the Mongols he was known as the Holy Warrior, and not unlike the Jews, who continued to see hope in a conquering king (messiah) like David, Mongols were to continue to believe that one day Genghis Khan would rise again and lead his people to new victories.

Into Afghanistan and Persia

Tribes as far away as Kazakhstan and Kyrgyzstan heard about the Great Khan, and overthrew their Buddhist rulers in order to join his growing empire. By 1219, Genghis Khan ruled from northern China to the Afghan border, and Siberia to the border of Tibet. Genghis Khan wanted trade and goods, including new weapons, for his nation. He sought a trade alliance with the powerful Khwarizm Empire, which controlled Central Asia from Afghanistan to the Black Sea. Sultan Muhammad II agreed, but then murdered the first Mongol trade convoy of 450 merchants, stealing their goods. The sultan there claimed that spies were in the caravan. Genghis Khan sent envoys. The sultan received them by having the chief of the envoys killed and the beards of the others burned, and he sent the other envoys back to Genghis Khan. Before the end of

that year, the wrathful Khan had captured every Khwarizm city, adding
lands from Turkey to Russia to his realm.

In retaliation, sending his army westward in the coldest of months
the Mongols rode across the desert to Transoxiana with no baggage,
slowing to the pace of merchants before appearing as warriors in front of
the smaller towns of the sultan's empire. His strategy was to frighten the
townspeople into surrendering without battle, benefiting his own troops,
whose lives he valued. Those frightened into surrender were spared violence. Those who resisted were slaughtered as an example for others,
which sent many fleeing and spreading panic from the first towns to the
city of Bukhara. People in Bukhara opened the city's gates to the Mongols
and surrendered. Genghis Khan told them that they, the common people,
were not at fault, that high-ranking people among them had committed
great sins that inspired God to send him and his army as punishment.
The sultan's capital city, Samarkand, surrendered. The sultan's army surrendered, and the sultan fled.

Genghis Khan and his army pushed more deeply into what had been
the sultan's empire -- into Afghanistan and then into Persia. It is said that
the caliph in Baghdad was hostile toward the sultan and supported Genghis Khan, sending him a regiment of European crusaders who had been
his prisoners. Genghis Khan, having no need for infantry, freed them,
with those making it to Europe spreading the first news of the Mongol
conquests.

Genghis Khan had 100,000 to 125,000 horsemen, with Uighur and
Turkic allies, engineers and Chinese doctors -- a total of from 150,000 to
200,000 men. To show their submission, those his army approached offered food, and Genghis Khan's force guaranteed them protection. Some
cities surrendered without fighting. In cities the Mongols were forced to
conquer, Genghis Khan divided the civilians by profession. He drafted
the few who were literate and anyone who could speak various languages.
Those who had been the city's most rich and powerful he wasted no time
in killing, remembering that the rulers he had left behind after conquering
the Tangut and Jurchen had betrayed him soon after his army had with-
drawn.

Torture

Lest we Americans forget. Modern America's advocate for torture
was the former Vice-President Dick Cheney who amassed a fortune
through his insider buying as Secretary of Defense primarily. He was also

a key 'Decider' in the Bush Administration. Egypt under the un-elected 'President' Mubarak was a collaborator of American captured and detained "Security Suspects' who were sent to Egyptian prisons for torture sessions.

It is said that the Genghis Khan's military did not torture, mutilate or maim. But his enemies are reported as having done so. Captured Mongols were dragged through streets and killed for sport and to entertain city residents. Gruesome displays of stretching, emasculation, belly cutting and hacking to pieces was something European rulers were using to discourage potential enemies -- as was soon to happen to William Wallace on orders from England's King Edward I. The Mongols merely slaughtered, and preferred to do so from a distance.

Politics and economics

> [As mentioned earlier,] the Mongol Empire was governed by a civilian and military code, called the Yassa, created by Genghis Khan. The Mongol Empire did not emphasize the importance of ethnicity and race in the administrative realm, instead adopting an approach grounded in meritocracy. The exception was the role of Genghis Khan and his family. The Mongol Empire was one of the most ethnically and culturally diverse empires in history, as befitted its size. Many of the empire's nomadic inhabitants considered themselves *Mongols* in military and civilian life, including Turks, Mongols, and others and included many diverse Khans of various ethnicities as part of the Mongol Empire.
>
> There were tax exemptions for religious figures and, to some extent, teachers and doctors. The Mongol Empire practiced religious tolerance to a large degree because Mongol tradition had long held that religion was a very personal concept, and not subject to law or interference. [18]

Various Mongol tribes were Buddhist, Muslim, Shamanist or Christian. Religious tolerance was thus a well-established concept on the Asian steppe.

> Modern Mongolian historians say that towards the end of his life, Genghis Khan attempted to create a civil state under the Great Yassa that would have established the legal equality of all individuals, including women. However, there is no con-

---

[18] http://en.wikipedia.org/wiki/Genghis_Khan

temporary evidence of this, or of the lifting of discriminatory policies towards sedentary peoples such as the Chinese. Women played a relatively important role in Mongol Empire and in family, for example Töregene Khatun was briefly in charge of the Mongol Empire when next male Khagan was being chosen. Modern scholars refer to the alleged policy of encouraging trade and communication as the Pax Mongolica (Mongol Peace).

Genghis Khan realized that he needed people who could govern cities and states conquered by him. He also realized that such administrators could not be found among his Mongol people because they were nomads and thus had no experience governing cities. For this purpose Genghis Khan invited a Khitan prince, Chu'Tsai, who worked for the Jin and had been captured by the Mongol army after the Jin Dynasty were defeated. Jin had captured power by displacing Khitan. Genghis told Chu'Tsai, who was a lineal descendant of Khitan rulers, that he had avenged Chu'Tsai's forefathers. Chu'Tsai responded that his father served the Jin Dynasty honestly and so did he; he did not consider his own father his enemy, so the question of revenge did not apply. Genghis Khan was very impressed by this reply. Chu'Tsai administered parts of the Mongol Empire and became a confidant of the successive Mongol Khans.[19]

Commerce

He emerged to alter the then known civilized world significantly in the field of commerce and which became his primary vision- opening up commerce mainly through removing severe superstitious restrictions often generated by the various organized religions of the times. Jewish, Nestorian Catholic, Buddhist, and Islam –which were prominent. He was democratic however; all of these faiths were represented as generals or commanders of his various army units. His other passion was of course unifying Mongolia with the domain his thousands of warriors captured all the way to the gates of Western Europe. In Eastern Europe, his armies defeated the many adversaries they confronted. According to Jack Weatherford's book, *Genghis Khan*, based mostly upon material offered to him from modern Mongolia's archives, he discarded the idea of invading Western Germany, France and Great Britain primarily because they had

[19] Ibid.

little enough wealth (commerce), in his estimate to be worthy of engaging his army in the field. As mentioned his mounted archers riding equestrian style upon their swift ponies with both hands free easily dispatched the bit and rein holding Hungarian, Russian and German knights in Eastern Europe whose supporting archers could not be mounted. Firepower, most often wins! Yet, as time went on and the Mongol armies returned (They did not retreat.) to Mongolia or for southern missions into China, Western Europe enjoyed a greater opening of commerce with other trading nations never before enjoyed.

Some of the new commercial laws Genghis Khan enforced were the rights of women to work as merchants, removal of religious based restrictive selling and buying taboos, tariff removal, and outlawing restrictions and impediments enforced upon certain classes of societies within his realm. A concerted attempt to eradicate caravan banditry was no doubt one of his greater commercial accomplishments for that era. The merchant class became elevated and artisans were free to travel and work their arts and crafts outside of their birthplaces. Caravan routes were policed and bandits hunted down and executed. Courts were created to hear and settle disputes. Mongolian law was applied equally from the lowest herder to the nobility. Religious clerics, mullahs, clergy and priests were considered exempt from capital punishment. Lawbreakers were punished but torture was forbidden. Organized Religion was allowed but it could not subvert or claim first allegiance over the Domain of Mongolia. He emphasized to his generals and field commanders of various faiths, that their first allegiance was to Mongolia and then to their God concept! Obviously such a command was not disputed. God or the Higher Power was revered and respected but Genghis Khan, who remember, went out in solitude to beseech the Higher Power as did the American Indian leaders who are of Mongolian extract; the Supreme leader held an attitude that such a Higher Power didn't need human's worship. It was obviously the Supreme Provider of all and so powerful; what benefit could mere human convey upon it? Thoughts of allegiance in this world, therefore, was to Mongolia as a whole-- all dutifully working together for greater harmony which cultural characteristics have carried into present China today. I find myself not adverse to such a pragmatic consideration and would much rather have a leader so devout that they would go out for several days alone spiritually respecting much more deeply, in my opinion, than an hour's charade on the seventh day. Our sun dances last for four days without food and water under a hot July/August Badlands sun while we beseech to our Higher Power concept thanking IT that we live. Needless to say, Commerce flowed freely in early medieval times, not only westward to Europe but south to the Chinese and on into the Mid-east and India.

Modern Terrorism, however, must be dealt with in a more violent manner, my opinion for we have fanatics involved. What? With human so religiously inebriated that they get so carried away to blow themselves up among harmless innocents? Communication will never reach these extremists.

It goes without saying that Organized Religion can be extremely disruptive to a smooth running, efficient Democracy. G. K. would not tolerate its interference nor does modern China nor present Mongolia today yet citizens are allowed their religious/spiritual participation – as long as they do not proselytize. Wherein Religion should truly respect 'Mystery,' fanatically, zealous human has proven repeatedly that Religion is too often dangerous for the existence of True Democracy and spawns poor, narrow-minded political candidates. We simply can observe the political candidates in the 2012 and 2016 primary presidential election process. Which are more inept? Why has Donald Trump risen so popularly and is not classified as a politician. No doubt the public is finally awakening. In 2012, Three candidates; a Congresswoman, a former governor and a former Senator all were elected to their office mainly through a single themed religious issue. They were obviously ill equipped to administer a much broader form of direly needed policy making based on far more important issues. Congresswoman Bachmann of Minnesota even called for Organized Religion to be a major portion of national policy. Not unlike presidential aspirant Ted Cruz, four GOP Primary years later, she also advocated an abolishment of Church/State Separation. The horrendous damage such a political philosophy can wreak upon freedom seeking citizens is evident in Congress today. We are becoming like the splintered parties of Europe.

CHAPTER 5
LEADERSHIP

Four great leaders would come to the fore among the Sioux after the entry of the nineteenth century: [20]

Red Cloud (Makpiyah Luta)

Crazy Horse (Tahshuunka Witko)

Sitting Bull (Tatanka Iyotanka)

Black Elk (Hehaka Sapa)

All were spiritual men as mentioned was Genghis Khan. Also mentioned before, Mongolian tactics delivered from their 'archer cavalry' were far superior to European strategy. 'Fire Power' – the deliverance of overwhelming weaponry - is a key ingredient for victorious battle which the Sioux would later pick up on utilizing Mongolian spawned tactics unbeknown to them. Maybe it was in their Mongolian genes and of course the availability supplied by the Winchester rifle company who offered the best cavalry weapon of its times.

The attacking Sioux rider fired a 12 shot repeater Winchester lever action rifle held with both hands for accuracy from a superbly conditioned mount that could be steered without reins by the rider's balance and knees. Sioux horses were well adjusted to gunfire from frequent buffalo hunting, while cavalry horses were not and often threw their riders in fear when engaged in initial gunfire with the Sioux and Cheyenne. The

---

[20] This material is from, *Crazy Horse and Chief Red Cloud*. Four Directions Publishing, Hill City, SD, 2004).

Sioux/Cheyenne horse and rider was too overwhelming for the single shot, 'Sharps .45 seventy' rifles that the U. S. Army utilized. This single shot rifle was also employed by Sioux riders not possessing the preferred Winchester due to its abundant availability from repeatedly defeated Army forces starting with the earlier battling Chief Red Cloud. The .45 – 70 would also jam its second fired shot often on a hot day due to its copper casing which would swell due to fired powder heat. After the breech would cool it could be extracted but not immediately during the midst of battle.

Winchester was turned down by a corrupt war department choosing to be bought off by the competing Springfield Arms Company, maker of an inferior rifle. Red Cloud's Sioux warrior's obtained the rifle through eager traders.

Why should one study Sioux leadership in order to seek knowledge regarding Spirituality and hence a more thorough avoidance/reduction of Terrorism? Fairly simple! Each man's track record speaks for itself. They were spiritual living examples and not religious followers. The four men on Mt. Rushmore led exemplary lives. George Washington could have easily become a military dictator but chose not to. Jefferson believed strongly in separation of church and state and encouraged Benjamin Franklin and Thomas Paine to study the non-religious but spiritual influenced Iroquois for their government that offered incorporated freedoms that eventually swept through Europe as well no thanks to deadly, blocking religious hindrance. Lincoln fought a war to free the slaves and Teddy Roosevelt clamped down on corporate greed that is running amuck within these modern politicians who are owned by the 1 % which we have now. Of course, it helped that the Native Americans' surroundings were of Creator's Nature and not Nature covering steel and concrete. Does the

White Man not tell of his military engagements to expound upon leaders back in biblical times? The lives of the Sioux leaders may be found to be just as interesting, and for many readers, more so. The caliber of a nation's moral and ethical leadership guidance should reflect the high degree of expectation an all truthful exhibiting Higher Power would want from mere human – would it not? Weatherford tells of the deep spirituality Genghis Khan held for his concept of his Higher Power. As stated earlier, Genghis Khan would at times disappear for several days alone into the high hills of a Mongolian hinterland to beseech to his concept of Creator. Obviously, such solitude helped create a democratic leader unusual for his time despite the false claims and accusations by the errant vilifying Eurocentric writers of later times.

By studying the four Sioux leaders, we will immerse ourselves deeper into the 'natural' living and nature blended mind and hence come closer to honing our own abilities. These men demonstrate honor, bravery, self-sacrifice, decision making and always kept a deep spirituality. Example is a powerful teacher. In these perilous environmental times, our country is in dire need of such leaders. If we look at these modern political leaders in America they are at the bottom of the frequent public polls. Not one single military veteran has run for the highest office if we look at the recent presidential primaries. Why? Because Congress has a history of financial self-promotion and continues to pass such self-promoting laws besides absolving themselves from certain tax and duty burdens imposed upon the populace. None of them immerse themselves in Creator's soothing, calming, educating mystical Nature.

Life is not a pharmaceutical supermarket wherein one can purchase a quick-fix to serenity and happiness. At least not from what I have observed. Nature does not condone or allow the encapsulated, 'ready-made' approach to life's journey. Isn't it obvious that we are here to 'prove ourselves' over the long haul for hopefully a higher purpose in a Beyond? This holding is not my exclusive thought, by no means. It seems to be a universally accepted viewpoint. The danger laden attempts through drugs or alcohol and/or over-materialism, greed and selfishness demonstrate the futility of human's foolish short-cuts to real happiness, character building, exemplary track record and true confidence let alone striving to protect the planet. We do have a planet to save! And now we have the added burden of overcoming Modern Terrorism besides exponential Over-Population, Planetary Heating, Climate Change, runaway Atomic Weaponry, too much or too little Water and Gone Resources – the major malefactors threatening human's survival.

Warrior Chiefs

Three of the above were warrior chiefs. Their bravery upon the field of battle was unquestioned. That means that they were willing to risk their very lives in the field of combat to protect their tribal constituents. Very few of the Congressional members in Congress are combat military veterans despite the many wars America becomes involved in allowing them many opportunities to volunteer for the military and go out into the field of battle. The presidency rarely has a leader who has been a combat experienced veteran.

The Sioux leaders sun danced, vision quested, sweat lodged and smoked the sacred pipe to beseech to their Creator and Creator's Six Powers. Chief Red Cloud was known to pull back his troops in the midst of a military engagement and ride away to participate in the annual sun dance. Obviously his commitment to God was more important than fighting with other men. No American or European military leader would ever think of doing such an act. Their culture would not condone it.

Chief Red Cloud, Oglala-Teton Lakota Sioux, (1821- 1909).

Red Cloud had an Army fort surrounded and was starving out the occupants. It was in the hot summer of the 1860s out on the Great Plains. The occupants were out of water and suffering from dehydration. No re-supply was able to rescue the doomed occupants and they were planning to surrender and capitulate.

The next morning Chief Red Cloud's warriors were gone. Yes, simply vanished. The fort commander sent out a rider upon the strongest horse to summon help and supplies. A detachment hurriedly went to a water point - a creek that still bore precious water. The soldiers rejoiced and lived.

Years later, Chief Red Cloud was asked why he left a sure victory. He calmly stated, "I had a date with God. That is more important than killing men." A Sun Dance had been scheduled to meet with other tribal bands to hold a Thanksgiving ceremony to their concept of the Higher Power.

Sun Dance

The primary ceremony for the Sioux was the annual Sun Dance which is mentioned by most all past writers in regard to Chief Red Cloud, Chief Crazy Horse and Chief Sitting Bull. I do not believe any of these writers had the depth to explore why this was such an important event to stop fighting their campaigns or at least placing their combat on hold. Something this important would certainly seem to bear some scrutiny, some curiosity, some probing; would not one think? Did not any of these leaders go into the Sun Dance before their Creator concept and ask Wakan Tanka to spare them one more time, one more battle, feed them one more winter, bring the Wahshichu to the treaty table? Would not these issues be heavy on their minds? I have participated as a Sun Dance Pledger in six sun dances. Many sun dancers have taken part in many more sun dances than I but as a writer, I believe I have taken part in at least six more sun dances than most all the rest of the related subject writers of Native extraction, with the exception of my fellow authors, Manny Two Feathers and Dr. Chuck Ross.

Chief Red Cloud was born in 1821; therefore he bore the brunt of the major fighting with the Army during the turbulent 1860s. He was the Commander in Chief for five years of constant battle from 1862 to 1867 although he began fighting the American Army while in his thirties. His superb fighting tactics were dependent upon well-conditioned, well trained mounts whose riders repeatedly defeated the U. S. Cavalry culminating in his winning the famous Treaty of 1868. At present one billion dollars is within a bank endorsed to the Sioux Nation because of the fighting efforts, mostly of the Oglala and Sichangu tribes. Red cloud and Spotted Tail (Sichangu) had their warriors train their mounts to be ridden equestrian style. This meant that the rider guides the horse with his knees and weight shifting, allowing both hands to be free: Such an advantage for aiming a rifle. The U. S. Cavalry clumsily tried to aim their rifles while mounted with only one arm free while the other had to guide the horse with bit and reins. No wonder Genghis Khan swept through the armies of Europe with his mounted archer cavalry riding the same method, letting loose a hail of arrows at close range. Hence the name, 'Mongolian style': to ride a horse with both hands free. Maybe it was the Mongolian blood within the Sioux that allowed them to readily adapt to the horse and use the Mongolian battle tactics so successfully in less than a hundred years of experience with the horse. Why the American generals could never adapt to this proven strategy is easy to understand: sheer, foolish, disastrous Eurocentric ego. Eventually the Army had to submit to the burning down of their three forts on the Bozeman Trail because of Red Cloud's leadership tactics and strategy. Sioux horse herds grew significantly under Red Cloud as did their weaponry and ammunition supply which was mostly captured from the U.S. Cavalry. This solid fact, historians are loath to admit. How else could the Sioux mount so many warriors and effectively arm them?

The signing of the Treaty was supposed to guarantee to the Indians that the land west of the Missouri River to and including the Black Hills of South Dakota whose western boundaries include into the state of Wyoming; North to the Cannonball river (North Dakota); and as far south to the Nebraska Sand Hills; this land would remain to the Sioux: for as long as the grass will grow, for as long as the rivers will flow and for as long as the Sioux dead lie buried. This meant forever to the Indian and was thus their battle won grant under Chief Red Cloud for ceasing to fight (and thoroughly beating) the U. S. Army.

At this point I have to add one more battle tactic of the highly skilled chief. He had Sioux youth ride the warrior's battle mounts every day to keep them exercised and in top physical shape. Army horses were no match for such firmly conditioned Sioux mounts, many of which were captured Army horses; no doubt probably the majority of them. These horses were also well adjusted to gunfire from the many buffalo hunts they experienced (and enjoyed, no different than the energetic reaction we experience with good hunting dogs in modern day shooting of pheasant and quail.). Native mounts did not throw their riders, bolt and run at the first volleys of attack as did many of the inexperienced Army mounts. Believing that the U.S. Government would keep their word regarding the Treaty of 1868, Red Cloud took an oath that he would not fight again.

Chief Sitting Bull, Hunkpapa-Teton Lakota Sioux (1831- 1890).

Sitting Bull of the Teton Saones (Northern Lakota) was born 10 years after Red Cloud – 1831. After many battles with neighboring tribes, mostly Crows, his bravery and daring led him to become chief of the Hunkpapa tribe of the seven tribe Tetons. The Oglala and Sichangu were also members of the Teton group but further south upon the Great Plains, still teeming with buffalo. Sitting Bull was so brave, notably his specialty was to crawl daringly into enemy campsites at night trailing his own mount where the horse herds were and steal many of them if not driving the whole herd off. This feat would result in a sure death warrant, should they become discovered and/or captured by patrolling night sentries.

Among the old-time Sioux, there were two kinds of chiefs. The Nacha was a war chief who was in command of the group of warriors only when they were outside the camp on a war party. While in the camp, he was just one of the boys like anyone else. The other kind of chief was the Itanchan, or camp chief who ruled in the camp and was responsible for the welfare of the people. Sitting Bull was both kinds of chiefs in one. A chief, Itanchan, or camp chief, had to have a great heart. He had to be generous, always understanding, and above all spite or selfishness. He had to keep his temper always and had to constantly share with those who, he knew, could never repay him. Sitting Bull was all of this and more. He was a spiritual leader as well as he was a military leader.

Stanley Vestal (Author) said Sitting Bull was "A man who was a peacemaker in the camps, and never quarreled. A generous man, who was always capturing horses from the enemy and giving them away, a man who constantly shared his kill with the poor and helpless when hunting, a man who could not bear to see one of the Hunkpapa Lakota unhappy. Sitting Bull was an affable, jocular, pleasant man, always making jokes and telling stories, keeping the people in a good humor, a sociable man who had tried to please everybody all his life, and was not in the least haughty or arrogant--in spite of his many honors. A man who . . . was devoutly religious, whose prayers were strong, and who generally got what he prayed for."

Toward the end of his days, he was to write in a letter one of his convictions that he had carried all his life, ". . . all Indians pray to God for life, and try to find a good road, and do nothing wrong in their life. This is what we want, and to pray to God . . . who made us all." He was known to state frequently, "I pray to God every day."

In the beginning, the idea of making war against the non-Indians and the non-Indian soldiers never entered his mind. It was only later when the military became a threat to the land he had fought to take, and a threat to his people, that he did turn his fighting forces against the soldiers, and this was out of sheer self- defense. It was, to his way of thinking, the only way to solve his problem of protecting his people and his country. The time would come when he would have not only his traditional Indian enemies to hold off, but strong military forces of soldiers.

General Sibley

In 1863 Sitting Bull had his first skirmish with the Army. After a Mormon cow incident wherein some Sioux killed and butchered a wandering cow belonging to some Mormons, a migrating religious sect, U. S. soldiers over retaliated by killing some Indians over the incident. These were Oglala and they promptly retaliated by killing the lieutenant commanding and his men. The Hunkpapa usually gave the Army troops a wide berth afterwards and fought only in self-defense. The chief ranged from northern Wyoming across northern South Dakota to the Missouri River and had been relatively free of contacts with the emigrants and military. Because of drought conditions, he had to hunt east of the Missouri in 1863. General Sibley, who had put down the Dakota Sioux in the Minnesota uprising, was out patrolling the same area. Sibley, without warning, opened fire on a Hunkpapa hunting party. In retaliation, Sitting Bull attacked Sibley's wagon train at Appel Creek. To show Sibley he was unafraid of him, Sitting Bull rode in within easy range of the Army rifle fire and returned with a government mule.

General Sully

In 1864, the Hunkpapa again faced the U. S. Army under General Sully who was all the way into Wyoming attempting to run down a large group of Yanktonai and Santee Sioux who were fleeing Minnesota. This group attached themselves to Sitting Bull's warriors and attracted a running battle wherein the Hunkpapa had their first taste of cannon fire. They wound up having their camp, including the tipis and winter's supply of meat, destroyed. The soldiers then turned back eastward leaving the Hunkpapa the task of working extra hard to get in a new supply of meat, clothing and make new tipis for the coming winter.

The following year, Sitting Bull made General Sully pay dearly by chasing him all the way across Wyoming, this time westward from the Little Missouri River crossing clear to the Yellowstone River. Sully lost hundreds of horses and mules due to the extreme drought and grasshoppers destroying the grass at the time. It came out later that the soldiers had thought that none of them would survive the hunger, thirst and attacking Sioux. They barely survived by reaching the Yellowstone River where steamboat supplies saved them. Sitting Bull broke off his attack and went home feeling some retaliation against Sully for destroying his tipis the year before.

Sitting Bull's skeptical; wait-and-see attitude after the Laramie treaty in 1868 was fully justified only four years later. In 1872 Colonel O. S. Stanley commanded a military escort for a surveying party of the Northern Pacific Railroad. The survey placed the railroad on the south bank of the Yellowstone River, in clear violation of the Laramie Treaty. Stanley promptly had a run-in with Chief Gall and his warriors, and when word of this reached Sitting Bull at his camp on the Powder River, he immediately rode out with a large party of his Hunkpapa, accompanied by Oglala, Minicoujou, Sans Arc, and Blackfeet Sioux warriors. He tangled with Major E. M. Baker and his four hundred men in the valley of the Yellowstone below Pryor Creek on August 14, 1872. Losses were relatively light on both sides, but Sitting Bull had made his point that no one was to come into his territory without being hit. The most notable feature of this battle occurred when Sitting Bull got off his horse, gathered together his war pipe and smoking equipment, and calmly walked up to within easy rifle range of the soldiers. Here he sat down, lit his pipe, and smoked the tobacco all the way down to the bottom of the pipe, with the bullets of the soldiers whizzing past his ears and kicking up dust all around him. When he had finished, he quietly cleaned the pipe, put it back into its bag, and sauntered back to his own lines. Having shown his lack of fear of the soldiers, he called his men together and went home.

Lt. Colonel Custer

The years of 1873 and 1874 were relatively quiet, as far as fighting was concerned, but Sitting Bull was busy, hunting and supplying food for his people. He kept a wary eye toward the east, however, because he still had his wait-and-see attitude. Again, his suspicions were justified when Lt. Col. George Custer led a large force of over 1,100 men and 110 wagons to explore the Black Hills in 1874. This was in clear violation of all the treaties and resulted in large numbers of non-Indians filtering into the Black Hills area - many of them lured there by the reports of gold that Custer had brought out. Sitting Bull knew that the non-Indians were closing in around him and that a showdown would have to be coming soon.

The Unrealistic Order

The next year, 1875, found Sitting Bull and his people in their winter camp at the mouth of the Powder River. He and his Hunkpapa had camped here for years during the winter, but further treaty modifications had placed the western boundaries of Indian Territory just east of the Black Hills which is now in Western South Dakota. For this reason, Sitting Bull and his people, in the eyes of the military, were off reservation boundaries and were, therefore, 'hostile'. The government had long been annoyed that the various tribes would wander off reservation boundaries in order to hunt. On the basis of a report filed with the Commissioner of Indian Affairs by a U. S. Indian Inspector named E. C. Watkins, in the fall of that very year, November 1875, the Secretary of the Interior issued an order that all the bands had to return to their respective reservations by the end of January 31, 1876 or the Army would come after them.

This was an unrealistic order. No one including the Army could move during that very brutal winter. Most bands never received the message because no one dared travel or rather could not travel once the winter snows came fiercely in December and way into March. General Crook attempted to march his troops out of Ft. Laramie in that month and barely made it back by eating his mules and horses let alone receiving a severe mauling from Crazy Horse and Cheyenne allies.

Sitting Bull's Little Big Horn Battle Dream.

Sitting Bull had been far to the north of the Oglala and Sichangu during the heavy fighting in the 1860s. He would stay out of the 60's era conflicts in the southern Dakota Territory and North Platte/Powder River battles but he would be as mentioned, fighting his own with the Army, first General Sibley and then General Sully. It would be after the signing of the Treaty of 1868 and the breaking of that treaty's agreements that the northern Tetons, Hunkpapa and Minicoujou mainly, would rise up with the southern Oglala and Sichangu.

Sitting Bull's spirituality is highly exemplary; he prayed almost daily and had powerful prophetic dreams. About a week before the famous Little Big Horn battle, at the huge encampment where the attack would soon take place, Sitting Bull had a powerful dream of soldiers falling into the camp upside down. This vision predicted that enemy soldiers would come and be defeated as the dream symbolized by having them fall upside down.

The Battle of the Little Big Horn was fought. Sitting Bull's powerful dream, the prediction, was quite accurate. After that battle, Sitting Bull and many of his Hunkpapa finally ended up in Canada in 1877, but they were very unhappy there. The Canadian Mounted Police (the red coats) watched them too closely and, in 1881, after four years there, Sitting Bull decided to return to his reservation. He became a friend of Buffalo Bill Cody and even joined his Wild West show that toured the East for a period of time.

Chief Crazy Horse, Oglala-Teton Lakota (c.1842 – 1877)

Twenty years (approximately) after Red Cloud's birth, Crazy Horse, also an Oglala would be born. Crazy Horse was renowned for isolating himself in Creator's Nature for days and nights. I would assume that Crazy Horse was Vision Questing to Creator. He shunned publicity or the public limelight despite his fame and military prowess. Hence, no photographs exist of him unlike Chief Red Cloud and Sitting Bull. During the 60's era fighting with the Army, Crazy Horse would be a young warrior under Red Cloud's command. He counted over eighty coups during the earlier era of tribal combat. His rise to acclamation as one of the greatest of warriors was culminated with his victories in his last three battles with the Army during the spring and summer of 1876. A coup can be described as one committing a brave deed or action during the heat of battle. Often, a coup would be an act of extreme bravery as in reaching out and touching an enemy and not killing him.

The Battle of the Little Big Horn in what is now the state of Montana is regarded as the greatest battle of the Sioux. Several thousand warriors fought back against a foolish attack by an egocentric George Armstrong Custer, commander of less than 700 soldiers and Crow Indian scouts. Many historians believe he had his sights set on the Presidency of the United States. By 'Riding through the Sioux Nation' which he occasionally proclaimed, he thought such an act would send him through politics to eventual Commander in Chief of the Nation.

Military intelligence predicted that a large gathering of the Sioux would take place during the late Spring/early summer of 1876 in the Big Horn plateau country where the last of the once enormous buffalo herds were still ranging. This area is to the east of the Rocky Mountain range and referred to as the Big Horns. Three military forces were dispatched to encircle the encampment, attack and force the surviving Indians back onto their reservations, mostly in the States of North and South Dakota. General Crooks would set out from Ft. Laramie with approximately 1440 cavalry mounted soldiers and Crow scouts. General Terry and Custer would come from a fort in what would become North Dakota and Colonel Gibbon would come down from a fort farther west in what would eventually be Montana. This was called the Three Pronged Attack strategy.

Tongue River Battle

This battle was far more 'famous' in my opinion because it truly displayed the superior fighting ability of the Sioux in that less than half as many warriors easily defeated the advancing forces of the White A bit over a week before the Custer battle, General Crook was advancing northward toward the Big Horn Mountain range from Ft. Laramie which is now in the state of Wyoming. Sioux scouts reported he had a contingent of well over a thousand men including Crow Indian scouts advancing upon the large Sioux encampment along the Little Big Horn River which was also bolstered by their allies the Northern Cheyenne and the Arapaho. U. S. Army records list Crook's forces at 1440. Chief Crazy Horse of the Teton Oglala Lakota was selected to stop the invading force. Crazy Horse picked fewer than 700 younger warriors, blatantly avoiding over a thousand of the older, more experienced warriors. Before he left southward, Chief Sitting Bull of the Hunkpapa Lakota approached him to chastise his selection. "Why are you –picking such few warriors, less than half than the approaching enemy and leaving out most of the veterans?"

According to the warriors whom Dr. Bryde interviewed in Lakota when he was a young Jesuit priest, they told him that Crazy Horse laughed and picked up a Winchester rifle. "I pick young men because they do as I tell them!" He aimed the weapon and pretended that he was mounted on a horse. "I do not like to waste men. Why should I take too many and have their women crying after the battle? I will stop him," he remarked confidently. "You will see." Which he did! In less than two days of his encounter with Crook, the General's badly mauled forces were sent fleeing back to Ft. Laramie. The advantage of a repeating, rapid firing rifle and the 'Mongolian'/Equestrian ability to ride and fire with both hands free proved out the outcome in less than two full days of engagement. The Army with 'Bit and Reins' could not fire accurately from a moving horse. Even the Army's records admit this defeat but it was too difficult for the white man's newspapers to admit or later white authors to write about and it is mostly lost in the recording of true history.

Crazy Horse's preference for young warriors was also because most were yet unmarried as it was Sioux custom that a man would not marry until well after he had been a proven warrior and a meat providing hunter. Usually it would not be until a man was in his thirties before he would marry and begin to raise offspring.

Battle of the Little Big Horn

About a week later after the Tongue Battle which is also termed, 'Battle of the Rosebud,' Lieutenant Colonel George Armstrong Custer foolishly neglected to utilize Reconnaissance when he set out with his 650 mounted men along with pack handlers and Crow scouts. Fearing that

General Crook was in the area and would reach the Sioux encampment ahead of him and steal his imagined glory, he hurriedly marched his troops on tiring horses. The night before the battle he marched all night which would spell doom for later chance to escape. All in all, approximately almost 2/3rds of his command would be lost.

After sighting a portion of the huge Sioux encampment, Custer split his forces sending Major Reno and Captain Benteen toward the river in separate forces. Major Reno would attack from crossing the river. Custer would attack the opposite end of an encampment much larger than they could imagine and teeming with warriors within quick reach of loaded rifles. These rifles, when not carried, were always within easy reach from rifle racks outside each tent made from a pair of supporting twigs holding a cross branch for the standing rifles; Winchesters and the single shot '45-70'.

As he approached, the encampment remained mostly hidden by the rolling bluffs until he came over the last crest when it was too late to make a wise retreat for later arriving forces. Likewise at the same timing, Custer had waved to Reno to begin his charge across the river. Reno was also blinded by the sloping and shielding view of the opposite river bank his horses would have to ride over. As soon as the Indians reacted to the short lived attack, the immensity of Sioux, Arapaho and Cheyenne fire power would bring such a foolish move to an abrupt end.

The battle was quickly over. Custer was one of the last to die with his men behind a hasty makeshift barricade of dispatched horses. Most reports state that he received two gunshot wounds, either of which could prove fatal. Despite his ignorance and many flaws, both character wise and military deficient, he is buried in the U. S. Army cemetery at West Point Military Academy near the Hudson River, New York.

Dr. John Bryde

Bryde was a former Jesuit priest who could speak fluent Lakota Sioux. My mother spoke the language fluently as did my father. Both grew up speaking Lakota. She stated that he spoke the language well after they conversed in Lakota. Over a decade, Bryde interviewed the last of the remaining warriors mostly from the Oglala reservation where I was born. These men, mostly in their 80s and 90s, were anxious to talk to a White Man who spoke their language. According to Bryde, they had the unusual ability to reflect back upon their past with clarity and would not speak of battlefield events unless they had a fellow 'verifier' to add to the accuracy of their recollections. The Sioux lifestyle provided a healthy environment indeed compared to our present modern day living. Bryde stated that the mind debilitating diseases of Arthritis, Parkinson's and Alzheimer's disease were rare among the old time warrior.

The time it takes to eat a meal.

The Battle of the Little Big Horn was over within less than an hour; closer to a half hour if Dr. Bryde's combat experienced Sioux interviewees were listened to. "In less than the time it takes for a man to eat a meal," is the way they described its duration. Most of the numerous 'Custer Battle' books, both non-fiction and fiction, have the battle advancing into flanking movements and time consuming battle strategy, all obviously made up by the authors of course; primarily for Hollywood fomented entertainment is my suspicion and hence – selling of the books. To the effect: "A Chess match of battle strategy as Custer and Crazy Horse maneuvered back and forth." Two Sioux Indian authors have also joined those ranks. One is a non-fiction writer and the other more popular, a fiction writer and both quite patterned after the most notorious error filled story teller of them all- Maria Sandoz. She, who wrongfully vilified and damaged Chief Red Cloud, the leader who wisely obtained the essential, critical, battle winning Winchester. In my historic non-fiction book, *Crazy Horse and Chief Red Cloud*, I quote Author Larry McMurtry eight times who points out Sandoz among others; her writing deficiency. Without that weapon procurement, the Sioux would never have won the Treaty of 1868. I honor and respect McMurtry's writings. He criticizes other writers as well for not bothering to quote from the only sources surviving to truly and reliably report the main portion of the battle. These sources were the Indians who were there! He no doubt would criticize just as severely the two Sioux Indian writers as well.

Black Elk

Black Elk (born 1863) was not a military leader but was a powerful visionary. His revealing vision which is applicable to our present day environmental dilemma we will study in the following chapter. It took place close to the Little Big Horn River, where Sitting Bull would later receive his vision just prior to the famous Custer Battle. Black Elk out lived all of the leaders mentioned above. He remained basically unknown throughout his life time, except among his own people where he was regarded as a powerful healer. His healing abilities took place while the Sioux were in containment on the reservations after the turn of the century.

In just one lifetime, these leaders were upon the planet at the same time period. It is needless to doubt that the Natural Way produced equivalent selflessness from other leaders before them who were elected and led selflessly. So much contrast, their exemplary contact compared to the greedy selfishness that modern elected officials now display. Simply look at the list of benefits the American Congress has provided for itself compared to the laws they have cast upon the populace. This was said earlier but the gravity of the lack of true leadership in America and the majority of other countries as well make it well worth repeating. On the contrary! What passes for leadership today in the U.S. is a combination of entitlement, egotism, greed, racism, xenophobia, and misogyny.

It seems that the White Man's religion has not produced comparable leaders- has it?

CHAPTER 6
BLACK ELK'S VISION

Much of my Black Elk material is from a close friend who gave me both my child's and my adult warrior's Indian names- Ben Black Elk, the son of the Visionary, Nicholas Black Elk. His picture holding my pre-school daughter is in my book, *Warrior's Odyssey*. As Interpreter of every word of the original *Black Elk Speaks* from his father to John Neihardt, the interviewer, those questions and comments back to old Black Elk went through Ben. Needless to say: Ben knew the Vision backwards and forwards. He was a valuable mentor for my knowledge of the world acclaimed book.

Dec. 2004, an earthquake struck off Indonesia's Sumatra Island and triggered a devastating tidal wave that cost 230,000 lives. 131,000 lives were lost in Aceh Province alone. The outer island people, those who were first exposed to the deadly onslaught, were mostly not members of Organized Religion. The island folk were Nature based in their beliefs and readily noticed the unusual actions of the birds and other animals that took to the high ground immediately when the earthquake happened. The outer Island people reacted to Nature's warnings and survived. Thousands of Organized Religion's adherents did not.

The 10 Commandments

Thousands of years ago (suppositional at least by many), Creator appeared to a leader of a Jewish tribe on a mountain top to give him 10 commandments. The first of these commandments was that man shalt not have strange (or false) gods before him. Creator, (It is believed by many) did appear in non-human form to issue these edicts obviously to guide human toward a more harmonious lifestyle as the animals of the world so enjoyed. Before man's domination, the animals certainly preserved a pristine, comfortable, compatible planet. Most Dominant Society adherents believe the Ten Commandments were so issued by Creator but few know of Black Elk's Vision and most who do know no doubt find such a supposed happening as nothing more than a myth or fairy tale, such is their insulation toward other cultures than their own.

Religious Prophet

Do Indians have religious prophets? I would consider the Oglala

Lakota (Sioux) named Black Elk as more of a visionary than a prophet upon which the White Man, both the Christian and the Islamic, seems to place a greater reliance. Indians I have known, mostly Sioux, shy away from all-knowing prophecy because they truthfully admit that when dealing with Mystery there are simply too many unknowns. I say that not looking for argument. It is simply the way we have observed our own life journeys. Our spiritual direction comes from what we view daily, termed simply, Direct Observation. We also prefer to have a verifier if possible when we attempt to relate what we believe to be a profound observance or discovery. To us, the Creator is all encompassing. Like many religious beliefs, we think It knows whether we are being Truthful or not. Creator's Spirit helpers also know. Embellishment, exaggeration, even telling a lie to promote one's own religion or spirituality is still a lie and can bear consequences for one's soul or, as we prefer, 'our Spirit.'

Now the above is an attempted description of what we term as a Traditionalist; a North American Indian ancestrally rooted from Northeastern tribes and later migrated out to the Great Plains, mainly to escape the invading whites and their deadly diseases. Approximately over half of my fellow Sioux tribal people are Traditionals, especially since Martin Luther King's Civil Rights Movement allowed us to return spiritually to our old beliefs.

Knowledge

What is knowledge? I believe knowledge mainly comes from what one experiences. The other part of knowledge can come from truthful associates who impart their knowledge. If it happened, then, why would not some knowledge come from what one observed? Millions of books have been written on observations or what one 'thought' had happened

One should attempt to verify what one hears or reads from another especially when considering the Religious or Spiritual; reasoning out the circumstances, background, feasibility, if you might. Black Elks Vision is a bit too immense for a fairy tale to be invented especially from one only ten years. Could there be Six Powers? Do the Four Directions exist? I think they are a bit more plausible than an Adam without a mate and then a woman named Eve is made from his rib. They live comfortably in a plush Garden of Eden. A talking snake comes along and Eve is coerced by the snake to eat God's forbidden fruit. They are cast out and eventually these 'First Parents have children. Oddly these children grow up and go over a hill and find their mates. Unless these mates are monkeys I have to utilize my God designed and given, common sense mind and begin to doubt the White Man once more regarding his 'First Parents' claim. I also have to doubt The Noah's Ark and 'Great Flood' and saving every animal story. The various aspects of Darwinism I was offered in a prestigious Catholic University raises verifiable question as well of the ecumenical Christian sects who even post on Highway billboards denouncing Darwin's approach to Creationism. What about the meat eaters on board? Could they fast for 40 days plus the staging time while waiting to be taken on board? Such fallacy we humans feed each other.

Conversely the Six Powers are actually visible to this day. From a Creator concept, it is not difficult to hypothesize their extensive powers regarding the operations of our Universe. Why does egotistical human attempt to deny or downplay that Creator could not or would not utilize what IT has made to demonstrate what It seeks to foretell? Western man seeks only to accept what emanates from himself. The resolute Scientific Laws within these Six Powers as God's laws are not that difficult to understand either, at least in my Nature influenced mind. Better such than having to accept some bearded Leviticus Duck Dynasty types who swore the world was flat.

Black Elk's Vision

Upon this hemisphere over a century ago, in league with respecting the vision of Moses, a similar spiritual occurrence took place. Creator did not appear in human form or speak directly but most certainly allowed its created entities to deliver a supreme warning of a devastating danger to the planet. Only the Supreme Maker could allow such a vision. In these modern times, each successive year exponentially verifies the accuracy of the predictive warnings – environmental and social- therein.

Creator warned through Six Powers, the Six Powers that control our Universe. It is difficult for European descended man so steeped in his man-created-God imagery to decipher these nature based entities even though they are observable and not dependent on man's history

Indigenous utilize respectful ceremony directed to Creator ultimately to connect, visualize and even communicate into that beyond world which organized religion warns its followers as some sort of 'evil' and have fabricated as a colluding contrivance their equally fabricated 'Satan' or 'Master Devil'. At most, some sects, only certain members of hierarchal church leadership are allowed or qualified to repel or 'cleanse' such imagined 'evil' through ceremony i.e. the Catholic Church's demon removal ritual- Exorcism.

. One dark night, a Jesuit missionary kidnapped Black Elk from a healing ceremony and hauled him off in a wagon to have an accomplice conduct an Exorcism at the reservation mission on a bewildered and fearful Black Elk. Odd! Black Elk's Sioux beliefs do not recognize or admit to Devils, Satan's or such superstitious creations. The term 'Evil' or 'Sin' is also rather foreign to them. Ignorance or 'not knowing' would be their term for such. The term 'being born into or with Sin' was rather difficult for them to understand or accept as well, from the insistent missionaries.

Vision Quest is a lone individual participated ceremony. I must add that it is an incredible confidence creating experience. Most all Sioux sun dancers who endure for four long hot summer days will Vision Quest and Sweat Lodge before such a spiritual enhancing endurance. It is my understanding that the Christ of Christianity went out into the desert, the wilderness, some say. One chooses a lengthy period of isolation while fasting to enhance the attempt to commune with one's Higher Power concept. Did not Moses seek a lone, isolated mountain top for such related communication? Odd, that the leaders of these adherents avoid such similar personal sacrifice. If I were to be on my way down from vision questing upon Spirit Mountain in the Black Hills, I would never expect to encounter an ascending Pat Robertson, Billy Graham or his protégé son, rosy cheeked and now bankrupt Pastor Bob formerly of the San Francis-

co Glass Cathedral nor a host of the intense television evangelicals, Bishop O'Brien, Norman Vincent Peale's offspring and of course, mega preacher, Joel Osteen. At the bottom of the mountain I could expect several medicine men or medicine women waiting for adherents they had placed near the upper solitude of the historic projection rising from the Dakota plains. Never would I expect to meet a Pope, Bishop or a Cardinal on their way up a mountain to humble themselves and endure a bit of discomfort to emulate Christ's Vision Quest vigil. From their electronic pulpits they could later 'describe' an attempting 'Devil' or was it "Satan' itself planning to lure or subdue Christ's vision quest vigil without food and water in a hot, hostile desert inhabited back then by large carnivorous beasts. It is not difficult for me to believe that such a brave and harmoniously concerned man for the world back then did or would seek out such a spiritual vigil. It is a very powerful ceremony for the participant. Counting the many sun dances now held on various reservations, some thousand or so of those participants endure vision quests prior to the four day Sun Dance. I must give credit, however to a few Jesuit reservation assigned priests influenced by native Spirituality and their Christ, who have bravely endured what Indians commonly do, to come closer to their God concept. One of those exemplary priests will have his own chapter later.

Bill Moyers and Joseph Campbell

We have experienced some powerful Natural Way ceremonies and now know the history of the people who kept their Natural Ways alive, even up to this time of so-called 'Modern Living'. Now let us explore a powerful happening that is most revealing of the word – 'Spiritual Imagery.'

Bill Moyers is a noted American interviewer of various people, mostly those who have explored the various realms of life experiences, philosophies and those who champion environmental causes and stance. He interviewed Joseph Campbell who explored worldwide the various tribes and Indigenous who still followed their Natural Way. Moyers asked Campbell, "You speak of Spiritual Imagery often. What is the best example, in your opinion of it?"

Without a second's pause, Campbell replied abruptly. "Black Elk Speaks!" *Black Elk Speaks* is the title of a famous book, authored by John Neihardt, a White Man, first published in 1934. It has been printed in many languages and reprinted several hundred times in the English language.

1873 or 1874

It is now the 1800s, around 1873, 1874. Having migrated westward from close to the Atlantic Ocean, the Sioux Indians entered the vast grasslands of the Great Plains and now followed the buffalo and often the buffalo followed a great circle of their own. A river coursing through the eastern plateau of the Big Horn Mountains country, just east of the higher Rocky Mountain Range, the Greasy Grass wandered and meandered, bound and obedient to Creator's gravity, silently flowing its powerful course eventually toward the Yellowstone, the Missouri, the Mississippi River and hence to the sea. But a few years later a great battle by

two-legged (human) would be fought by those who respected the teeming herds which grazed its meadows and those two-legged in blue who did not. Newspapers would soon make this river as historically immortal as Bastogne, Kasserine Pass, Guadalcanal and the Chosen Reservoir, terming it – the Little Big Horn.

The Battle of the Little Big Horn would soon echo worldwide. But for the moment, the winter counts would term the slow paced river as the Greasy Grass. A young boy named Black Elk, a Teton Oglala, had a powerful vision here on its banks as would a great chief named Sitting Bull, but a few years later. His vision, Sitting Bull's, however was for the moment; the men in blue would be falling, helplessly head first, down, into a great Sioux, Cheyenne and Arapahoe camp and they would be swallowed up. Considering these two visions that happened there, maybe this Greasy Grass, like Bear Butte Mountain or the Pipestone Quarries, is a special place for those who quest. I would have to consider the boy's vision as the more profound, however. Maybe one could claim that it held more of a world view. For Sitting Bull, his vision or dream soon bore truth. The soldiers did 'fall' fatally for them, into the Sioux camp. In 1876, Colonel Custer lost his entire immediate command when he foolishly attacked the large, well-armed Sioux encampment supported also by Cheyenne and Arapahoe warriors. Black Elk's vision is indeed puzzling, yet thanks to Neihardt's book, millions have become aware of what the boy experienced, after he journeyed into a strange Spirit World. The boy was innocent and it would have been difficult for him to make up such a vivid portrayal. His lifelong actions following this great event insured this vision as surely as the river's journey would end at the sea.

This event occurred several years before that famous battle. It was a time when the tribe enjoyed the freedom of the Great Plains. The boy named Black Elk was a young boy when he had such an open, understandable vision as it pertained to all of Creator's Nature which surrounds us. It began with the Wamaskaskan, the animal creations, finned, flying and four-legged, all in a myriad of gracious display. Yes, whatever was responsible for such a powerful vision did include the Wamaskaskan (the Animal Brothers and Sisters). His vision took him into a Rainbow Covered Lodge of the Six Powers of the World.

The Vision

Two spirit men carried this young boy upward to the spirit world. On a cloudy plain, thunder beings leaped and flashed. A bay horse appeared and spoke: "Behold me!" Twelve black horses appeared showing manes of lightning and nostrils that rumbled thunder. The bay horse wheeled to the white north and there Black Elk saw twelve white horses abreast. Their manes flowed like a blizzard wind and their noses roared. White geese soared around these horses. The bay wheeled to the east and there, twelve sorrels (red horses) appeared abreast. Their eyes glimmered like the day-break star and their manes were like the red dawn of morning. The bay wheeled to the south and there, twelve buckskins (yellow horses) stood abreast bearing horns and manes like living trees and grasses. The horses went into formation behind the bay horse. The bay spoke to Black Elk: "See how your horses all come dancing!" A whole sky full of horses danced and pranced around him.

Black Elk walked with the bay and the formation of horses marching four abreast in ranks. He looked at the sky full of horses and watched them change to other animals and winged. These fowl and four leggeds then fled back to the four quarters of the world from where the horses had come. He walked on toward a cloud that changed into a teepee with a rainbow for an open door. Within, he saw six old men sitting in a row. He was invited to go into the rainbow door lodge and told not be fearful.

He went in and stood before the six old men and discovered that they were not old men but were the Six Powers of the World. Of the powers, the West Power, Wiyopeyata, spoke first. When the West Power spoke of understanding, the rainbow leaped with flames of many colors over Black Elk. The West Power gave him a wooden cup filled with water and spoke. "Take this, it is the power to make live." The West Power gave him a bow and spoke. "Take this, it is the power to destroy." The West Power then left and changed to a black horse but the horse was gaunt and sick.

The second power, Waziya, the Power of the White North, rose and instructed Black Elk to take a healing herb to the black horse. The horse was healed and grew fatter to come back prancing. The horse changed back to Wiyopeyata and took his place in the council.

The North Power spoke again. "Take courage, younger brother," he said, "on earth a nation you shall make live, for yours shall be the power of the white giant's wing, the cleansing wind." When the North Power went running to the north, he became a white goose wheeling. Black Elk looked around and saw that the horses to the west were thunders and the horses to the north were geese.

The third power, the East Power, Wiyoheyapata, spoke. "Take courage, younger brother," he said, "for across the earth they shall take you." Wiyoheyapata pointed to two men flying beneath the daybreak star. "From them you shall have power," he said, "from them who have awakened all the beings of the earth with roots and legs and wings." The East Power gave Black Elk a peace pipe that bore a spotted eagle. "With this pipe," the power said, "you shall walk upon the earth, and whatever sickens there you shall make well." A bright red man appeared standing for good and plenty. The red man rolled and turned into a buffalo. The buffalo joined the sorrel horses of the east. These horses then changed into fat buffalo.

The fourth power to speak to Black Elk was the yellow South Power—Itokaga, the power to grow. "Younger brother," he said, "with the powers of the four quarters you shall walk, a relative. Behold, the living center of a nation I shall give you and with it many you shall save." In

Itokaga's hand, the power held a bright stick that sprouted and sent forth branches. Leaves came out and murmured and birds sang in the leaves. Beneath the leafy stick, in the shade, Black Elk saw the circled villages of people and every living thing with roots or legs or wings, and all were happy. "It shall stand in the center of the nation's circle," Itokaga said, "a cane to walk with and a people's heart; and by your powers you shall make it blossom."

Then when he had been still a little while to hear the birds sing, he spoke again. "Behold the earth!" Black Elk looked down and saw the earth and in the center bloomed the holy stick that was a tree, and where it stood two roads crossed, a red one and a black one. "From where the giant lives (the north) to where you always face (the south) the red road goes, the road of good," the South Power said, "and on it shall your nation walk. The black road goes from where the thunder beings live (the west) to where the sun continually shines (the east), a fearful road, a road of troubles and of war. On this also you shall walk, and from it you shall have the power to destroy a people's foes. In four ascents you shall walk the earth with power."

Black Elk thought that an ascent was a generation and that he was seeing the third ascent (generation) when he revealed his vision in the fourth decade (1930 to 1940 approximately) of the twentieth century.

Itokaga rose and stood with the buckskin horses (yellow horses) at the end of his words. The South Power became an elk and the buckskin horses changed to elks.

The fifth power, the Sky Spirit, which was the oldest of the Six Powers, was the next to speak. Makpiyah Ate, Father Sky, became a spotted eagle hovering. "Behold," he said, "all the things of the air shall come to you, and they and the winds and the stars shall be like relatives. You shall go across the earth with my power."

The sixth power, the Earth Spirit spoke, "My boy, have courage, for my power shall be yours, and you shall need it, for your nation on the earth will have great troubles. Come."

The Earth Power rose and went out through the rainbow door. Black Elk followed, finding himself on the bay horse that had appeared at the beginning of his vision. The bay faced the black horses of the west, and a voice said: "They have given you the cup of water to make live the greening day, and also the bow and arrow to destroy."

The bay faced the sorrels of the east, and a voice said: "they have given you the sacred pipe and the power that is peace, and the good red day."

The bay faced the buckskins of the south, and a voice said: "They have given you the sacred stick and your nation's hoop, and the yellow day; and in the center of the hoop you shall set the stick and make it grow into a shielding tree, and bloom."

All of the horses now had riders and stood behind Black Elk, and a voice said: "Now you shall walk the black road with these; and as you walk, all the nations that have roots or legs or wings shall fear you."

Black Elk rode east, down the fearful road and behind him came the horsebacks (horses with riders). He came upon a place where three streams made a river and something terrible was there. In the flames rising from the waters a blue man lived. Dust floated all about him, the grass was short and withered, trees were wilting, two legged and four-legged beings were thin and panting and the winged were too weak to fly.

The black horse riders shouted "Hokahey!" and charged down to attack and kill the Blue Man but were driven back. The white troop riders shouted "hokahey!" and charged down but were driven back; then the red troop and the yellow. When each failed they called to Black Elk. Black Elk's bow changed to a spear and he charged on the Blue Man. His spear head became lightning. It stabbed the Blue Man's heart and killed him. The trees and grasses were no longer withered and every being cried out in gladness.

Black Elk thought that it was drought that he had killed with the power that had been given to him. At the time that he related the vision, he was understanably unaware of the great environmental dilemma that the Blue Man was symbolizing.

John Neihardt

Black Elk intended that the world should know of his vision. Several writers had earlier attempted to secure Black Elk's story but he was not satisfied with them. When John Neihardt came to his cabin, he told Neihardt that he was the one he was waiting for. "Where have you been? You should have been here earlier." It was in the fall. Black Elk said that it was too late that year to relate his vision. "You come back when the grass is so high," the holy man held out his hand to indicate the height of spring grass, "and I will tell you my story."

Ben Black Elk, son of Nicholas Black Elk, interpreted between Neihardt and the holy man, who the missionaries would later give the name, Nicholas Black Elk. As mentioned, Ben was well satisfied with the finished writing, *Black Elk Speaks*. As mentioned, I personally knew Ben, beginning as a child. He gave me my child's name, 'Wanblee Hokeshilah – Eagle Boy'. Later he was instrumental in changing my name to Wanbli Wichasha- Eagle Man, after I returned from war in Vietnam and was in the Sun dance. The book was published in 1932, but at that time there existed so much prejudice and ignorance against Indians let alone their culture, true history as expressed by them and definitely a rejection, denial and outright accusation of heretical heathenry - their Spirituality that it went into remainder and copies were sold for 45 cents apiece. It wasn't until thirty years later that the importance of such a profound vision would be rediscovered, thanks to the interest of Carl Jung and Dick Cavett. The book has now sold well over a million copies and has been printed in many languages, including Japanese. But now it has been severely altered by denying commentary placed within two revisions of the book and a host of other diluting writers not unlike the evangelicals of today who deny Climate Change, Planetary Heating and Over Population Peril. Corruption and Greed also stimulate such impending disaster along with the root cause of Terrorism which can be found within the Six Powers console to the young boy when he entered the Great Rainbow lodge. A vivid portrayal of a sinister, powerful, scheming Blue Man surrounded by his environmental evidenced disaster is predicted at the end of the vision. Unfortunately for the worldwide reader audience, the ending of the Vision is covered up by later versions of the book Black Elk Speaks and ongoing academic commentary from other non-Indian writers. This errant final focus of the vision has forced me to write my counter rebuttal- *Black Elk Speaks – IV* (Amazon & Kindle). In justice to John Neihardt, the interviewer and author of Black Elk Speaks back in the early 1930s, such was a time when this Blue Man warning was absolutely unnoticeable. Both of the Black Elk's, interpreter Ben, his revealing Father and also Neihardt were completely innocent of predicting future environmental disaster. It was the early 1930's and the words 'Planetary Heating and Climate Change' had not been coined yet. The greatest dictator of them all in Germany was not yet within his destructive power. Reservation missionaries, mainly the Jesuits no doubt realized to some degree the power of the vision and set about to dilute and deny the essence of the Vision. They turned on Black Elk. The blatant kidnapping and exorcism was no small initial effort. Investigative details supported by first hand interviews of related victims, Ben Black Elk and a personal audience with Neihardt's daughter are within my BES IV book for the reader who seeks a much fuller and accurate expose not found in the writings of Anthropologist Raymond DeMallie who refers to Black Elk as a Conjuror (One who realms upon or within the 'Dark side.). DeMallie narrates the two latter versions of BES. I term those two as Black Elk Speaks II and Black Elk Speaks III. Despite the obvious world change both environmentally and Blue Man deceit, corruption, untruth and deception the commentary and added narration within these two books needs to be exposed. Neither of the altered edition's commentary or DeMallie's narrating favorably mention the heart of the Vision (the Blue Man Warning). DeMallie has allowed his overwhelming contrary religious beliefs to distract and worse purposefully deny and vilify Indigenous Spirituality. He shouldn't be narrating a Native American spiritual book.

With Our Own Kind

The reservation missionaries made a strong attempt to dislodge Black Elk's vision and were almost successful. Why? All that I can surmise on their behalf is that it intruded on their belief system as this writing will be judged. It was also quite convincing if one would rely on direct observance of what all surrounded us. Many Sioux know little about it, or they believe the detracting dogma perpetuated against it. That is their loss; my opinion. I harbor little remorse for those who deny direct observation. It is the choice they made while on their Earth journey; a foolish choice; my opinion. Hopefully, there exists a Spirit World in which we can be with our own kind. That categorization, also hopefully, will not be a separation by race or worldly accomplishment, but one of how well we utilized our mind while here upon this journey. How much did we place into this greatest of gifts which Benevolent Creator has designed specifically just for us? Courage, bravery, generosity and sharing - the four cardinal virtues of the Sioux may also have their importance toward our final destination. I deeply hope that when one enters the Spirit World, one will be able to go or be placed with one's own kind. 'According to your truths!' This could be the real 'Heaven or Hell' most of us wonder or ponder about, if we are at all truthful.

There are many from all walks who are taking a serious look at this vision. Joseph Campbell's remark that this vision is the best example of spiritual imagery is very appropriate. There are many people who have discovered the visible Six Powers of this earth and who are now relating these daily entities in balance, acknowledgement and kinship to their everyday lifestyle. Black Elk lived at a time when Chief Crazy Horse, Chief

Red Cloud and Chief Sitting Bull were alive and in power. As I said earlier, I believe that these three leaders we have studied were spiritually respectful men who believed that it was the Six Powers (Shakopeh Ouyea) who regulated the known world to the Sioux under the laws, actions and powers of the Creator, Wakan Tanka, as those leaders understood it.

Direct Observation is far more meaningful to me for my spiritual advancement than mostly foolish words by white men based too heavily on sheer superstition especially now in this age when I notice that what the White Man has claimed has now no proof or veracity as the seas rise, the Arctic melts, Glaciers retreat and over-population soars. His Black Book offers nary a warning. Black Elk's Vision does explicitly: the Blue Man of Environmental Destruction, Pollution, Greed and Untruth at the vision's ending despite the extreme cover up by the descendants of Neihardt who have allowed in line with an opiating pied piper anthropologist named Raymond DeMallie who altered the original interview in versions II and III. His brazen, destructive meddling into our culture with no respect or spiritual experience has cheated the literary world out of serious needed knowledge. Ego is indeed dangerous on an immense scale. Not a dime's worth of book royalties have the Neihardt's shared with the Black Elk Family either which is typical anytime a White exploiter deals with an Indian.

The Six Powers:

Many of you will want a greater depth to explore regarding this powerful happening; this Spiritual Imagery; so I will continue with it.

West Power. We acknowledge the life-giving rains as the power to make live. The thunder and the lightning are the power to destroy. As the sun goes down in the west, darkness comes to the land. The color for the west is black. The spirits who enter ceremony appreciate less distraction in the darkness when two leggeds seek to communicate with them, therefore the spirit beseeching ceremonies are usually held when the west power has allowed darkness to come forth. The spirit world is associated with the west power in this regard but are not confined to a direction

North Power. We think of endurance, cleanliness, truth, rest, politeness and strength as associated with the North. The cold north has Mother Earth rest beneath the white mantle of snow. She sleeps and gathers up her strength for the bounty of springtime. When the snows melt, the earth is made clean. When native people wintered over, often confined to a small area for a lengthy time while they waited for the spring thaw, they learned to be extremely polite, to be truthful and honest with each other. They kept clean by using the sweat lodge to take winter baths and to beseech to the spirit world. The power of the cold white north taught them to endure. The cleansing white wing within Black Elk's great vision emphasizes endurance and cleanliness.

East Power. The third power brought him the red pipe of peace. Peace begins with knowledge. To have peace, one must first become aware of knowledge, which comes forth out of the red dawn, the east, with each new day. When you have knowledge and it is discussed and considered, it can become wisdom. Others share their thoughts, their observations and their needs. A widow can add much wisdom to a council that is deciding to make a war, or planning to send out a war party. She can tell of the loneliness of the children and her own grief when they learned that their father and her husband was slain on the last war party. When lands are to be taken from a people by financiers or politicians the people's voices should be heard. Communication and knowledge of what is happening can lead to the wise decision that the people's interest must be seriously considered and they must be adequately compensated, or the project may be halted. Especially when sabers rattle and threats are being made, wisdom can lead to understanding and understanding can bring peace to the land. The pipe of peace and the red dawn that brings new experience each day is symbolic of knowledge, wisdom and communication coming together in this day and age.

This is the beginning of the age of communication. We have seen great progress from communication that allows new knowledge to come into people's lives. The red dawn rises to bring a bright new day in which we can add knowledge to our lives on a daily basis as long as we walk this planet. Now we have modern communication that is allowed by the mystery of the radio waves, the television waves and other mysterious gifts. These created and allowed forces, put here for our use, give us optimism that our planet can be saved from past practices of destruction. We have no choice. We have seen in Rwanda and the "ethnic purity" cleansing of Bosnia what can happen when humans refuse to communicate.

South Power. Medicine from roots, stems, herbs and fruits are associated with the south power. Today, many species are beginning to disappear and these medicines can soon be lost. The sun rises higher and higher as the South Power advances with summer. Eventually plants such as corn and wheat will bring forth yellow or golden kernels that will sustain much life through the long winter. Abundance is the primary gift from this power, for it makes all things grow and we are allowed to take that which grows. In the summer, buffalo fattened on endless grasses. During the heat of summer, buffalo hunts provided meat to cure in the hot, blowing wind for long winters. During this time of plenty, dances and gatherings of thanksgiving would happen. The annual summer Sun Dance is to thank creator for all its benevolence. To be thankful for what you receive adds strength to your search for sustenance, provisions and shelter.

Sky Power. Father Sky spoke and said the things of the air would be with Black Elk to help him in his struggle. He warned that a time would come when the Earth Mother would become very sick but the 'things of the air' would be there to help her. Could these "things of the air" also be the open space of communication which now can transcend across the globe? Can it also be the satellites—"things of the air," beaming back video and radio waves so we may see and talk directly across the skies? Communication is a powerful tool to bring understanding and prevent costly, wasteful and polluting wars. If so, Truth will be more difficult to distort. Now we have modern communication that is allowed by the mystery of the radio waves, the television waves and other mysterious gifts. No doubt there are new mysterious waves yet to be discovered. The computer stores vast information and transmits volumes in an eye wink. None of this could so perform were it not allowed by a Powerful Vastness! These communicative forces, created for our use, foster optimism that our planet can be saved from past practices of destruction.

I perceive that what the Sky Power said could be closely associated with the advance of more communicative people upon the earth because the things of the air are helping to promote peace and harmony. Distortion, lies, falsehoods mainly over greed can be combated with immediate, exposing communication. It is happening right before us.

Earth Power. Mother Earth, the Sixth Power, spoke little and instead took Black Elk to the danger that was confronting the earth. Direct observation she exhibited. This danger was the Blue Man of greed and deception that was already harming the living things. This Blue Man symbolizes the corruption, insensitivity, greed and ignorance which constitute a blight upon the Earth. The Blue Man would wreak great destruction using lies and untruths and would have to be addressed or else all creatures including two leggeds would perish. Untruth is the Blue Man. In America, every day we observe much deception by those who lobby our political leaders in Washington with disregard for the environment and the ongoing dilemma. As the situation worsens, more eyes will be opened and eventually the old ways of real Truth will have to be accepted in order to finally destroy the Blue Man. Hopefully, it will be in time for the planet to have a chance to regain the old harmony. Two leggeds will discover that there is no other choice. Religious fundamentalists will no doubt keep on praying and waiting for miracles but the realistic and workable solution will be to return to the values that actually worked. The population spiral will not wait for miraculous curing. Some tragic consequences will be learned along the way. Climate Change- Planetary Heating is now upon us. Just ask those who experienced Hurricane Katrina in New Orleans and then afterwards the huge Hurricane coupled with two other storms that devastated New York City and surrounding states. Fewer Scientists and naysayers of Climate Change exist now except for the ultra-religious who will not admit its happening because this scenario would circumvent their Bible or Koran which says nothing about the greatest catastrophe ever setting up against the planet bringing more dangerous storms, melting Arctic Sea ice and Greenland's ice cap as well as glaciers throughout the world. Oceans are rising, yet blind Organized Religion Zealots refuse to take heed.

The Six Powers were all mounted on horses. Black Elk himself sat upon a horse and carrying the bow gifted to him by the West Power. Down below three rivers flowed toward each other. Where they met a man stood in the confluence of waters that grew foul and putrid. Fish were dying and floating in deathly form. Water birds suffocated as they flew through the putrid haze. This danger was the Blue Man of greed and deception that was already harming the living things in more ways than just drought which the rains could cure as always, down through time. This Blue Man symbolized the corruption, insensitivity, greed and ignorance which are now upon the Earth. The Blue Man would wreak great destruction using lies and untruths and would have to be addressed or else all creatures including two leggeds would perish: Perish through their greed and over consumption. The reality of Creator's warning given to Black Elk is among us now. Terrorism was not predicted but is an off shoot of the circumstances evolving from the vision.

"Come," cried Mother Earth. "We must charge this Blue Man! Hokahey!" With that call, the Six Powers flew down upon their mounts and attacked the Blue Man but he beat them back. After a furious battle they stood panting. They called up to Black Elk, exhorting him to join in the fray. His bow turned into a spear giving him confidence. The bay horse beneath him reared and snorted fire. Horse and rider charged down and killed the Blue Man with the spear. * Note: The original Black Elk Speaks holds the 6th Power as masculine in gender. DeMallie titles his book, *The Sixth Grandfather* and changes the Earth Power to Black Elk, himself. A bit pompous and ostentatious would not one think and brazenly placing oneself into another tribes/Nation sacred historic culture? Such is the false sense of Superiority of the Wahshichu. I asked Ben if the Earth Spirit is regarded as usually feminine. He agreed. He said – "Those Powers took the form of two-legged probably so as not to scare a little kid compared to how 'Lelah Ataaah' ('Immense')- they really are." Hence, I refer to Earth Spirit as Feminine for she certainly does give birth.

The Blue Man. The Six Powers attacked the Blue Man but were beaten back. They called on Black Elk for his help, which was the knowledge he had received and had the power to communicate, now that he had learned of the Six Powers. His bow changed to a spear and when he attacked, he killed the Blue Man. The Six Powers demonstrated the need for two leggeds to destroy the corruption, lies and greed of humankind which in turn is destroying our environment. His bow changing to a spear and thus giving him the ability to destroy the Blue Man, I interpret as symbolic that he now had new knowledge and it was a very powerful knowledge, which enabled him to kill the Blue Man who was causing unnatural and chaotic suffering and destruction. Is it the Natural Knowledge from his vision that is really the spear which can save the world environmentally and give it a more peaceful perspective, free from war-fomenting greed and wasteful detraction which is not working? By learning to be peaceful, two leggeds can devote their energy to the environment.

Interpretation

Everyone is free to their own interpretations, even Raymond DeMallie's, whom the Neihardt foundation's new Director, Coralie Neihardt, has now designated to add his narrations within the very pages of the second alteration printing of the book (New York University Press) after the death of her Mother, Hilda Neihardt: such a sacrilegious insult to the Spirituality of the Lakota Sioux People who revere the Great Vision. My interpretation vastly differs from Professor Raymond DeMallie. DeMallie has never Sun Danced, never Vision Quested, never conducted a Sweat Lodge, never visualized a Yuwipi Ceremony nor personally known the real narrator of *Black Elk Speaks*- Ben Black Elk as I have known since I was a child and participated within the aforementioned mind and culture expanding ceremonies. What belief system is DeMalle? I highly doubt that he follows or champions the Way of the Traditional Lakota! DeMalle was also severely criticized by Hilda Neihardt before me and her son, Robin one day when I paid her a friendly visit in Nebraska. Thankfully I believe in a Spirit World where all Truth shall reign and we all will be called 'upon the carpet' so to speak for the ignorant and wrongful actions we have imposed on others. In this case it is a serious insult upon an entire nation- the Lakota people. It is also long overdue that the Neihardt Trust compensate the descendants of Black Elk and Ben Black Elk's descendants in particular. Yes, long overdue for a book that could never have been printed without the words of Old Black Elk and translating by Ben Black Elk and since has reaped thousands of dollars in Royalties. This is typical greed as mentioned, employed in America against Indian people.

The Six Powers are quite observable yet it is almost impossible for Dominant Society folks, including their converted Indians to understand them. This is merely my perspective and we shall wait and watch how the succession of new political administrations worldwide shall deal with the Blue Men that surrounds them daily. I expect little from them and I hope that they prove me wrong. I have more faith in the people rising up with a renewed spiritual imagery and consequently destroying the Blue Man, along with the corrupt politicians and their supporters. Organized Religion will never admit that too often, it was their backing and support that has allowed too many Blue Men to rise to such powerful control. The sore has turned into a wound with this ongoing jihadist, superstition based Terrorism where religious ISM opiates the human mind to carry out suicidal death, destruction and maiming.

Organized Religion supported more than one decadent dictator such as Francisco Franco of Spain. In time, if Real Truth does not come from humankind, Mother Earth will act. Over Population generating pollution according to the non-failing Scientific Laws of Physics will mathematically force her to react and she is now steadily so doing. No 'Leviticus, Lucretius, Corinthians, Thessalonian, Mohammed, Bwana Sahib Lord Big Jim, Joel Osteen, Oral Roberts or Momma Bwana Big Lulu prophetic pronouncement will alter Nature's oncoming reactions. Nature based people assume that Creator has endowed Mother Earth, the Sixth Power, with far more corrective power to survive than what mere two-legged can employ. Real Truth will return one way or the other when Mother Nature severely reacts. It is possible, that supreme suffering occasioned by the

'Four (Nature-based) Horses of the Apocalypse' will finally bring Human to a true reckoning of their situation and hence, dramatic change, politically, socially and even Religious-wise! These Four forces are beginning now, though an inadequate few are recognizing them. As mentioned earlier and in light of the encompassing world dilemma they are well-well worth re-repeating - Heating of the Planet, Water Shortage, Gone Resources and Too Many (Over Population): quite possibly we should add-Uncontrolled Water as well (Floods, wasted water)!

Canton Asylum

The Canton Indian Insane Asylum was created in 1902 while Red Cloud was in his eighties; a time when the United States' official Indian policy was assimilation.[21] The Federal Canton Indian Insane Asylum was built out of brick at Canton, South Dakota, in the eastern part, south of Sioux Falls, the largest South Dakota city. I even have a picture of it sent to me by a Canton township person. It demonstrates how brutal and primitive the mindset of the government officials was as well as the church people who lobbied for it. Leonard Bruguier says whatever the intent behind the asylum; it was a convenient tool for reservation agents. Bruguier is a member of the Yankton Sioux and former Director of the Institute of American Indian studies at the University of South Dakota.

"Many Indians who went into Canton, simply disappeared. A large graveyard is now part of the Canton golf course. 121 bodies, and possibly more, former patients, are buried between the 4th and 5th fairways." [22]

Bruguier: "So in order for the Indian agent to feel more comfortable being surrounded by yes-people, it would be very easy for him to say "This person's insane," and have him shipped to Canton to be administered by a whole different set of rules. Basically you'd just be able to get rid of 'em." [23] It is alleged that medicine men were also incarcerated with no symptoms whatsoever of 'insanity.' This too was a method to wipe out the old religion.

Black Elk was no doubt threatened by the Jesuits in league with the Government administrators and feared he would be sent to Canton. He underwent the Exorcism in fear for his children whose mother had died

---

[21] Todd Leahy, They Called It Madness – The Canton Insane Asylum for Insane Indians 1899 – 1934 (Baltimore, : Publish America, 2009).
[22] www.hiawatha.historicalasylums.com
[23] Ibid.

and he had to raise them alone. He had to succumb to their conversion demand but after a decade or so he slowly went back to his old spiritual beliefs. He gave his story to Neihardt without asking or notifying his religious captors the coming event. What few friends he held as verifiers were obviously sworn to secrecy all the following winter while they waited for Spring and Neihardt's return. Upon his death bed he called for his peace pipe. He held it high and stated to Ben and his daughter Lucy Looks Twice, "This was my Way, all along."

CHAPTER 7
GREAT INQUISITION

Two murderous Dominican Order inquisitors, Heinrich Kramer and James Sprenger, who went on to live out comfortable, acclaimed lives, published their infamous *Malleus Maleficarum* ("Witches Hammer") outlining a lurid litany of imagined magical acts performed by witches and their imps, familiars, phantoms, demons, succubi, and incubi. It described how the evil women blighted crops, devoured children, caused disease, and wrought spells. The book was filled with witches' sexual acts and portrayed women as treacherous and contemptible. "All witchcraft comes from carnal lust, which is in women insatiable," they wrote. "Why is it that Women are chiefly addicted to Evil Superstitions? Why Superstition is chiefly found in Women."[24]

Malleus Maleficarum - best seller in Europe and Imprimatur 'supportively blessed' by reigning Popes for at least five centuries. Five long, horrible centuries of murderous terror, superstition based – ruled unmercifully. Biblical quotes verify and support the papal hierarchy atrocity allowances within. The authors, Sprenger and Kramer, were granted carte blanche by the Popes among other religious order terrorists. Papal Writs allowed them to be let loose to roam Europe, mostly Northern Germany and seek out mostly young attractive women to torture and murder.

> Concerning Witches that copulate with Devils, why is it that women are chiefly addicted to Evil Superstitions?[25]
> Whether witches may work Prestidigitatory Illusion so that the Male Organ appears to be entirely removed and separate from the Body.[26]
> Of the Continuing of the Torture, and of the Devices and Signs by which the Judge can recognize a Witch; and how he ought to protect himself from their spells. Also how they are to be shaved in those parts where they use to conceal the

---

[24] Montague Summers, *Malleus Malificarum of Heinrich Kramer and James Sprenger*, (New York: Dover, 1945, 1971), 41
[25] Ibid, Contents, Part One, Question VI.
[26] Ibid, Part One, Question IX, 58.

Devil's Masks and Tokens; together with the due Setting Forth of Various Means of Overcoming their Obstinacy in Keeping Silence and Refusal to Confess. [27]

An entire religious organization unleashed maiming, torturing and murder for centuries justifying their horrid acts from their 'God Inspired' Bible. The entire church hierarchy dictated the accusation of heresy against any would be dissenters and recommended torture and death sentence for non-compliance. Such superstition based policies are even worse than ISIS if duration is considered. St. Johns University, (Minnesota), my Alma Matter- offered less than two pages within my semester long Church History class text to 'Cover' the Great Inquisition.

Modern psychology easily perceives the sexual neurosis of these priests—yet for centuries their sanctioned book bearing numerous papal Imprimatur was the official manual used by inquisitors sending mostly innocent women to horrible deaths.

Council of Nicaea

Constantine, a dictator, conveyed a council of Christian bishops in 325 A. D. to declare with the purpose of defining the nature of God for all of Christianity and eliminating confusion, controversy, and contention within the church. The Council of Nicaea over-whelming affirmed the deity and eternality of Jesus Christ and defined the relationship between the Father and the Son as "of one substance." It also affirmed the Trinity—the Father, Son, and Holy Spirit were listed as three co-equal and co-eternal Persons. - Wow! Really? Human beings could actually do what-back then? They (mere humans) could actually define Creator? And worse, insert their own tailored concepts or was it cooperation with the dictator's cunning concepts to remain in power? Will modern man, hopefully advancing toward a new intellect mainly through advanced communication, will He/She someday question this new theological 3 in 1 status or as Thomas Jefferson aptly queried, "1 in 3"?

If we presume to maintain real Truth, we must accept that Man is extremely fallible. Here, in this situation, Man again is flirting with Mystery. Regardless of the magnanimous attempt, realistically can Man truthfully make such wordage come to fruition? Or is their declaration, merely an-

---

[27] Ibid., Part Three, Question X, 227.

other one of organized religion's edict that clearly would never come to fruition like the rest of the obvious mysteries of each religious sect's proclamations from the world over? Is Creator directly observed regarding verification of such an edict? Where is Creator's verification? Is Moses and the 10 commandments verified by a Supreme Power? Is Black Elk's Vision verified? A gathering of all the Wizards of the Ku Klux Klan or Joseph Stalin's Politburo can also make binding declarations but theirs also are simple human defined ultimatums. I, however, do not choose to be that gullible. Organized Religious Man, at least those of one of the world's major religions, will not change this 3 in 1 hypothesis, theory and now absolute dogma. Only a dreadful chaotic destruction either from Man himself, his atomic weapons or exponential Over Population- Nature's advancing scenario will effectively catalyze serious questioning, by some at least. Despite planetary chaos many will not question their faith and will go to their graves expecting the Resurrection, 'the Second Coming of Jesus to save them'- is my supposition.

Creator's nature reactions upon the planet are not mere man's often foolish declarations, however. Nature's reactions are solid, unquestionable scientific fact based on direct observation as tenable as the rising tide could be if it comes in far too high for escape and which has happened. Most in this world will hold that the declarations of ISIS are untenable declarations, especially their victims, yet their supporters declare the contrary and even willingly blow themselves up over their cause. Such is their resolve. 30 or 300 voting bishops or 30 ISIS Mullahs makes little or no difference as to the veracity of such declaring what they may decide.

Constantine, one of many dictators who claimed conversion to Christianity, called for a meeting of bishops to be held in Nicaea to resolve some escalating controversies among the church leadership. The issues being debated included the nature of Jesus Christ, the proper date to celebrate Easter, and other matters. The failing Roman Empire, now under Constantine's rule, could not withstand the division caused by years of hard-fought, "out of hand" arguing over doctrinal differences. The emperor saw the quarrels within the church not only as a threat to Christianity but no doubt, more importantly for his survival. His rule was endangered therefore he had to act to save his reign. Therefore, at the Council of Nicaea, Constantine commanded the church leaders to settle their internal disagreements and become Christ-like agents who could bring new life to a troubled empire. Constantine felt "called" to use his authority to help bring about unity, peace, and love within the church.

The main theological issue had always been about Christ. Since the end of the apostolic age, Christians had begun debating these questions: Who is the Christ? Is He more divine than human or more human than divine? Was Jesus created or begotten? Being the Son of God, is He co-equal and co-eternal with the Father, or is He lower in status than the Father? Is the Father the one true God, or are the Father, Son, and Spirit the one true God? What occurred at the council of Nicaea? [28]

The matter was settled and the Christian adherents adopted the Nicene Creed in 325. Human's overwhelming desire to have a man-God overrode his practical reasoning as to sheer Mystery. The Church grew into Europe's largest and without question, controlling organized religion.

Inquisition

Very little has been written in fact about the truth of the Holy Inquisition, which was an awesome, utter terroristic time which sent Europe backwards in respect to technology and scientific advancement for at least five to six centuries. Such was its horror that the ruling Church did a thorough job of covering up endless atrocities. The victims however, mainly the smaller sects who differed with the controlling church authorities maintained records and art of such extremes. In fact, our present generations are suffering today by the fact that it set mankind back at least a half millennia in needed technological advancement for today's environmental dilemma. Scientific research wasn't allowed. Such is the power of Organized Religion to suppress the truth or delay/curtail needed advancement. Where would we be at had we not been dead ended technologically for over half a millennium? How much farther advanced would we be had we nurtured and gleaned environmental research for this day and age? If you do not believe me regarding the centuries upon centuries of reigning terror, then go to your local library and see how little you can find regarding informative resources. There is plenty of detouring/distracting focus on the Aztec and Inca alleged human sacrifice but little information on medieval victimization. Death is Death regardless of its categorization- murderous, heretical alleged punishment or religious

---

[28] (1/22/2016 www.gotquestions.org/council-of-Nicaea.html)

sacrifice. Why should this information be swept under a rug? Because real truth diminishes the image of Christianity? It is a threat toward increased membership. Truth is Truth. It most certainly did have an effect upon history. We in these modern times should allow this knowledge to fortify our intellect so that these happenings will never occur again. Man will always have differing, contesting views on the Mystery of Creation will he not? The Separation of Church and State Clause becomes highly essential and preventive of Man's most dangerous ability to wreak havoc against fellow Man – murder, torture and following disaster far beyond than just ISIS terror once True History is understood thoroughly. Odd, how most evangelicals feel threatened by the clause which allowed them their initial protection to thrive and begin in America once they fled here: The Pat Robertsons, Michele Bachmanns, Santouris, Huckabees, and Palins to name a few. As a congressional member, Bachmann wanted to initiate a law banning and impending removal of the secular protective clause. Likewise the Republican Party presidential aspirant, Ted Cruz seeks the same.

The Jewish people are so very right to reveal the Holocaust in all its intensity. Down through time they have suffered repeated holocausts. This Christian backed betrayal to the harmony of Creator's ultimate de-sign is well hidden in post war cover up and obvious secrecy. Authors who exposed the blatant denial and prejudice of the sanctified wartime reigned Pope Pius Pacelli have been decidedly, falsely vilified by the Catholic hierarchy and opiated minions. John Cornwell and James Carroll and Susan Zucotti exposed Pacelli from their own Vatican archive rec-ords. The RCC (Roman Catholic Church) took extreme issue with John Cornwell, unleashing an all-out war of their own making effort to vilify him for his *Hitler's Pope*. They are not pleased either with James Carroll, a former priest and author of *Constantine's Sword*. Both men set out to write positively about the wartime pope when the usually secretive Vatican, surprisingly, opened up its files due to a newly elected open minded pope who did not last long. As I write this, we have what appears is the great-est pope of them all. I only hope Pope Francis does not depart us early. These two authors, Cornwell and Carroll, were so shocked at what they discovered that they could not and would not lie about the clear evidence within the wartime records. Susan Zucotti, author of *Underneath His Very Windows*—Pius XII's cowardly refusal to save, at least make a humanitarian attempt, 4,200 Jews, corralled and bound for Auschwitz to be gassed. Sporadic gunfire raged to round up recalcitrant Vatican neighborhood Jews and yet the Vicar of Christ never intervened, not even a phone call to the German commandant in Rome and now, beatified by the resigned Pope Ratzinger for canonization.

Less than a century ago was it the last holocaust? Israel now, will not allow it. Hopefully this age of communication will put an end to such awesome tragedy. The orchestrated terror of WW II was all blamed on the 'Nazis,' however, as though the entire exuberant 'Sieg Heiling of the supporting Christian nation had nothing to do with the carrying out of the holocaust- its enslavement, persecution and actual death of millions. How effectively, however, will Man deny actuality and real Truth? 'Resolve', 'My Way only!', 'To Hell with yours.' The healing, mental health promoting deep meaning of the word- Introspection – is not accepted within the mind of the religious zealot, however. The persecuted, the survivors of all this idiotic carnage, however, do not want its reoccurrence and most certainly believe in the value of knowledge and portrayal. Introspection respects Creator's Truth and promotes Its desired social and environmental Harmony. Those who deny Introspection will find out their error of denial, at least, in the Beyond World… my mere supposition.

*   *   *   *

James Haught, author of the unusual books, *Holy Horrors* and *Holy Hatred-* Prometheus Books, describes in detail the human sacrifice within the Great Inquisition.[29] Over 500 years is quite a timespan and even reached into the New World to punish Indians who adhered to their native beliefs. "Efforts to establish heresy led to the establishment of the Holy Inquisition, one of mankind's supreme horrors. In the early 1200s, local bishops were empowered to identify, try, and punish heretics. When the bishops proved ineffective, traveling papal inquisitors, usually Dominican priests, were sent from Rome to conduct the purge." [30]

> Pope Innocent IV authorized torture in 1252, and the Inquisition chambers became places of terror. Accused heretics were seized and locked in cells, unable to see their families, unable

[29] James Haught, *Holy Horrors*, (Amherst, NY: Prometheus Press, 1990).
[30] Ibid, p.61

to know the names of their accusers. If they didn't confess quickly, unspeakable cruelties began.

Swiss historian Walter Nigg recounted. "So that the torturers would not be disturbed by the shrieking of the victim, his mouth was stuffed with cloth. Three-and four hour sessions of torture were nothing unusual. During the procedure the instruments were frequently sprinkled with holy water. [31]

The victim was required not only to confess that he was a heretic, but also to accuse his children, wife, friends, and others as fellow heretics, so that they might be subjected to the same process. Minor offenders and those who confessed immediately received lighter sentences. Serious heretics who repented were given life imprisonment and their possessions confiscated. Others were led to the stake in a procession and church ceremony called the "auto-da-fé" (act of the faith). A papal statute of 1231 decreed burning as the standard penalty. The actual executions were performed by civil officers, not

priests, as a way of preserving the church's sanctity.

Some inquisitors cut terrible swaths. Robert le Bourge sent 183 to the stake in a single week. Bernard Gui convicted 930—confiscating the property of all 930, sending 307 to prison and burning forty-two. Conrad of Marburg burned every suspect who claimed innocence." [32]

Haught includes numerous paintings and drawings from medieval

---

[31] Ibid, pg.62
[32] Ibid, p.62-64

artists which portray torture scenes to add further proof that these ago-nizing horrors did happen. Some illustrations exhibit a pope or a bishop looking on with their cortege and often wearing a halo. Examples of the descriptions are as follows:

"Albigenses, Christians, also called Cathari and Publicani, were burned by Catholic bishops in the late 1100s, before the pope declared a military crusade against them."[33]This painting was a courtesy from the Lancaster Mennonite Historical Society. The memory of the purged vic-tims, now organized themselves and becoming the fastest growing por-tion of Christianity – the evangelicals have their museums exposing such victimization.

> St. Dominic wears a halo in this church painting as he presides over an Inquisition session deciding the fate of two accused heretics stripped and bound to posts at lower right.[34]
>
> Pope Pius V and his cardinals (background) watch the Roman Inquisition burn a nonconforming religious scholar, about 1570." [35]
>
> Ceremonious burning of convicted heretics at a religious "auto-da-fé" (act of faith) climaxed the Inquisition process. Engraved in 1723 by Bernhard Picart [36]``

---

[33] Ibid, p.55
[34] Ibid, p.63
[35] Ibid, p.65
[36] Ibid, p.67

Accused "witches" first were stripped and searched for "devil marks"—then the torture began. The process usually ended in execution.[37] This painting depicts an attractive woman in terror, bound and nude before two male torturers, one who is reading a manual on torture.

"About 2,000 Waldensian Protestants in Calabria, southern Italy, were massacred in 1560 by Catholic troops under Grand Inquisitor Michele Ghislieri, who later became Pope Pius V and was sainted."[38]

"Burning at the stake was the chief fate of accused witches, but others were hanged, drowned, or crushed."[39] This portrait portrays an accused woman repentantly holding a crucifix as she looks to the heavens

[37] Ibid, p.75
[38] Ibid, p.57
[39] Ibid, p.77

while tied to a burning stake. This picture I find the most stunning regarding terroristic horror along with page 75, of Haught's *Holy Horrors*. (Artist- Jose Brito, Library of Congress print collection.) The process usually ended in execution. It is no wonder that so many Christians have a fear of their religion or their concept of God. The DNA blueprint which all, might beings have, would surely carry over some of that fear implanted in such a horrible age of ignorance that lasted down through generations. Imagine! Superstition ran so rampant that entire countries believed fervently that a woman wearing a pointed hat could sit on a stick and thus fly around freely, most often at night. So much do we owe to Iroquoian earth based Democracy that initiated the rejection of such sheer, terroristic superstition idiocy. Some background for the largest sect in Christianity.

* * * *

The Inquisition was divided into three phases: the medieval extermination of heretics; the Spanish Inquisition in the 1400s; and the Roman Inquisition, which began after the Reformation.

> In Spain, thousands of Jews had converted to Christianity to escape death in recurring Christian massacres. So, too, had some Muslims. They were, however, suspected of being insincere converts clandestinely practicing their old religion. In 1478 the pope authorized King Ferdinand and Queen Isabella to revive the Inquisition to hunt "secret Jews" and their Muslim counterparts. Dominican friar Tomas de Torquemada was appointed inquisitor general, and he became a symbol of religious cruelty. Thousands upon thousands of screaming victims were tortured, and at least 2,000 were burned. [40]
>
> The Roman period began in 1542 when Pope Paul III sought to eradicate Protestant influences in Italy. Under Pope Paul IV, this inquisition was a reign of terror, killing many "heretics" on mere suspicion. Its victims included scientist-philosopher Giordano Bruno, who espoused Copernicus's theory that planets orbit the sun. He was burned at the stake in 1600 in Rome. [41]
>
> The Inquisition blighted many lands for centuries. In Portugal, records recount that 184 were burned alive and auto-da-

---

[40] Ibid, pp.65-66
[41] Ibid, p.66

fé processions contained as many as 1,500 "penitents" at a time. The Inquisition was brought by Spaniards to the American colonies, to punish Indians who reverted to native religions. A total of 879 heresy trials were recorded in Mexico in the late 1500s.

The horror persisted until modern times. The Spanish Inquisition was suppressed by Joseph Bonaparte in 1808, restored by Ferdinand VII in 1814, suppressed again in 1823, and finally eradicated in 1834.

Lord Acton, himself a Catholic, wrote in the late 1800s, "The principle of the Inquisition was murderous. The popes were not only murderers in the great style, but they also made murder a legal basis of the Christian Church and a condition of salvation." [42]

Women were special targets of the Inquisition:

During the 1400s, the Holy Inquisition shifted its focus toward witchcraft, and the next three centuries witnessed a bizarre orgy of religious delusion. Agents of the church tortured untold thousands of women, and some men, into confessing that they flew through the sky on demonic missions, engaged in sex with Satan, turned themselves into animals, made themselves invisible, and performed other supernatural evils. Virtually all the accused were put to death. The number of victims is estimated widely from 100,000 to 2 million.[43]

Pope Gregory IX originally authorized the killing of witches in the 1200s, and random witch trials were held, but the craze didn't catch fire until the 15th century. In 1484 Pope Innocent VIII issued a bull declaring the absolute reality of witches—thus it became heresy to doubt their existence. Prosecutions soared. The inquisitor Cumanus burned forty-one women the following year, and a colleague in the Piedmont of Italy executed 100.[44]

As mentioned before but well bears repeating for memories sake by James Haught- "All witchcraft comes from carnal lust, which is in women insatiable," they wrote.[45] Modern psychology easily perceives the sexual

---

[42] Ibid, pp.66-68
[43] Ibid, p.73
[44] Ibid, p. 73
[45] Ibid, p.74

neurosis of these priests—yet for centuries their book was the official manual used by inquisitors sending women to horrible deaths.

> Witch-hunts flared in France, Germany, Hungary, Spain, Italy, Switzerland, Sweden, and nearly every corner of Europe— finally reaching England, Scotland, and the Massachusetts Bay Colony. Most of the victims were old women who roused suspicion of neighbors. Others were young, pretty women. Some were men. Many in continental Europe were simply citizens whose names were shrieked out by torture victims when commanded to identify fellow witches. [46]

Such horridness against humanity needs to be emblazoned within every sound human beings memory.

The standard Inquisition procedure of isolating and grilling suspects was followed—plus an added step: the victims were stripped naked, shaved of all body hair, and "pricked." The *Malleus Maleficarum* specified that every witch bore a numb "devils mark," which could be detected by jabbing with a sharp object. Inquisitors also looked for "witches' tits," blemishes that might be secret nipples whereby the women suckled their demons.[47]

> A profound irony of the witch-hunts is that they were directed, not by superstitious savages, but by learned bishops, judges, professors, and other leaders of society. The centuries of witch obsession demonstrated the terrible power of supernatural beliefs. [48]

As I have said over and over, an elevated priesthood that does not recognize the balance of woman and her leadership can prove to be a very dangerous thing. Human sacrifice is a horrendous example of extreme zealousness. People get too carried away with "knowing" that they are right and the others, the outsiders, "are definitely wrong." This idea— that God does not care if the zealous exterminate the victims of their choosing—has been a tragic part of human history. Pretending that this past did not exist or blaming it all on the Incas and Aztecs is not beneficial knowledge if we seek balanced harmony amongst all creeds. Such

---

[46] Ibid, p.74
[47] Ibid, *Holy Horrors, Witch hunts* pp.73-76.
[48] Ibid, p.79

history assures me that my mere perspective—"I do not know" and "It is all a mystery,"—seems like a harmless butterfly flitting through the woods, in comparison. I believe there is a spirit world. Those poor medieval victims are quite possibly in that spirit world and they just might be reminding their tormentors for an eternity how wrong they were.

*   *   *   *

I sat in a Perkins, on Veterans Day, it was cold outside and I wore my colorful Marine aviation flight jacket with its many military patches and insignia. The flight jacket has gold military aviator's wings embossed on a leather name tag as all Navy/Marine pilots wear. I was finishing off a Biscuits and Gravy breakfast. My 110 combat Missions Vietnam patch is just above the leather embossed name plate. The waitress walked up to me, a pretty girl. She stammered, crossed her hands and awkwardly took a stance looking down on me. She pointed to a couple a few booths away to tell me they were picking up my bill. This also happens occasionally when I have been in a restaurant wearing my flight jacket or summers when I wear my Korea/Vietnam Veterans ball cap which sports gold Marine pilot's wings. After a nervous shifting she sporadically blurted out, "Thank you for my Freedom." A slight tear formed as she spoke and hurried away. Yes. We all cherish Freedom.

I had to think of the same pretty girl, back several millennia. Actually many were 'comely lasses' as they were referred to in that best-selling book of the times, *Malleus Maleficarum*. Pervert Monks, as mentioned, carried copies throughout Europe, mostly Dominican, their papal papers allowing free entrance into any village to search for the Devil hiding among fictitious' Devil Spots, presumably upon a woman's body. Of course to more fully satisfy the sexual perverts, they were urged by the manual in its —'How to torture a woman and find the Devil's spot, chapter' - it offered that 'most likely', the Devil hid among the most comely lasses.' Can any one of you women, especially those who are favorably blessed looks wise- can you imagine two perverts seeking you out and legally hauling you away to some barn to apply torturous, brutal suffering death! Most often as a result? Yes- your sexually arousing, horrible death! Simply for being pretty and appealing as ISIS no doubt does now after satiating rape and so far- Feb 1, 2016- our POTUS is too cowardly and politically minded to do so little and will not immediately put a quick ending to such and has the power to do so. Instead, the CIA had influenced him to fight the regime that is fighting for survival against ISIS. Granted, I am no friend of the Syrian dictator- Assad, but he is no ISIS. If I was POTUS, I would definitely take out ISIS first which shall be covered in a latter chapter —Fighting Terrorism.

Obama was no Warrior. It was not in his genes! We had elected a blatant coward for a leader. Who, what will be next?

Aztecs and Incas

What about sacrifices? North American spirituality never had the human sacrifices which are attributed to the Christian Inquisition or the Central and South American Aztec and Inca sacrifices. Within the same time span, the medieval Christian and the major Central and South American tribes similarly had an organized religion, a priesthood and a class system controlled by a nobility that co-existed in league with the supporting priesthood. Like the Inquisition, the Aztec and Inca priesthood originated human sacrifices which utilized fear and superstition to enhance or perpetuate their power. I must acknowledge however- Some Aztec scholars are disputing the child sacrifice accusations as presumably the imaginations of the conquering Christians so as to spread their conversion operandi more effectively. We Sioux have had our experiences with exaggerating devious missionaries whose final solution was to send off innocent medicine/spiritual leaders via death warrants to Canton Insane Asylum- same option- upon our culture and Spirituality.

Charles Van Doren's book, *A History of Knowledge*, tells us: "Sacrifice, one of the most fundamental and ubiquitous of religious rituals, was or is practiced in almost all of the religions that have ever existed. Great latitude is found in the types of living beings or other things that are or have been sacrificed, as well as in the ritual itself.

> Human sacrifice seems to have originated among the first agricultural peoples. Apparently rarely practiced by the hunter-gatherers who preceded them, it existed in all of the most ancient religions. The early Greeks and Romans, the earliest Jews, the Chinese and Japanese, the Indians, and many other ancient peoples sacrificed human beings to their gods. The victim was often dressed in magnificent garments and adorned with jewels so that he or she might go in glory to the god. The victims, often chosen for their youth and beauty (the god wanted the best), were drowned or buried alive, or their

throats were cut so that their blood might bedew the ground, fructifying it, or be spattered upon the altar. The throats of bulls, rams, and goats were also ritually cut, their blood spilled upon the ground in the effort to please the god or produce a communion between the god and those who sought his help.[49]

Van Doren chose the example of the Aztecs and the Incas to illustrate, in gruesome, but believable detail, the practice of human sacrifice within a religion. "Why were the Spaniards able to destroy two flourishing civilizations so quickly and easily, so that today little is known of them and hardly anything survives except the monumental buildings, a few gold ornaments out of the millions that were made, and the foods that they grew? (The last is far from insignificant.) The answer may lie in the principles by which both empires were organized. [50]

> Fear and force ruled both empires. Both the Aztec and the Inca were relative arrivistes. In each case a ruthless, semi barbarian minority had taken over a previous, probably decadent civilization. These new rulers, having conquered by the merciless use of military power, saw no reason not to rule by it, too. They did not bother to try to acquire the love and loyalty of those they ruled. They had nothing they wished to give their subjects, except a measure of security against want and external enemies. But the enemy within—the rulers themselves—were more fearsome than any foreign foe. And the price exacted for freedom from want, turned out to be very high.[51]
> It was paid in the blood of children and young people. Human sacrifice was practiced by both these unregretted civilizations of the recent past. Among the Aztec, the toll of sacrifice stuns the mind. In the last years before the Spanish conquest, a thousand of the finest children and young people were offered up each week. Dressed in splendid robes, they were drugged and then helped up the steps of the high pyramids and held down upon the altars. A priest, bloody knife in hand, parted the robes, made a quick incision, reached in his other hand and drew forth the heart, still beating, which he held high before the people assembled in the plaza below. A thousand a week, many of them captured in raids among the

[49] Charles Van Doren, *A History of Knowledge*, (New York: Ballantine Books, 1991), p. 13.
[50] Ibid, p.12.
[51] Ibid, p.12.

neighboring tribes in the Valley of Mexico. A thousand a week of the finest among the children and youth, who huddled in prisons before their turn came. It is no wonder that all the enemies of the Aztecs rushed to become the allies of the conquering Spaniards and helped overthrow that brutal regime. Not that doing so helped these fervent allies. They were also enslaved by the victorious conquistadores.

The Inca did not regularly sacrifice large numbers of human beings, but whenever an Inca emperor died, the toll was terrible. Hundreds of maidens would be drugged, beheaded, and buried with the dead ruler. Hundreds of others would die whenever the state faced a difficult problem or decision. Stolid priests proclaimed that only thus would the gods be pleased to help, and so the beautiful boys and girls died on the reeking altars."[52]

Van Doren goes on to state that following the example of Abraham and his son, the Jews were the first to decide that human sacrifice was wrong, that God did not desire it. He states that the Christians, following the traditions of the Jews, never practiced human sacrifice. No details of the Great Inquisition nor of the thousands (or more than likely, several millions) of victims who were sacrificed in Europe over the centuries is to be found in his biased book subtitled: *The Pivotal Events, People, and Achievements of World History*. Introspection is foreign, un-utilized thought to fanatic organized religionists, not just Christians alone. When you bring these historically proven facts up before them, expect a reply, "Why do you have to pick on our religion?" or "Don't you believe in God?" *"Our Way."* They most likely want to add. I take solace in a belief that a Spirit World awaits beyond where hopefully the deep seriousness of this life will be corrected, if need be, according to God's Ultimate Truth.

<hr>

[52] Ibid, p.12.

CHAPTER 8
[ISLAM] WHAT WENT WRONG? BERNARD LEWIS

In Lewis' view, the "by now widespread terrorism practice of suicide bombing is a development of the 20th century" with "no antecedents in Islamic history, and no justification in terms of Islamic theology, law, or tradition."[53] By all standards of the modern world—economic development, literacy, scientific achievement—Muslim civilization, once a mighty enterprise, has fallen low. Many in the Middle East blame a variety of outside forces. But underlying much of the Muslim world's travail may be a simple lack of freedom.

From *The Atlantic* , January 2002 Issue, Bernard Lewis

> Muslim modernizers—by reform or revolution—concentrated their efforts in three main areas: military, economic, and political. The results achieved were, to say the least, disappointing. The quest for victory by updated armies brought a series of humiliating defeats. The quest for prosperity through development brought in some countries impoverished and corrupt economies in recurring need of external aid, in others an unhealthy dependence on a single resource—oil. And even this was discovered, extracted, and put to use by Western ingenuity and industry, and is doomed, sooner or later, to be exhausted, or, more probably, superseded, as the international community grows weary of a fuel that pollutes the land, the sea, and the air wherever it is used or transported, and that puts the world economy at the mercy of a clique of capricious autocrats. Worst of all are the political results: the long quest for freedom has left a string of shabby tyrannies, ranging from traditional autocracies to dictatorships that are modern only in their apparatus of repression and indoctrination.[54]

Lewis offers that, "Many remedies were tried—weapons and factories, schools and parliaments—but none achieved the desired result."[55] The increasing imbalance between Islam and the Western world moved

---

53 Bernard Lewis and Buntzie Ellis Churchill, *Islam: The Religion and the People.* (Indianapolis: Wharton Press, 2008), 153, quoted in "Bernard Lewis," *Wikipedia,* accessed April 8, 2017, https://en.wikipedia.org/wiki/Bernard_Lewis.
54 https://www.theatlantic.com/magazine/archive/2002/01/what-went-wrong/302387/
55 Ibid.

onward. They would continue to fall backward from their historic leadership role to free fall downward in comparison to a host of rising Nations, and not just the Christian based ones. Expansion to the West took a sea going Navy of galleons and equivalent sized vessels and not coastal hugging Arab Dows. France, England, Spain, Portugal and even tiny Holland in comparison ventured seaward exploring, conquering and settling the new hemispheres. The Arab leadership, post Columbus, remained disinterested. The Industrial Revolution would sweep forward with little Arabic participation. Eventually Japan, and later Korea, Indonesia, the Philippines would go Western while a lethargic China took its time to arrive where it is now- a vast world power of production. The West – would lead the exploration and initial tapping of vast oil reserves which has saved the Arab world from utter poverty. Oil revenue pays for the foreign technology, construction and even military weaponry supplied by Westernized nations. In these fields the Arab world still remains stagnant. They have become reduced to the role of followers of the West. Now, their major ware, Arab oil has to be transported by foreign shipping let alone having to hire foreign contractors and technicians because their own are apparently incapable. Comparing the standards that matter in the modern world—economic development, mobile transit, (auto, rail, ocean going, aviation), literacy, educational and scientific achievement, political freedom and respect for human rights—what was once a mighty civilization is no more.

I agree with Bernard Lewis- "Western progress is the separation of Church and State and the creation of a civil society governed by secular laws."[56] The abandonment of such laws and resulting rise in the power of the Islamic clergy remains the primary deterrent toward democratic progress. When the future tragedy of Planetary Heating and Climate Change arrives in full force via the church sanctioned, generated 'Multiply and dominate Mother Nature' mentality; if their mythically acclaimed Resurrection doesn't happen, exponential suffering worldwide will catalyze angry, miserable humans to end church/mosque influence. Re: Organized Religion's fanatic denial of Over-population which is the major cause of planetary heating. Equally destructive for the Mid-east regarding civilization's advancement is the relegation of women to an inferior position in Muslim society, which deprives the Islamic world of the talents and ener-

---

[56] Ibid.

gies of half its people and entrusts the other half's crucial early years of upbringing to illiterate and downtrodden mothers. The products of such an education, grow up either arrogant or submissive, and unfit for a free, open society. Is there some hope within Turkey, Egypt or even Iran for the secularists and feminists? Israel is the only nation in the Mid-east where a woman enjoys the basic freedoms found in the West. Right now it is my belief that such are major faults withholding progressive Democracy. Religious backed male dominated Fanaticism, a term we can truthfully utilize if we compare to our American society's secular and feminine freedoms, is the major reason for Arab stagnation.

Religions, of all man's creations, have the most difficulty when it comes to truthful, harmonic promoting, soul studying introspection. "Who did this to us?" and not "How did I do this to us?" is a common human response in the Middle East. It is easier to blame others for one's mistakes. For a long time the Mongols were the favorite villains. The Mongol invasions of the thirteenth century were blamed for the destruction of both Muslim power and Islamic civilization, and for what was seen as the ensuing weakness and stagnation.

If one would read Jack Weatherford's *Genghis Khan*, based on the Mongol history found in the libraries of Mongolia a vastly opposing view is portrayed than what revengeful western authors present. Genghis Khan was far more democratic including advanced secularism along with opening feminist freedoms. Khan was also far more a Spiritualist than he was a religiously led proponent and not one to be led by a man created religious society or belief system to control his empire. Many an Islamic city state he confronted before his path, he conquered by overthrowing from within and hence without a single casualty. He simply pointed out the despotic sultan rulers and gave the besieged a choice. Join with his forces by throwing out the said despot who often wisely fled beforehand. He even offered the besieged a share in the sultan's spoils. Unfortunately for an early democracy to take root, the Mongols moved on leaving but a temporary reign mainly to protect commerce rather than to demand the change or alteration of religious belief and its resultant political control. The Mongols overthrew an empire of the despotic caliphs that was already fatally weakened by such savage treatment of its citizens who often chose to support the invading force.

Following the Mongols, Turks were customarily blamed for Arab troubles who had ruled them for many centuries. Turks could lay the blame for the stagnation of their civilization on the Arab past, which slowed the creative energies of the Turkish citizens. Persians blamed the loss of their ancient glories on Arabs, Turks, and Mongols.

Blaming Western Imperialism followed rather than one's religious inhibiting, denying, civil rights suffocating control. Islam's change for the worse began long before and continued unabated afterward. Anglo-French rule and American influence, like the Mongol invasions, were not a cause of their modern civilization lack of progress for the Middle Eastern. Finding targets to blame serves a useful, essential, purpose for despotic leadership—to explain the poverty that they have failed to alleviate and deflect the misery of their unhappy subjects.

Of course the Jews would be blamed. A democratic secular country (Israel) within the Mid-east should hardly be the culprit of retarding the necessary democratic freedoms required for the fruits of an industrial revolution.

> Another European contribution to this debate is anti-Semitism, and blaming "the Jews" for all that goes wrong. Jews in traditional Islamic societies experienced the normal constraints and occasional hazards of minority status. Until the rise and spread of Western tolerance in the seventeenth and eighteenth centuries, they were better off under Muslim than under Christian rule in most significant respects. With rare exceptions, where hostile stereotypes of the Jew existed in the Islamic tradition, Islamic societies tended to be contemptuous and dismissive rather than suspicious and obsessive. This made the events of 1948—the failure to prevent the establishment of the state of Israel—all the more of a shock. As some writers observed at the time, it was humiliating enough to be defeated by the great imperial powers of the West; to suffer the same fate at the hands of a contemptible gang of Jews was intolerable. Anti-Semitism and its image of the Jew as a scheming, evil monster provided a soothing antidote....
>
> For most of the Middle Ages it was neither the older cultures of the Orient nor the newer cultures of the West that were the major centers of civilization and progress but the world of Islam. There old sciences were recovered and developed and new sciences were created; there new industries were born and manufactures and commerce were expanded to a level without precedent. There, too, governments and societies achieved a freedom of thought and expression that led persecuted Jews and even dissident Christians to flee Christendom for refuge in Islam....

For those known nowadays as Islamists or fundamentalists, the failures and shortcomings of modern Islamic lands afflict those lands because they adopted alien notions and practices. They fell away from authentic Islam and thus lost their former greatness. Those known as modernists or reformers take the opposite view, seeing the cause of this loss not in the abandonment but in the retention of old ways, and especially in the inflexibility and ubiquity of the Islamic clergy, who, they say, are responsible for the persistence of beliefs and practices that might have been creative and progressive a thousand years ago but are neither today. The modernists' usual tactic is not to denounce religion as such, still less Islam in particular, but to level their criticism against fanaticism. It is to fanaticism—and more particularly to fanatical religious authorities—that they attribute the stifling of the once great Islamic scientific movement and, more generally, of the freedom of thought and expression....

At present two answers to the question of what went wrong command widespread support in the Middle East, each with its own diagnosis and corresponding prescription. One attributes all evil to the abandonment of the divine heritage of Islam and advocates return to a real or imagined past. That is the way of the Iranian revolution and of the so-called fundamentalist movements and regimes in various Muslim countries. The other condemns the past and advocates secular democracy, best embodied in the Turkish Republic, proclaimed in 1923 by Kemal Atatürk.

To a Western observer, schooled in the theory and practice of Western freedom, it is precisely the lack of freedom—freedom of the mind from constraint and indoctrination, to question and inquire and speak; freedom of the economy from corrupt and pervasive mismanagement; freedom of women from male oppression; freedom of citizens from tyranny—that underlies so many of the troubles of the Muslim world. But the road to democracy, as the Western experience amply demonstrates, is long and hard, full of pitfalls and obstacles.

If the peoples of the Middle East continue on their present path, the suicide bomber may become a metaphor for the whole region, and there will be no escape from a downward spiral of hate and spite, rage and self-pity, poverty and oppression, culminating sooner or later in yet another alien domination—perhaps from a new Europe reverting to old ways, perhaps from a resurgent Russia, perhaps from some expanding superpower in the East. But if they can abandon grievance and

victimhood, settle their differences, and join their talents, energies, and resources in a common creative endeavor, they can
once again make the Middle East, in modern times as it was in
antiquity and in the Middle Ages, a major center of civilization.
For the time being, the choice is theirs. [57]

It is some years now since Bernard Lewis wrote such a revealing, solidly portraying article for *Atlantic Monthly*. Time has moved on, however.
Unfathomable developments have progressed positively and appear to
strengthen democratic principles. We have now been able to com-
pare/equate Atrocity of both of the world's most populous religions. If
Terrorism remains a major consideration we shall attempt a glimpse of
another vast portion of Islam and compare the explicit hatred for the
West of mid –Eastern Islam accurately brought forth by Bernard Lewis
and compare to a much mellower far- Eastern Islamic attitude. Islamic
Indonesia which is deeply engaged in world trade sufficiently to rival its
neighbors Japan and China has a competitive edge as well in agriculture
and ocean products for U. S. markets. Less restrictive religious rules (notably for its female population) abide in comparison. Hatred for the West
cannot be exemplary if their economic success is to continue. Indonesia's
productive citizens are not about to relinquish the abrupt upturn in their
living standards. The Islamic hierarchy holds less control over a freedom
enjoying populace tasting a new democratic emerging and leaning lifestyle
contrary to the mid-East's suffocation/eradication of democratic government held down by brutal dictatorships in league with the cooperating
Ayatollahs. Yes, this window from afar will be an important scenario to
study. Fanatic, self-serving religious rules for the controlling hierarchy are
the bane of True Democracy and opens the door for corrupt dictatorships.

---

[57] Ibid.

CHAPTER 9
PEDOPHILIA AND RAPE ARE TERRORISTIC TOO!

Native American Boarding School victims filed their Class action law suit in South Dakota. The Catholic Bishops of the Dakotas lobbied the South Dakota Legislature to shorten the Statue of Limitations. Governor Mike Rounds signed the bill which granted amnesty to the perpetrators. Unlike other states wherein the pedophile and rape victims were compensated, the South Dakota victims were left with only their life damaging memories.

Jesuit Gonzaga University, State of Washington pedophile and rape victims suffered as students in church run Indian boarding schools but won their lawsuits.

For decades, Churches were immune to recompense for rape and pedophile crimes against Christian educated children in the Dakotas, Minnesota and surrounding states with more numerous Indian populations. Bishops would simply cover up and usually transfer church priests or ministers to other parishes where they usually sought out new victims. Many catholic priests had numerous transfers until their retirement.

I was accepted at St. Johns University after a two year stint in the U. S. Marine Corps (Korean tour). Monsignor Costigan, Chancellor of the Diocese of Rapid City opened the door to St. Johns University (MN) if I would attend the seminary school there initially as it was the only way I could get into the rather prestigious school. I soon discovered, however, I just did not fit in with by far, most of my seminary peers. I believed at first it was my Native American blood and background that was the usual shunning by peers but it turned out to be that I still held a degree of interest for the opposite sex not far down the road at the women's college-St. Benedicts. Cars were limited at St Johns. Only a second semester junior with a B average was eligible to bring a vehicle on St. Johns campus or a senior in good standing. Veterans of the military were allowed however, regardless of grade. Due to full dormitories at mid-semester when I arrived I temporarily lived in a make shift clinic 'sick bay' room and later, since I had a vehicle, I was granted permission to live off campus in the nearby, small town where the women's college was located. Needless to say, this 'seminarian' transported many a carload of 'Bennies' to various Friday and Saturday evening 'watering hole' night spots for entertainment. Naturally, I became fairly popular and not because of any appreciable looks I might have imagined or hopelessly fantasized I possibly carried. It was the car- pure and simple. My seminary peers frowned on any conversation about the ladies I had met when we would gather in various dormitory rooms and socialize mostly after the noon meal. I had very little to contribute otherwise from their points of view and eventually figured out that I just did not fit in with them. Being a former Marine and having spent time in freewheeling Asia especially on two R & R vacation eye opening experiences in Japan out of war torn Korea was no doubt less pleasing or prudent conversation among my opposite valued, fellow seminarians. I was no longer in the company of Marines in an eight man squad tent in Korea where girls were a pastime conversation item. Females were a taboo subject among these seminarians, I soon learned.

I knew so little about Church history. In fact I was so illiterate that I did not even understand what the Old Testament versus New Testament was all about. Where did this Moses fit in? Was he more important than Jesus? Who appointed a human as a God, at least a three in one God? Seems such an important event would have been a pretty big decision and not just for humans alone- that Nicea Council when they came up with it sometime back in the 300s. Seems Creator lay back and let all those White, know-it-all Bishops come up with that one. What did Creator have to do with it is a puzzling question at least for my Sioux brain? Will I go to Hell or get thrown in a Lake of Fire for simply asking? Is the Church's Devil making me so curious and making me do all this insane wondering? Are we Indians wrong or 'Sinful' to dare think our God concept is so powerful and truthful that IT just will not allow any Untruth (Which obviously, a Devil, Satan is!) in its Beyond World reign? Could be however, those '3 in 1' folks and Devil believers are in a helluva lot more trouble than I might be - come 'Stepping into the Beyond' Day. Creator's Nature exhibits no Superstition. Where does superstition (Grandiose, tailored claims) come from? Certainly not my Indian Creator who does not allow it in all Its Creation. Judging from his ethical lacking track record, I just can't buy into all of what Wahshichu is trying to push onto me.

One other observation that turned me against becoming a priest was my religion class instructor, a Benedictine monk who began the class with a discussion as to whether or not Mary and Joseph, God's, I mean Jesus's Mom and Dad, had sexual relations before or after his birth. I should say step-dad, right? This teacher had a real fetish over this sex supposition.

We'd spend a good ten to fifteen minutes on the subject. Of course, whether or not whatever, nothing was solved. Personally I didn't care. The Moses question nagged me but I was too embarrassed to let everyone know just how utterly dumb I was. Then we'd go to another related subject as to whether or not we should look at our penises when we went to the restroom urinals to relieve ourselves. I know all this is rather silly, actually weird, but this was my experience in that class. A good half and sometimes all the class period was sexually related in one way or another. I got to thinking that if misogyny and the holy vow to remain celibate does that much weirdness to one then I had better bail the hell out of Divinity.

Eventually I had to sit down and discuss my plight with the Dean of Men who was a former Army major and sympathetic possibly because I was a military veteran. I wound up dating his pretty blonde niece who was a Bennie (nearby St. Benedicts Woman's College). I was freed from my seminarian interest and transferred to the rest of the student body. I continued to remain friendly with certain Bennies until graduation. Seems that blondes always treated me a bit better than the non-blondes. I had bad luck with just about every Indian girl I met. They were pretty hard to find in colleges back then. I had a crush on two of them from high school before I went off to Korea and they never wrote back after sending several letters. One I cut her picture out of a high school annual and pretended she was my girlfriend while in Korea. Another stood me up in college. One borrowed $100.00 while I was summer Ironworking and disappeared on me. Yet, blondes seemed totally opposite so that is why I mostly dated them. Isn't or wasn't my fault. I developed a motto. Never go with anyone unless they like you and I fairly well have stuck by such self-advice which wound up with what I consider were healthy, pleasing for the most part- harmonic relationships.

I enjoyed my years at St Johns. It was not until years later that some of the seminarians that were not very friendly to me, wound up on a 23 member Benedictine monk, Abbey published confessional list before the entire student body for pedophilia allegations including Abbott John Eidenschink who died before victim justice could be applied. A convenient boy's prep school was administered on campus as well during the abbot's reign. A former monk who quit the Benedictines' to become a law firm's pedophile victim's investigator contributed to the following Northwest Jesuit expose.

"Pedophile's Paradise" by Brendan Kiley , *The Stranger* - Feb 5, 2009

Alaska Natives are accusing the Catholic Church of using their remote villages as a "dumping ground" for child-molesting priests—and blaming the president of Seattle University for letting it happen.

One spring afternoon in 1977, 15-year-old Rachel Mike tried to kill herself for the third time. An Alaska Native, Rachel was living in a tiny town called Stebbins on a remote island called St. Michael. She lived in a house with three bedrooms and nine siblings. Rachel was a drinker, depressed, and starving. "When my parents were drinking, we didn't eat right," she says. "I just wanted to get away from the drinking."

Rachel walked to the bathroom to fetch the family rifle, propped in the bathtub with the dirty laundry (the house didn't have running water). To make sure the gun worked, Rachel loaded a shell and blew a hole in her bedroom wall. Her father, passed out on his bed, didn't hear the shot. Rachel walked behind their small house. Her arms were too short to put the rifle to her head, so she shot herself in her right leg instead.

Rachel was found screaming in a pool of blood by her Auntie Emily and flown 229 miles to a hospital in Nome. The doctor asked if she wanted to see a priest. She said yes. In walked Father James Poole—a popular priest, radio personality on KNOM, and, according to allegations in at least five lawsuits, serial child rapist. Father Poole has never been convicted of a crime, but the Jesuits have settled numerous sex-abuse claims against him since 2005, in excess of $5 million, according to an attorney involved in four of those five lawsuits. Exact figures aren't available because some of the settlements involve confidentiality agreements. The Jesuits have never let a single case against Father Poole go to trial.

In a 2005 deposition, Rachel testified that she had been molested by Father Poole in 1975, while in Nome for her second suicide attempt, an attempted overdose of alcohol and pills. He'd come sit by her bed, put his hand under the hospital blanket, and fondle her, she said.

She traveled between Stebbins and Nome several times in the late 1970s, spending time in hospitals and receiving homes. By 1977, Rachel testified, Poole had given her gonorrhea, and by 1978 she was pregnant with his child. In an interview with *The Stranger*, she said Poole encouraged her to get an abortion and tell the doctors she had been raped by her father. She followed his advice. "He brainwashed me," she said. "He messed up my head, man."

Rachel Mike's father died in 2004. A year later, she heard Elsie Boudreau, another survivor of Poole's abuse, being interviewed on the radio. Listening to Boudreau, Rachel was moved to finally tell the truth.

"He's gone, and I'll never have a chance to tell him in person," she said, talking about her father between heaving sobs. "I was scared. In a way he knew, but—he never even touched me."

"This man," says Anchorage-based attorney Ken Roosa, referring to Poole, "has left a trail of carnage behind him."

The only reason Poole is not in jail, Roosa says, is the statute of limitations. And the reason he's still a priest, being cared for by the church?

"Jim Poole is elderly," answered Very Reverend Patrick J. Lee, head of the Northwest Jesuits, by e-mail. "He lives in a Jesuit community under an approved safety plan that includes 24-hour supervision."

Roosa has another theory—that Poole knows too much. "They can't put him on the street and take away his reason for keeping quiet," Roosa says. "He knows all the secrets."

Father James Poole's story is not an isolated case in Alaska. On the morning of January 14 in Seattle, Ken Roosa and a small group Alaska Natives stood on the sidewalk outside Seattle University to announce a new lawsuit against the Jesuits, claiming a widespread conspiracy to dump pedophile priests in isolated Native villages where they could abuse children off the radar.

"They did it because there was no money there, no power, no police," Roosa said to the assembled cameras and microphones. "It was a pedophile's paradise." He described a chain of poor Native villages where priests—many of them serial sex offenders—reigned supreme. "We are going to shine some light on a dark and dirty corner of the Jesuit order."

The suit, filed in the superior court of Bethel, Alaska, the day before, accuses several priests of being offenders and conspirators. Among the alleged conspirators is Father Stephen Sundborg, who is the current president of Seattle University and was Provincial of the Oregon Province of Jesuits from 1990 through 1996. (The Oregon Province includes Washington, Oregon, Montana, Idaho, and Alaska; as Provincial, Sundborg was head of the entire province.) The suit alleges that while Sundborg was head of the Northwest

Jesuits, he had access to the personnel files of several
pedophile priests, including one named Father Henry
Hargreaves, whom he allowed to remain in the ministry. "As a
direct result of Father Sundborg's decision," the suit alleges,
"Father Hargreaves was able to continue molesting children,
including but not limited to James Doe 94, who was raped by
Father Hargreaves in 1992, when James Doe was
approximately 6 years old."

Roosa and his associate Patrick Wall (a former
Benedictine monk who once worked as a sex-abuse fixer for
the Catholic Church) said they knew of 345 cases of
molestation in Alaska by 28 perpetrators who came from at
least four different countries.

This concentration of abuses is orders of magnitude
greater than Catholic sex-abuse cases in other parts of the
United States. Today, Roosa said, there are 17,000 Catholics in
the diocese of Fairbanks, though there was a much smaller
number during the peak of the abuse. Roosa compared this
lawsuit to the famous Los Angeles suits of 2001, which
claimed 550 victims of abuse in a Catholic population of 3.4
million.

These abusers in Alaska, Wall said, were specifically sent
to Alaska "to get them off the grid, where they could do the
least amount of damage" to the church's public image.

One by one, the Alaska Natives—including Elsie
Boudreau, the woman whom Rachel Mike had heard on the
radio—took their turns before the cameras and microphones,
talking softly and nervously and choking back tears. "I am Flo
Kenny," a woman with a gray ponytail and sunglasses said
carefully. "I am 74 years old. And I've kept silent for 60 years.
I am here for all the ones who cannot speak—who are dead,
who committed suicide, who are homeless, who are drug
addicts. There's always been a time, an end of secrets. This is
the time."

Alphonsus Abouchuk, wearing a black leather jacket and
sunglasses, talked about how poor his family was and how the
priests used to give him quarters after abusing him.

Rena Abouchuk, his sister, cried while she read a letter to
a Franciscan monk named Anton Smario (currently living in
Concord, California) who taught her catechism classes. "You
did so many evil things to young children," she read, gripping
her letter in one hand and an eagle feather tied to a small red
sachet in the other. "God will never forgive you. You took a
lot of lives." Six of her cousins, she later said, committed

suicide because of Brother Smario.

The lawsuit states that Brother Smario offered children food and juice to coax them to stay after class: "He then would unzip his pants, and completely expose his genitals to these children, and masturbate to ejaculation as he walked around the classroom. He would ask the girls to touch his penis and would rub his erect penis on their backs, necks, and arms. Sometimes he would wipe or rub his semen on the girls after he ejaculated."

According to the allegations, Father Joseph Lundowski molested or raped James Does 29, 59–71, and 73–94, plus Janet Does 4–7—a total of 40 children—giving them "hard candy, money he stole from the collection plate, cooked food, baked goods, beer, sacramental wine, brandy, and/or better grades (silver, blue, or gold stars) on their catechism assignments in exchange for sexual favors."

The lawsuit also alleges Father George Endal raped and molested several boys—and, as Smario and Lundowski's boss, was the person who put Lundowski in charge of the boys dormitory in the Holy Rosary Mission School in Dillingham, Alaska, where catechism classes were split between Smario (in charge of the girls) and Lundowski (in charge of the boys). On separate occasions, Father Endal and another priest named Norman E. Donohue—who allegedly raped James Doe 69—walked in on Lundowski while he was molesting children and either quietly left the room or did nothing to stop it.

Father Francis Fallert, principal of the Copper Valley School and head of the all the Alaska Jesuits from 1976 to 1982, is accused of molesting Janet Doe 6.

The sheer concentration of known sex offenders in these isolated communities begins to look less like an accident than a plan. Their institutional protection looks less like an embarrassed cover-up than aiding and abetting. And the way the church has settled case after case across the country, refusing to let most of them go to trial for a public airing, is starting to look like an admission of guilt.

When Patrick Wall wore monk's robes, he must've looked like Friar Tuck. A former all-state football lineman, Wall has broad shoulders, a brawny neck, short reddish hair, and a habit of calling people "bro."

We met last week in Sea-Tac Airport's Alaska Airlines Board Room—a two-story business lounge, just past the security check, with conference tables, ergonomic chairs next to computer stations, and free espresso. He and Ken Roosa were there to meet with a client. Wall lives in California, Roosa lives in Anchorage, and many of their clients are on the West Coast, so they've done a lot of business in the Board Room. "I like to spend the night at home," Wall says, setting his airplane reading—*The Name of the Rose*—on the conference-room table.

Wall's first call as a sex-abuse fixer knocked on his door one morning in 1991, while he was brushing his teeth. Wall was not yet a priest, just a monk studying at St. John's University in Minnesota. The abbot came to his room before class with an urgent matter regarding another monk and said Wall would be moving into the boy's prep-school dormitory—immediately. The other monk "had an incident with a 14-year-old in the shower." Wall was to take his place.

Taken aback, Wall threw up every objection he could think of. He didn't own a computer and used the communal ones in the monastery. "We'll buy you a laptop." He helped with mass at a local parish. "We'll reassign you to campus ministry." He was on call for the volunteer fire department. "Not anymore." The abbot wouldn't take no for an answer.

So Wall packed up, moved into the boys dormitory, quickly intuited who else on the floor had been abused (5 out of the 90 residents), and coaxed them into talking about what had happened. Those cases never became public and were settled out of court. "If you're good," Wall says, "the assignments build." Wall was so good, he was ordained a year early and kept busy, working as many as 13 cases per month.

The job was harrowing and frustrating. "If you're the cleaner, you rarely find out the resolution to these things," Wall says. "Because survivors had to sign confidentiality agreements." The ultimate objective, for a cleaner, was to keep things quiet so the details never became public or went to trial. Wall slowly came to believe that his superiors were more concerned with protecting their public image than caring for survivors. It was, he says, a dark time, not least because he was struggling with his own vows of celibacy. In 1998, he asked to be laicized. By 2001, he was married to a ballet dancer and had a newborn daughter. By 2002, he was hired as a full-time researcher for the law firm Manly and Stewart investigating clerical sex-abuse cases.

Since then, he and Roosa—who often collaborate on cases with attorney John Manly—have worked over 250 cases together, all of them settled without going to trial. "I would like to see any of these cases go to trial to expose the corruption of the system," Wall says. But the church would rather pay the money than subject itself to public scrutiny, and survivors generally prefer to avoid the increased emotional turmoil of a trial. "There was one survivor who went through 11 days of questioning, of deposition," Roosa says. "The defense lawyers can make it so painful."

"If you bend a young plant, it grows at an angle," Roosa says. "Child sex abuse bends the character and maturation of a person—the abuse isn't the injury as much as the effect it has on people."

Father Poole's alleged abuses are particularly egregious, earning him a special place in Roosa's and Wall's hearts. He is their archetypal bad guy, their Dr. Mengele of the clerical sex-abuse world: Their clients have described, in sworn testimony, Poole pressing his erections against girls during junior-high dances, being caught by his own mother while masturbating in front of young girls, and much worse. "The defense lawyers have been so disgusted with Poole," Roosa says, "that they've told me off the record, 'anything you tell me about Poole, I'd believe.'"

According to a victim identified as Jane Doe 5 in a 2006 complaint, Poole first raped her during a private catechism class when she was 6 years old. From a direct transcript of her testimony:

> He started fidget—finger—started to touch me digitally with his fingers. And at that time, when he started getting closer to me, I—there's a picture—I'm on the desk, a picture to the left of me is a picture of Jesus who's at the rock praying, and to my left I look at the picture to my left, and I look into James Poole's eyes. I turned away from the picture, looked into his eyes, and asked 'Not in front of Jesus, please.' He kept telling me that in order to be a good little girl for God, I had to do this. That God wanted me to do this. And I remember a burning.

Then, she says, he raped her.

Roosa tells a story about Poole molesting a 9-year-old girl in Portland, Oregon, while simultaneously having an affair with the girl's mother. Poole supposedly told the girl's mother he would quit the priesthood and marry her, but abruptly returned to Alaska. The girl's mother committed suicide. According to Wall and Roosa, that same girl says she was molested by another priest, one who has been listed in at least three settlements in cases that reach back to the 1960s. They say that, in one incident, this priest was called to a house in

Yakima to administer last rites to a dying woman in 1989. "He raped the woman on her deathbed," Roosa says. "He told the family to go into the other room, the husband heard a weird noise, went into the bedroom, and caught him raping his unconscious wife."

The woman didn't die, and by the time Roosa and Wall caught up with her family last May, the church had offered the family half a million dollars. The family said they'd file a legal complaint if Roosa and Wall could guarantee more than half a million dollars in compensation.

"No," Wall said. "Take it, bro."

Within hours of the press conference on the sidewalk in front of Seattle University on January 14—which essentially alleges that Father Stephen Sundborg allowed molester priests to minister freely as members of the Northwest Jesuits when it was his responsibility, as Provincial, to keep them away from children—Sundborg denied having any information about the Jesuit "dumping ground" in Northwest Alaska:

> The allegations brought against me are false. I firmly deny them. I want the victims and the entire community to know that. The complaint filed by the plaintiffs' lawyers represents an unprincipled and irresponsible attack on my reputation. Let me be clear—my commitment to justice and reconciliation for all victims remains steadfast.

On January 31, Father Sundborg, through his spokesperson, responded to questions from *The Stranger* with this statement:

> I want to be very clear: As Provincial of the Oregon Province of the Society of Jesus, I would never have put a child at risk. I was never aware of any claim of child abuse concerning either Fr. James Poole or Fr. Henry Hargreaves.
>
> As I have said repeatedly in the past, as a member of the Society of Jesus, I personally and sincerely apologize for the pain that has been suffered through the actions of some members of our order.
>
> I am disappointed that the plaintiffs' attorneys are attempting to use falsehoods and innuendo to fuel a media campaign. Their attack on my reputation is unprincipled and irresponsible.
>
> Nonetheless, I remain firm in my resolve to seek justice and reconciliation for all victims.

With the exception of Father Hargreaves allegedly raping
James Doe 94 in 1992, no abuses—at least none that have
been reported—occurred while Sundborg was Provincial.

Still, Wall says, "Stevie has a little problem."....

[I]n 1992, Father Boly wrote an essay for a book called
Jesuits in Profile: Alive and Well in the U.S. about his attraction to
high-school girls:

> I remember being reprimanded more than once for
> spending too much time with visiting coeds from other
> local high schools. My rationalization was that if attractive
> young women brought their problems to me, it must be an
> opportunity for apostolic service. What I neglected to
> consider was what needs of my own the interactions with
> the women students were meeting.

Sundborg also contributed an essay to *Jesuits in Profile*, but
testified in 2005 that he had no recollection of reading the
book.

Dr. Greenberg—the counselor to whom Sundborg had
sent Poole, Laudwein, Boly, and others for evaluation—was
arrested in the summer of 2007 for surreptitiously filming staff
members and patients using the bathroom at his office and,
according to Roosa, filming himself masturbating while
watching the films. A few weeks later, he rented a room at a
motel in Renton, where he committed suicide. Police found
him with a bunch of bottles of prescription pills and two
slashed wrists.

"I wish I could offer you some adequate explanation," his
suicide note read. "I just don't know. I deeply and profoundly
apologize."

This isn't Sundborg's first go-around with fending off a
sex-abuse case. In 2006, the Jesuits settled a $350,000 suit
against Father Michael Toulouse, a philosophy professor at
Seattle University accused of abusing a 12-year-old boy in his
residence in 1968. At the time of the settlement, Father
Sundborg argued that Seattle University wasn't liable, even
though the abuse happened on campus, because the abuse
occurred outside of his official duties as a teacher—a rare
Catholic argument for the separation of church and sex.[58]

---

[58] http://www.thestranger.com/seattle/the-pedophiles-paradise/Content?oid=1065017

"Northwest Jesuits to Pay $166.1 Million to Native Abuse Victims".
The Circle, **Circle Staff, Mpls, April 12, 2011**[59]

"Hearings before a Subcommittee on Indian Affairs." Ed McGaa,
Warrior's Odyssey, **(Amazon- 2015, p. 292).**

> Physical Abuse of Children, Pine Ridge, South Dakota
> Senate, on S.R. 79, 71st Cong., 2nd sess., 1930, pp 2833-
> 2835.
> Examination by United States Senator Frazier
> Q. What is your name?
> A. Mrs. Rose Ecoffey.
> Q. Were you ever employed in the Indian Service?
> A. Yes. I was matron in the school, boys' matron tempo-
> rarily; I was there in August, September and part of October.
> Mr. Jermark asked me to go up there and take the matron's
> place.
> Q. And when they got a regular matron you went home?
> A. Yes.
> Q. Is that the only time you ever worked at the school?
> A. I worked as a nurse in the hospital.
> Q. What about the conditions at the school? How were
> the boys treated?
> A. Not good I would call it; runaway boys were whipped
> and a ball and chain was put on them and they were shaved
> close to their head; that is the way they punished them for
> running away.
> Q. Why did they do that?
> A. Because they run away and played hooky because they
> did not like the school.
> Q. Do you know of any specific instances where they
> done that?
> A. Yes; there was one little one 12 and another one 10,
> and they put a ball and chain on them and put them to bed
> and locked the door on them, and when I went in there I
> wanted to change their bed and the disciplinarian refused to let
> me; and it was not fit for anyone to see. They kept them
> locked up there for three or four weeks or a month. I asked
> Mr. Wilson, the disciplinarian about them—he was not here
> very long and he said to leave them there.

[59]http://thecirclenews.org/index.php?option=com_content&task=view&id=481&Itemid=51

Indian Boarding School – My Sister 'Chick' (Eldean) Ressl and Rosemon Goings.

Boarding School Memoirs

When I look in the mirror, I see an Indian

My sister, Chick and her best friend Rosemon stopped in one morning for coffee. I was just getting started on my writing. I had an old Macintosh that you had to put a disk into. They sat me down and Rosemon told most of this story.

We had read in the paper about another government research program. After Rosemon lit her cigarette, she sat back in her chair to blow a smoke ring at the ceiling. She waited for the smoke to dissipate before she spoke, "I'd like to see some of that grant money come up with a study on the boarding schools. I say a lot of Indians are alcoholics because they were taught to be ashamed of themselves. These studies and grants are always theorizin' about the Indian problem but they never take a look at the damage the boarding schools and missionaries did."

Those two have always been off limits for research," I remarked.

I remember when I was six, a bus picked us up in the fall," she continued, "We wouldn't see our folks for nine months. Can you imagine white kids in suburbia being sent off for nine months? And now they're bitching about busing. Hell, we had busing a long time ago, only it was a one-way trip. If you were lucky, you could go home Christmas vacation, providing your parents had money enough to come and get you or a round-trip bus ticket was sent in the mail. A one-way ticket, and they wouldn't let you go home.

Most research grants come from the government, through the BIA or the Education Department. The grants are controlled by non-Indians mostly, or Indians like that creepy Rosalie Carlson. She's been at this University longer than I can remember and she's attended every Indian conference in the country. If she ever graduates, she'll step into one of the BIA positions and continue to do nothing except take care of her crony friends who are just as phony as she is. Rosalie wouldn't know what to do with a shawl at a powwow, let alone know what a powwow is. You'll never see her at the Sun Dance either. The sociologists, anthros' and Indian experts work hand in hand with Rosalie's kind on the government grants. They aren't going to let the truth be told; hell no, because if you want to expose the truth, you don't receive the grant." She pursed a hard frown. "It's as simple as that. Telling the truth would put an end to their summer vacations."

I sat quietly, nodding my head to indicate agreement. I sure as hell would never receive a government controlled grant by Indian Bureaucrats except the GI. Bill, which I earned.

Then there are the do-gooders that will give money to the church for research. That church won't tell what really happened. Hell, they're so damn blind and bigoted, they can't believe their boarding schools did any damage. How could it be detrimental they say, as long as the people received Jesus? What more could the Indians want? Give 'em Geesus, even if we take their kids from them. But you know something? When you're six, seven or eight years old, lonely as hell, lying in your bed in a spooky dormitory with a bunch of black hooded nuns floatin' up and down the aisle stringin' their rosaries, you cry. Goddamn, you cry. Even animals have a family. God made families but they stole us from ours and they gave us…Jesus."

I cried for a couple weeks when I first got there," Chick chimed in. "But, what the hell good did it do?" She shrugged. "You had to toughen up to get through."

Chick reached for a cigarette. "The damned loneliness, especially the first nights away from home." She posed a sarcastic look. "They always offer that excuse—but they meant well."

Rosemon's reply was coldly emphatic. "Meant well! Hell, Hitler meant well for the Germans, they say. What the hell good was that for the Jews in the ovens and the concentration camps?" She continued with fervor, "A paper Jesus and 'meant well' can't replace human love, not when you're six or eight or eighteen, and lonely as hell in a cold goddamn institution." She paused to glance across the room. "You was lucky you didn't do much time in the boarding school. You went to school with the white kids. You came home every night to a mom and dad."

The remark evoked my response, "Some of the Rapid City kids at the public school made fun of us but I was fortunate. I played sports and had some baseball and basketball friends that stuck up for me." After a quiet moment of reflection, "Had big, tough, white kid, Curtis for a friend. (Both knew him.) He played basketball and didn't have much of a home life. He never knew what the hell a homemade cookie or a pie was until he came over to our house. Funny how a little thing like a homemade cookie can change your life," I said with a smile. "This guy was as tough as Brother Albert and he really liked our folks." My sister beamed. "They gave him the love that he never had at home. Before he came along I had trouble with some of the white kids at school." I frowned. "I knew some Indian kids a couple grades ahead of me, they were ridiculed so much they had to go back down to the boarding school." With that we held a discussion of the various family offspring that played summers along Rapid Creek in Rapid City.

"Rapid's getting better," Rosemon acknowledged, "but when I was going to school the missionaries had an iron grip. When September came, the buses would load up the kids, little ones and big ones and down to the reservations they'd go." She ground her cigarette into an ashtray before she continued.

"I was in grade school with your sister Elsie when she got pneumonia. She was real bad off. Albert wrote back to your folks and told them how sick she was. You must've been pretty small yet 'cuz they were still living on the reservation then. Well, in those days they even censored the letters at the boarding school and your folks never knew about it until Elsie was almost dead. The Indian grapevine finally got word to them. When they did get there, she was too far gone. She died two days later. Goddamn, even an animal gets comfort from its parent when it's dying. What was wrong with that little girl having her parents with her when she was sick?"

"Albert was never told about it until after she was dead. He was sitting in class and heard it from his teacher. 'Albert, your sister died. They buried her this morning.' He didn't even get to go to the funeral. God, talk about mean. Those frustrated things were cruel." She shook her head. "It wasn't just the missionaries that were mean," Rosemon went on. "Back in my time, they had a big federal boarding school just outside of Rapid. Some fourth grade boys ran away. They were headin' for their homes back on the reservation but they got caught on the railroad track by Creston. They brought those little fourth graders back and chained them together just like a chain gang, like we always hear about in the South."

"Fourth graders chained?" I looked at her.

"That's right...fourth graders! I hate to even tell about the boarding school. People think you're nuts or a big liar."

"I believe you. Go ahead."

"They had solitary confinement in all those schools, too. I did two days on bread and water, locked in a place as big as a closet and pitch black, too. Well, those little boys were chained together and they had to march off all the miles down to Creston and back, around the flagpole on the drill field. It was about fifty miles. They stayed chained together until they finished the fifty miles. They ate together, slept together and went to the bathroom together.

"They had a long punishment table and they would march in step. If one fell down, they all fell down. When it was time to feed them, they'd all sit down and the dining hall girls would bring their food over to them on trays.

"How would you feel if that was your little brother sitting there?"

I stared out the darkened window. Rosemon took a drink from her cup and continued. "It took a long time to march off those fifty miles." She motioned with her head toward the door. "I wonder how that would go over if you did that to some fourth graders in this college town? Fourth graders, and then people wonder why the Indians got so many alcoholics!"

"You know Indians were always a clean people, but they really tried to make us clean. We had to scrub, scrub, scrub when we worked in those boarding schools. I scrubbed a lot of floors in my day. We even scrubbed porches in the wintertime. We worked either a morning shift and went to school in the afternoon or the other way around.

"The girls worked in the kitchen, laundry, dining hall, dormitories, sewing room or clean up details everywhere. The boys were in the dairy, machine shop, barns and in the kitchen too. Everyone worked half a day and went to school the other half. We always laugh about how we really got only half an education."

The older woman paused to push her cup toward the center of the table. "Government and mission schools, they all operated the same way. We got less education from the missionaries. At the mission we'd get up at 5:30 every morning, get dressed and celebrate a goddamn boring mass every damn morning. You got slapped or had to kneel on the floor the whole time if you fell asleep or whispered. We'd go to church in the evening, too, and sometimes during the day. Hell, we were always going to church. Boys were separated from the girls. If you looked at a boy, you'd have to tell about it in confession. You couldn't even talk to your own brother standing in a mess hall line. We didn't get much education from the boarding schools, but we got all the work and religion we could handle. When we tried to go to college and compete with the white kids that had gone a full academic day, we couldn't get the same grades. The sociology and psychology experts claimed we had lower intelligence."

"We never got to read any books telling anything good about our leaders. They wouldn't even let us make a dance costume on our own time, let alone go to a powwow dance. If you spoke Indian you got your mouth washed out with soap. If you weren't a Christian you were a pagan and would go to hell. God help you if you was related to the holy men. Those kids really received a brainwashing. That's why so many of us don't know much about our ways. We never heard anything good about the Indian ways...only the white ways. Yet most of the white people at those boarding schools were cold and mean, and every morning we'd look in a mirror and still see an Indian." She rose to turn the burner on the coffeepot. She turned it to high then adjusted the controls for low. "We used to drill every day. Right flank, left flank, to the rear march. I know all that stuff." She managed a stifled laugh.

"Discipline, everything was discipline," she said as she sat back down. "When our men and women went into the war, we did okay in boot camp. We all knew how to march." She studied the blue flames under the coffeepot. "I didn't tell you everything. I couldn't. Even you wouldn't believe me."

"I believe you," I answered. She thought for a long while. She stared at the stove, then turned resolutely. "The last thing I'll mention about boarding school is hunger. You get so damn hungry that you'll do anything for just a little crust of bread. If you were smart or lucky, you'd be a waiter in the head nun's dining room or the head priest's table. Those people ate good. Hell, we'd be so damn hungry we'd eat off their plates, once we got them back into the kitchen. They ate a helluva lot better than the Indian kids ever did. The government schools were the same way. The employees stole them blind. When we unloaded the supply trucks, we saw butter and eggs but it never showed up on the tables for the Indian kids."

"You remember that old brother Herman down at Oglala?"

"Yeah, I remember him. You mean the one that limps. He used to hold kids down when Buchwald would put the belt to them. Course, now, I believe he was just following orders. I always think of him as being real scared, like a mean kinda' God was always watching him. Kyle told me he had that scared look, the last time he held Albert down and that big fight broke out...they ran away. Guess it was Kyle who crushed his foot with a big rock.

"I heard it was Albert or Kyle that made him limp." Rosemon said.

Chick shrugged. "When you are little you can't remember much." Her response was matter of fact. "They told me they were going to leave. I remember being scared...and then the fight broke out. Cross Dog and Albert planned it that way. Everything happened so fast." She paused, trying to reconstruct what seemed so far back in the past. "Kyle told me about the two big fancy stones that Buchwald had on his desk. He picked one up and crashed it down on a brother's foot. It took him out of action, so he reached for the other rock. It was a polished rock and flat on a couple of sides and big, like the other one. Albert mopped up by throwing that little prissy seminarian huddled and crying in a corner through a window. Kyle took the last brother out of action with that fancy rock and on the way to the railroad, Cross Dog and Albert were praising him. He said he felt like a Dog Soldier and warriors were singing kill songs over his exploit. He said he never was so proud in his life." A sad look shadowed her face. "I remember Cross Dog at the mission. Big and kind and sad, is how I remember him. That next summer, I heard he was dead and the war was going on. Train ran over Cross Dog that night they escaped. We were up at Rapid, the whole family. Dad had a job. It didn't take long for us to get out of the Indian camp. I was never separated from Mom and Dad again—not until I grew up. That's what I will always remember. No more boarding school."

"It almost seems like yesterday. I've seen that scared Jesuit brother a few times when I was watching you dance at the powwows. He seems okay."

"Yeah, he is, now maybe he is," Rosemon growled. "Back when he was young, your sister Elsie and I served him his meals. We'd get so goddamn starved, we'd let him feel our legs and he'd always leave a piece of meat and an extra piece of bread on his plate. We were just little girls though. I'd get so damn hungry that I'd let that horny son of a bitch feel my leg then damn near go nuts because I was afraid to tell about it in confession.

"It really bothered your sister and me. It got so damn bad that we decided to tell the head nun, especially when he'd come to feel us and he wanted to feel more than our legs. We got scared and we went to tell the head nun. We were both going to go in but I told Elsie to let me go first in case of a beating. 'No sense both of us getting beat up,' I told her.

"Well, I went in and told. I learned my lesson. I never was beaten so bad in all of my life. I can still see that nun. She called in two others to hold me down and she took off that big leather belt they always used to wear. That nun beat me and I can still hear her." Rosemon paused to look straight ahead at the refrigerator door. "Now you know brother would never do such a thing. You know he wouldn't. He's like a priest. He couldn't do such a thing. Tell us that you're lying. They beat me so damn bad that I said that I was lying."

"Not many people going to believe you, though. Not a helluva lot."

The older woman carried her coffee cup to the sink. "I'd better go. I said enough. You're right. Ain't nobody going to believe it." It happened.

"Put that in your book," she said with angry tears in her eyes.

Sister Chick was the same. "Nobody will believe it," she added.

South Dakota Pedophile Suit Denied

Native American church boarding school victims filed their Class Action law Suit in South Dakota. The Catholic Bishops of the Dakotas lobbied the South Dakota legislature to shorten the Statue of Limitations and Governor Mike Rounds signed the bill which granted amnesty to the perpetrators. Unlike other states wherein the pedophile and rape victims were compensated, the South Dakota victims were left with only their life damaging memories.

The greatest secret in South Dakota is Canton/Hiawatha All Indian Insane Asylum. Over several decades I have been the only author to expose Canton and - no-question the most prolific living author in that state. Yet the South Dakota State sponsored Humanities Commission purposely omits me from their annual three day South Dakota Authors Book Fair which touts the state's leading authors. Among the living I highly doubt if any author boasts a 50 times reprinted Harper/Collins work- my *Mother Earth Spirituality*.

Incidentally I have been honored recently by a huge crowd of Sichangu Rosebud Sioux at their annual Rosebud Fair - pow wow. Thousands of Sioux attend this event full of colorful and energetic dancers: the largest Indian gathering in the state. Twice, that memorable day, I was featured by Rosebud /Sichangu Medicine Man Leonard Crow Dog, see picture and publicly awarded an eagle feather for my books that do not hold back our struggles religious and social. After his complimentary speech, it took nearly an hour to circle the dance arena at the afternoon honoring to accept the hugs and tremolos from the women and handshakes of the men. Many women cried as they sang out their honoring tremolos. These sincere people, not cowardly Indian academics, appreciate a warrior that tells it like it is and one who fights for the Return of Our Way. They deeply appreciated that our own spiritual Way was allowed to come back. I am sure some of the respectful cheers and tears were for my participation in six sun dances besides just my books; four days under the hot Badlands sun without food or water.

The 'NDN' academics have to play 'close mouth' and never mention Canton or the Boarding schools nor were they out there even before and during the MLK days fighting for the return of our Spirituality, defying the government against their own un-constitutional Ban but mainly against the ever meddling and proselytizing missionaries. I never met an NDN academic at our grueling sun dances unless they came there to proselytize and we had to chase them off. We never go to their services and attempt to humiliate them. This is what Cheryl DeBoer, the Director of the Humanities Commission office at South Dakota State University, cannot and will not admit or realize that traditionalism among the Sioux has become a strong force and has to sprinkle her commission with non-humanitarian, truth covering NDN sheep lackeys. For that modus operandi she keeps her South Carolinian similar, Deep South attitude toward non-Christianized minorities and definitely we Traditional embracing writers. She will be interesting to chastise in the Spirit World eventually. *Mother Earth Spirituality* is at 50th reprint and a Book-of-the-Month Club printing makes it 51. I don't know of any living SoDak author earning such.

I called DeBoer's office at South Dakota State University. Her excuse was - "The Indians don't like you." Which is probably true- but limited to the academic sell out Indians, whom are sprinkled on her Commission. They won't say 'Boo' about South Dakota's red neck, good ole' Boy prejudice that elects mostly Republican legislators who roll back the Statue of Limitations to protect and exonerate the priests and ministers who administrated Indian Boarding schools while raping and pedophiling their youthful, helpless victims down through decades and now are encouraged more than ever. There is a sign as one enters South Dakota from the East. SOUTH DAKOTA is an AGRICULTURAL STATE and goes on to chastise the Animal Rights folk. Beside this sign an addendum should be placed the same size. South Dakota Protects Pedophiles and Rapists Instead: The legislative bill cite following in smaller letters. It wouldn't hurt to put several up for the nearly 2 million tourists who are headed for Mt. Rushmore- 'The Shrine of Democracy.'

After the Pedophile protecting bill was signed into law after meeting with the lobbying Bishops- Governor Mike Rounds, not one peep from those Commission board members including the Indians. One was South Dakota State University head of the Journalism Department named Doris Brewer Giago, a card carrying Oglala Sioux at that! The State University Journalism Department no less. The pedophile and rape victims never heard from her, to my knowledge. Are not journalists supposed to root out TRUTH to keep our nation safer- at least teach it if they do not have the courage to support honest journalistic Truth themselves? Sort of like a medical doctor not taking a Hippocratic Oath.

Indian author, Vine Deloria is DeBoer's hero and was a featured speaker at her loaded gathering many times. During his long employment in cushy academia, he never mentioned Boarding School atrocities, their victims over decades or Canton where many of our medicine people were sent away for life sentences. (Over 100 graves as proof.) The state of Washington however, set legal precedent by imposing heavy fines for such to distribute to lawsuit filing victims based on non-roll back law from their legislature.

Such is the power of Organized Religion stooge state administrators in red neck, evangelical or church controlled states and their alliance with cowardly Indigenous academics they can control through academic employment. The 'Church' can well afford to pay those Dakota victims. The same Jesuit order is paying from Gonzaga. Vine Deloria and his like lived comfortably by such to sustain their careers in Academia and deserve to be historically exposed. They were turncoat Quislings and not cultural protective heroes as academia wants to falsely, errantly portray them. Vine Deloria, now deceased, rates an annual remembrance honoring dinner in Washington State. Worse, most of the Deloria aficionados fought against we who were attempting to bring back our unconstitutionally Banned ceremonies. None in my warrior time supported AIM (American Indian Movement) who without AIMs strong, participating on- reservation support of the Sun Dance resurgence would have probably failed. Very few Indian Studies Directors have come out and forcefully challenged the ongoing and serious historic Native Indian issues that spotlight state prejudice and cover-up along with the Reservation missionary's constant proselytizing, negative meddling. They can't if they want to keep their jobs. University and DeBoer types will get them removed. A truthful warrior like me will never be hired.

Well…Dear Reader, maybe you can now understand why I go after the gutless, collaborating, traitorous quisling Indians who seek a higher perching and preening spot in the White Man's lice-infested chicken roost (Universities). A sadder, more tragic story would unfold had I had a poor relative confined within that all Indian, federally built and staffed, lobbied for by missionaries, Hiawatha Canton Insane Asylum I mentioned earlier. The non –Indian South Dakota Humanities Director is right along with them—scheming cowards all. They don't want you to know what really happened. I'm the bad guy however, like Kennedy. I just don't like what I see and not afraid to expose it! Pedophilia and denying State jurisdiction manipulation is Terrorism too!

As Black Elk declared. "To get to know me. You have to know my people." (And what happened to them.)

CHAPTER 10
GIVE THE NEW POPE A CHANCE!

Pedophiles and Popes: Doing the Vatican Shuffle[60] [*What Pope Francis will have to undo.*] **by Michael Parenti (posted 2010)**

When Pope John Paul II was still living in Poland as Cardinal Karol Wojtyla, he claimed that the security police would accuse priests of sexual abuse just to hassle and discredit them. (New York Times, 3/28/10). For Wojtyla, the Polish pedophilia problem was nothing more than a Communist plot to smear the church.

By the early 1980s, Wojtyla, now ensconced in Rome as Pope John Paul II, treated all stories about pedophile clergy with dismissive aplomb, as little more than slander directed against the church. That remained his stance for the next twenty years.

Today in post-communist Poland, clerical abuse cases have been slowly surfacing, very slowly. Writing in the leading daily Gazeta Wyborcza, a middle-aged man reported having been sexually abused as a child by a priest. He acknowledged however that Poland was not prepared to deal with such transgressions. "It's still too early. . . . Can you imagine what life would look like if an inhabitant of a small town or village decided to talk? I can already see the committees of defense for the accused priests."

While church pedophiles may still enjoy a safe haven in Poland and other countries where the clergy are above challenge, things are breaking wide open elsewhere. Today we are awash in a sludge of revelations spanning whole countries and continents, going back decades---or as some historians say--- going back centuries. Only in the last few weeks has the church shown signs of cooperating with civil authorities. Here is the story.

Protecting the Perpetrators.

As everyone now knows, for decades church superiors repeatedly chose to ignore complaints about pedophile priests. In many instances, accused clerics were quietly bundled off to

---

60 Michael Parenti, "Pedophiles and Popes: Doing the Vatican Shuffle," 2010, accessed on March 20, 2017, http://www.michaelparenti.org/VaticanShuffle.html.

distant congregations where they could prey anew upon the children of unsuspecting parishioners. This practice of denial and concealment has been so consistently pursued in diocese after diocese, nation after nation, as to leave the impression of being a deliberate policy set by church authorities.

And indeed it has been. Instructions coming directly from Rome have required every bishop and cardinal to keep matters secret. These instructions were themselves kept secret; the cover-up was itself covered up. Then in 2002, John Paul put it in writing, specifically mandating that all charges against priests were to be reported secretly to the Vatican and hearings were to be held in camera, a procedure that directly defies state criminal codes.

Rather than being defrocked, many outed pedophile priests have been allowed to advance into well-positioned posts as administrators, vicars, and parochial school officials---repeatedly accused by their victims while repeatedly promoted by their superiors.

Church spokesmen employ a vocabulary of compassion and healing---not for the victims but for the victimizers. They treat the child rapist as a sinner who confesses his transgression and vows to mend his ways. Instead of incarceration, there is repentance and absolution.

While this forgiving approach might bring comfort to some malefactors, it proves to be of little therapeutic efficacy when dealing with the darker appetites of pedophiles. A far more effective deterrent is the danger of getting caught and sent to prison. Absent any threat of punishment, the perpetrator is restrained only by the limits of his own appetite and the availability of opportunities.

Forgiving No One Else

The tender tolerance displayed by the church hierarchy toward child rapists does not extend to other controversial clergy. Think of those radical priests who have challenged the hierarchy in the politico-economic struggle for liberation theology, or who advocate lifting the prohibitions against birth control and abortion, or who propose that clergy be allowed to marry, or who preside over same-sex weddings, or who themselves are openly gay, or who believe women should be ordained, or who bravely call for investigations of the pedophilia problem itself.

Such clergy often have their careers shut down. Some are subjected to hostile investigations by church superiors.

A Law Unto Itself

Church leaders seem to forget that pedophilia is a felony crime and that, as citizens of a secular state, priests are subject to its laws just like the rest of us. Clerical authorities repeatedly have made themselves accessories to the crime, playing an active role in obstructing justice, arguing in court that criminal investigations of "church affairs" violated the free practice of religion guaranteed by the US Constitution—as if raping little children were a holy sacrament.

Church officials tell parishioners not to talk to state authorities. They offer no pastoral assistance to young victims and their shaken families. They do not investigate to see if other children have been victimized by the same priests. Some young plaintiffs have been threatened with excommunication or suspension from Catholic school. Church leaders impugn their credibility, even going after them with countersuits.

Responding to charges that one of his priests sexually assaulted a six-year-old boy, Cardinal Bernard Law asserted that "the boy and his parents contributed to the abuse by being negligent." Law himself never went to prison for the hundreds of cover-ups he conducted. In 2004, with things getting too hot for him in his Boston archdiocese, Law was rescued by Pope John Paul II to head one of Rome's major basilicas, where he now lives with diplomatic immunity in palatial luxury on a generous stipend, supervised by no one but a permissive pontiff.[61]

One of the most startling exposes is the Boston Globe's 'Teflon Removal' of Cardinal Law's Boston Diocese's pedophilia cover up which set off a long overdue world reaction to centuries of Church Denial. This work acknowledges and dedicates to both the Boston Globe and the revealing movie- Spotlight. Every reader needs to view this expose which will keep humanities fire of truthful hope very much alive.

A judge of the Holy Roman Rota, the church's highest court, wrote in a Vatican-approved article that bishops should not report sexual violations to civil authorities. And sure enough, for years bishops and cardinals have refrained from cooperating with law enforcement authorities, refusing to release abusers' records, claiming that the confidentiality of their

---

[61] Ibid.

files came under the same legal protection as privileged communications in the confessional---a notion that has no basis in canon or secular law.

Bishop James Quinn of Cleveland even urged church officials to send incriminating files to the Vatican Embassy in Washington, DC, where diplomatic immunity would prevent the documents from being subpoenaed.

Just a Few Bad Apples

Years ago the Catholic hierarchy would insist that clerical pedophilia involved only a few bad apples and was being blown completely out of proportion. For the longest time John Paul scornfully denounced the media for "sensationalizing" the issue. He and his cardinals (Ratzinger included) directed more fire at news outlets for publicizing the crimes than at their own clergy for committing them.

Reports released by the US Conference of Catholic Bishops (one of the more honest organizations in the Catholic Church) documented the abuse committed in the United States by 4,392 priests against thousands of children between 1950 and 2002. One of every ten priests ordained in 1970 was charged as a pedophile by 2002. Another survey commissioned by the US bishops found that among 5,450 complaints of sexual abuse there were charges against at least sixteen bishops. So much for a few bad apples.

Still, even as reports were flooding in from Ireland and other countries, John Paul dismissed the pedophilic epidemic as "an American problem," as if American priests were not members of his clergy, or as if this made it a matter of no great moment. John Paul went to his grave in 2005 still refusing to meet with victims and never voicing any apologies or regrets regarding sex crimes and cover-ups.

With Ratzinger's accession to the papal throne as Benedict XVI, the cover-ups continued. As recently as April 2010, at Easter Mass in St. Peter's Square, dean of the College of Cardinals Angelo Sodano, assured Benedict that the faithful were unimpressed "by the gossip of the moment." One would not know that "the gossip of the moment" included thousands of investigations, prosecutions, and accumulated charges extending back over decades.

During that same Easter weekend, Cardinal Norberto Rivera Carrera, archbishop of Mexico City, declared that the public uproar was an "overreaction" incited by the doings of "a few dishonest and criminal priests." A few? An overreaction? Of course, the picture now becomes clear: a few bad apples were inciting overreaction by engaging in the gossip of the moment.

The church seems determined to learn nothing from its transgressions, preoccupied as it is with avoiding lawsuits and bad publicity.

Really Not All that Serious

There are two ways we can think of child rape as being not a serious problem, and the Catholic hierarchy seems to have embraced both these positions. First, pedophilia is not that serious if it involves only a few isolated and passing incidents. Second, an even more creepy way of downplaying the problem: child molestation is not all that damaging or that important. At worst, it is regrettable and unfortunate; it might greatly upset the child, but it certainly is not significant enough to cause unnecessary scandal and ruin the career of an otherwise splendid padre.

It is remarkable how thoroughly indifferent the church bigwigs have been toward the abused children. When one of the most persistent perpetrators, Rev. John Geoghan, was forced into retirement (not jail) after seventeen years and nearly 200 victims, Cardinal Law could still write him, "On behalf of those you have served well, in my own name, I would like to thank you. I understand yours is a painful situation." It is evident that Law was more concerned about the "pain" endured by Geoghan than the misery he had inflicted upon minors.

In 2001, a French bishop was convicted in France for refusing to hand over to the police a priest who had raped children. It recently came to light that a former top Vatican cardinal, Dario Castrillón, had written to the bishop, "I congratulate you for not denouncing a priest to the civil authorities. You have acted well, and I am pleased to have a colleague in the episcopate who, in the eyes of history and of all the bishops in the world, preferred prison to denouncing his 'son' and priest." (The bishop actually got off with a suspended sentence.) Castrillón claimed that Pope John Paul II had authorized the letter years ago and had told him to send it to bishops around the world. (New York Times, 4/22/2010.)

There are many more like Cardinal Law and Cardinal Castrillón in the hierarchy, aging men who have no life experience with children and show not the slightest regard or empathy for them. They claim it their duty to protect the "unborn child" but offer no protection to the children in their schools and parishes.

They themselves are called "Father" but they father no one. They do not reside in households or families. They live in an old-boys network, jockeying for power and position, dedicated to the Holy Mother Church that feeds, houses, and adorns them throughout their lives.

From their heady heights, popes and bishops cannot hear the cries of children. In any case, the church belongs not to little children but to the bedecked oligarchs.

The damage done to sexual victims continues to go unnoticed: the ensuing years of depression, drug addiction, alcoholism, panic attacks, sexual dysfunction, and even mental breakdown and suicide—all these terrible aftereffects of child rape seem to leave popes and bishops more or less unruffled.

Circling the Wagons

The Catholic hierarchy managed to convince itself that the prime victim in this dismal saga is the church itself. In 2010 it came to light that, while operating as John Paul's über-hit man, Pope Benedict (then Cardinal Ratzinger) had provided cover and protection to several of the worst predator priests. The scandal was now at the pope's door---exactly where it should have been many years earlier during John Paul's reign.

The Vatican's response was predictable. The hierarchy circled the wagons to defend pope and church from outside "enemies." The cardinals and bishops railed furiously at critics who "assault" the church and, in the words of the archbishop of Paris, subject it to "a smear campaign." Benedict himself blamed secularism and misguided applications of Vatican 2's aggiornamento as contributing to the "context" of sexual abuse. Reform-minded liberalism made us do it, he seemed to be saying.

But this bristling Easter counterattack by the hierarchy did not play well. Church authorities came off looking like insular, arrogant elites who were unwilling to own up to a horrid situation largely of their own making.

Meanwhile the revelations continued. A bishop in Ireland resigned admitting he had covered up child abuse cases. Bishops in Germany and Belgium stepped down after confessing to charges that they themselves had abused minors. And new allegations were arising in Chile, Norway, Brazil, Italy, France, and Mexico.

Then, a fortnight after Easter, the Vatican appeared to

change course and for the first time issued a directive urging bishops to report abuse cases to civil authorities "if required by local law." At the same time, Pope Benedict held brief meetings with survivor groups and issued sympathetic statements about their plight.

For many of the victims, the pontiff's overtures and apologies were too little, too late. Their feeling was that if the Vatican really wanted to make amends, it should cooperate fully with law enforcement authorities and stop obstructing justice; it should ferret out abusive clergy and not wait until cases are publicized by others; and it should make public the church's many thousands of still secret reports on priests and bishops.

In the midst of all this, some courageous clergy do speak out. At a Sunday mass in a Catholic church outside Springfield, Massachusetts, the Rev. James Scahill delivered a telling sermon to his congregation (New York Times, 4/12/10): "We must personally and collectively declare that we very much doubt the veracity of the pope and those of church authority who are defending him. It is beginning to become evident that for decades, if not centuries, church leadership covered up the abuse of children and minors to protect its institutional image and the image of priesthood."

The abusive priests, Scahill went on, were "felons." He had "severe doubt" about the Vatican's claims of innocent ignorance. "If by any slimmest of chance the pope and all his bishops didn't know—they all should resign on the basis of sheer and complete ignorance, incompetence, and irresponsibility."

How did Father Scahill's suburban Catholic parishioners receive his scorching remarks? One or two walked out. The rest gave him a standing ovation.

*   *   *   *

Mother Teresa, John Paul II, and the Fast-Track Saints [62] - Michael Parenti (revised and documented, Atlantic Monthly, 27 October 2007)

Mother Teresa is a paramount example of the kind of acceptably conservative icon propagated by an elite-dominated culture, a "saint" who uttered not a critical word against social injustice, and maintained

---

[62] Michael Parenti, "Mother Teresa, John Paul II, and the Fast-Track Saints," 2007, accessed on April 8, 2017, http://www.michaelparenti.org/VaticanShuffle.html

cozy relations with the rich, corrupt, and powerful.

Mother Teresa

During his 26-year papacy, John Paul II elevated 483 individuals to sainthood, reportedly more saints than any previous pope. One personage he beatified but did not live long enough to canonize was Mother Teresa, the Roman Catholic nun of Albanian origin who had been wined and dined by the worlds rich and famous while hailed as a champion of the poor. The darling of the corporate media and western officialdom, and an object of celebrity adoration, Teresa was for many years the most revered woman on earth, showered with kudos and awarded a Nobel Peace Prize in 1979 for her "humanitarian work" and "spiritual inspiration."

What usually went unreported were the vast sums she received from wealthy and sometimes tainted sources, including a million dollars from convicted savings & loan swindler Charles Keating, on whose behalf she sent a personal plea for clemency to the presiding judge. She was asked by the prosecutor in that case to return Keating's gift because it was money he had stolen. She never did. She also accepted substantial sums given by the brutal Duvalier dictatorship that regularly stole from the Haitian public treasury.

Mother Teresa's "hospitals" for the indigent in India and elsewhere turned out to be hardly more than human warehouses in which seriously ill persons lay on mats, sometimes fifty to sixty in a room without benefit of adequate medical attention. Their ailments usually went undiagnosed. The food was nutritionally lacking and sanitary conditions were deplorable. There were few medical personnel on the premises, mostly untrained nuns and brothers.

When tending to her own ailments, however, Teresa checked into some of the costliest hospitals and recovery care units in the world for state-of-the-art treatment.

Teresa journeyed the globe to wage campaigns against divorce, abortion, and birth control. At her Nobel award ceremony, she announced that "the greatest destroyer of peace is abortion." And she once suggested that AIDS might be a just retribution for improper sexual conduct.

Teresa emitted a continual flow of promotional misinformation about herself. She claimed that her mission in Calcutta fed over a thousand people daily. On other occasions she jumped the number to 4000, 7000, and 9000. Actually her soup kitchens fed not more than 150 people (six days a week), and this included her retinue of nuns, novices, and brothers. She claimed that her school in the Calcutta slum contained five thousand children when it actually enrolled less than one hundred.

Teresa claimed to have 102 family assistance centers in Calcutta, but longtime Calcutta resident, Aroup Chatterjee, who did an extensive on-the-scene investigation of her mission, could not find a single such center.

As one of her devotees explained, "Mother Teresa is among those who least worry about statistics. She has repeatedly expressed that what matters is not how much work is accomplished but how much love is put into the work." Was Teresa really unconcerned about statistics? Quite the contrary, her numerical inaccuracies went consistently and self-servingly in only one direction, greatly exaggerating her accomplishments.

Over the many years that her mission was in Calcutta, there were about a dozen floods and numerous cholera epidemics in or near the city, with thousands perishing. Various relief agencies responded to each disaster, but Teresa and her crew were nowhere in sight, except briefly on one occasion.

When someone asked Teresa how people without money or power can make the world a better place, she replied, "They should smile more," a response that charmed some listeners. During a press conference in Washington DC, when asked "Do you teach the poor to endure their lot?" she said "I think it is very beautiful for the poor to accept their lot, to share it with the passion of Christ. I think the world is being much helped by the suffering of the poor people."

But she herself lived lavishly well, enjoying luxurious accommodations in her travels abroad. It seems to have gone unnoticed that as a world celebrity she spent most of her time away from Calcutta, with protracted stays at opulent residences in Europe and the United States, jetting from Rome to London to New York in private planes.

Mother Teresa is a paramount example of the kind of acceptably conservative icon propagated by an elite-dominated culture, a "saint" who uttered not a critical word against social injustice, and maintained cozy relations with the rich, corrupt, and powerful.

She claimed to be above politics when in fact she was pronouncedly hostile toward any kind of progressive reform. Teresa was a friend of Ronald Reagan, and an admiring guest of the Haitian dictator "Baby Doc" Duvalier. She also had the support and admiration of a number of Central and South American dictators.

Teresa was Pope John Paul II's kind of saint. After her death in 1997, he waived the five-year waiting period usually observed before beginning the beatification process that leads to sainthood. The five-year delay is intended to dampen impulsive enthusiasms and allow for a more sober evaluation. Claims made on behalf of a candidate are then subjected to critical challenge by an advocatus diaboli, a "devil's advocate" assigned to the beatification process. John Paul brushed aside all this. In 2003, in record time Teresa was beatified, the final step before canonization.

But in 2007 her canonization confronted a bump in the road, it having been disclosed that along with her various other contradictions Teresa was not a citadel of spiritual joy and unswerving faith. Her diaries, investigated by Catholic authorities in Calcutta, revealed that she had been racked with doubts: "I feel that God does not want me, that God is not God and that he does not really exist." People think "my faith, my hope and my love are overflowing and that my intimacy with God and union with his will fill my heart. If only they knew," she wrote, "Heaven means nothing."

Through many tormented sleepless nights she shed thoughts like this: "I am told God loves me—and yet the reality of darkness and coldness and emptiness is so great that nothing touches my soul." Il Messeggero, Rome's popular daily newspaper, commented: "The real Mother Teresa was one who for one year had visions and who for the next 50 had doubts---up until her death."

Another example of fast-track sainthood, pushed by Pope John Paul II, occurred in 1992 when he swiftly beatified the reactionary Msgr. José María Escrivá de Balaguer, supporter of fascist regimes in Spain and elsewhere, and founder of Opus Dei, a powerful secretive ultra-conservative movement "feared by many as a sinister sect within the Catholic Church." Escrivá's beatification came only seventeen years after his death, a record run until Mother Teresa came along.

In accordance with his own political agenda, John Paul used a church institution, sainthood, to bestow special sanctity upon ultra-conservatives such as Escrivá and Teresa---and implicitly on all that they represented. Another of the ultra-conservatives whom John Paul put up for sainthood, bizarrely enough, was the last of the Hapsburg rulers of the Austro-Hungarian empire, Emperor Karl, who reigned during World

War I. Still another of the reactionaries whom John Paul set up for sainthood was Pius IX, who reigned as pontiff from 1846 to 1878, and who referred to Jews as "dogs."

John Paul also beatified Cardinal Aloysius Stepinac, the leading Croatian cleric who welcomed the Nazi and fascist Ustashi takeover of Croatia during World War II. Stepinac sat in the Ustashi parliament, appeared at numerous public events with top ranking Nazis and Ustashi, and openly supported the Croatian fascist regime that exterminated hundreds of thousands of Serbs, Jews, and Roma ("gypsies").

In John Paul's celestial pantheon, reactionaries had a better chance at canonization than reformers. Consider his treatment of Archbishop Oscar Romero who spoke against the injustices and oppressions suffered by the impoverished populace of El Salvador and for this was assassinated by a right-wing death squad. John Paul never denounced the killing or its perpetrators, calling it only "tragic." In fact, just weeks before Romero was murdered, high-ranking officials of the Arena party, the legal arm of the death squads, sent a well-received delegation to the Vatican to complain of Romero's public statements on behalf of the poor.

Romero was thought by many poor Salvadorans to be something of a saint, but John Paul attempted to ban any discussion of his beatification for fifty years. Popular pressure from El Salvador caused the Vatican to cut the delay to twenty-five years. In either case, Romero was consigned to the slow track.

John Paul's successor, Benedict XVI, waved the five-year waiting period in order to put John Paul II himself instantly on a super-fast track to canonization, running neck and neck with Teresa. As of 2005 there already were reports of possible miracles attributed to the recently departed Polish pontiff.

One such account was offered by Cardinal Francesco Marchisano. When lunching with John Paul, the cardinal indicated that because of an ailment he could not use his voice. The pope "caressed my throat, like a brother, like the father that he was. After that I did seven months of therapy, and I was able to speak again." Marchisano thinks that the pontiff might have had a hand in his cure: "It could be," he said. Un miracolo! Viva il papa! [63]

[63] Editor's note: Be reminded that the full reference list for this article can be found at: http://www.michaelparenti.org/VaticanShuffle.html

Although a respected supporter of the Climate Change and Planetary Heating Theory, Pope Francis, during his first United States tour, never mentioned Over Population- the obvious cause. Dakota Bishops successful lobbied to shorten the legislative statue voiding payment to reservation boarding school victims. I ask this Pope to pay them rightfully out of the Vatican Bank. The Northwest Jesuit order was found guilty and millions of dollars were compensated to Alaskan and Washington state Native victims.

Minneapolis Tribune Nov. 2016 Church Cover up series.— Pope Francis has created a Vatican tribunal promising to punish senior churchmen (bishops, archbishops, cardinals) for sex abuse or cover-up. In November, 2016, he accepted the resignation of the embattled archbishop of St. Paul and Minneapolis and his deputy bishop, after prosecutors charged the archdiocese with having failed to protect children from unspeakable harm from a pedophile priest who was later convicted of molesting two boys.

Jennifer Haselberger, who was Archbishop John Nienstedt's archivist, alleged widespread cover-up of clergy sex misconduct and accused the church of using a chaotic system of record-keeping that concealed the backgrounds of guilty priests who remained on assignment. As a result of raising warning alarms, she was shut out of meetings about priest misconduct. Nienstedt denied misconduct and the archdiocese hired a firm to investigate. Both bishops eventually resigned. Separately, the Vatican indicted its own former ambassador to the Dominican Republic with sexually abusing minors in the Caribbean country — the highest-ranking Vatican official ever to stand trial for a sex crime.

With these resignations, there have been 18 bishops who have resigned after being publicly criticized for covering up for abusers, according to Anne Barrett Doyle of the online resource BishopAccountability.org. "All bishops must carry out their pastoral ministry with utmost care in order to help foster the protection of minors, and they will be held accountable," Francis declared. Pope Francis is a welcome leader to a horrid institution that focused on maintaining its dynasty down through centuries at all costs regardless of sexual predation rampant within its clergy. This age of modern communication has finally brought about needed exposure.

CHAPTER 11
HONORING - REV. WM. STOLZMAN, SJ

A Jesuit Priest Quests for a Vision

Father William Stolzman became the chairperson of the Medicine Men and Pastors' Meeting held at the Rosebud Reservation from 1973 to 1979. The meetings sought an exchange of information, spiritual discussion between the spiritual leaders and lay persons of the Sioux Tribe, and the pastors, priests, and laypeople of the white man's faith. It was well attended for a reservation function which met bi-monthly, nine months out of the year. Admittedly, it was a move initiated by reservation missionaries who were observing the fast resurgence of Native Spirituality sweeping across Sioux reservations following the Civil Rights movement and the Congressional 'Ban' removal by non-other than Congress in a 100% vote.

With Lakota relatives present, often there were as many as forty people present per meeting. My main mentor, Chief Eagle Feather, was a regular participant. Unlike most priests, Father Stolzman became a very open-minded priest through contact with the Traditionals. He discovered Natural ceremony, and described his own personal observations in his book, *The Pipe and Christ.*[64] Father Stolzman described the dark rain clouds that threatened his solitary vigil on the mountaintop as he faced the Four Directions and prayed.

> As I faced the West, the wind became more and more ferocious. The black flag in the West was long, and it whipped me and lashed me painfully. How hard and testing is the West! The wind became so strong that I seemed to lean 45 degrees into the wind to keep my balance. Finally when I could no longer stand, I descended into the pit and sat facing the West. The wind roared, the flags slapped, and the lightning flashed from the West overhead. Suddenly, 'Yehhhhhhhhhhh,' the most blood-curdling eagle scream I have ever heard! It was a thousand times louder than any eagle cry I had ever heard before. The wind immediately stopped! The sudden silence was shaking. There was only the snapping and crackling of the

---

[64] This book is available at Prairies Edge, Rapid City. SD. 57101. Also at Crazy Horse Museum gift shop, Custer SD. 57730

lightning in the West... and the lingering memory of that frightening eagle's scream. I sat and shuddered. It was the Wakiyan, the Thunder Bird, controller of storms.

The lightning then moved to the South. Something was wrong. This was contrary to the way it should be. It should have turned toward the North! Only later did I understand that this was a sign of the companion of the West, the contrary one, Heyoka, the Clown. With the wind quiet, I returned outside to pray. As the lightning moved to the South, the wind began to come from that direction. With it came a fine mist. As it touched my face, I could not help but think of tears. I did not want the mist to come into the square, so I prayed, and even the mist stopped. (This was amazing, for at the medicine man's house a mile away, the people were anxiously praying for me. They were having a downpour, and it hailed several times. In fact, the entire region suffered the worst hail storm in years that night.) On the hill, however, there were only wind, lightning, and thunder.

I began to hear voices coming out of the floor at the southern edge of the pit. There were thousands of voices resembling the drone of a crowd. I bent over and cupped my ear in order to pick up some words to discover if they were speaking to me in Lakota or English. After a few minutes the voices stopped. These were the voices of the dead who journey south to the place called Tate Makoce, what White men call the 'Happy Hunting Ground.'

I remained for quite a while in the pit, praying and feeling very close to the earth, to which the bodies of the souls had returned. Then I decided to go outside. As I got up to leave, the earth gave a great heave one direction and then the other. I was bounced back and forth from side to side in the pit -- gently. It seemed as if Grandmother Earth was showing her presence and love by rocking me back and forth in the 'arms' of the pit as a little child is rocked in the arms of its grandmother.

The rest of Father Stolzman's Nature based communication during his Vision Quest, is most informative of how the experience changed his life:

My prayers had been answered. In fact, every time I have gone to the spirits on the hill my prayers have been answered. Yet they are always answered in ways I have never expected. I have studied some psychology, and I know that a person can sometimes unknowingly program himself to see what he wants to

see or symbolically hallucinate events for the past. Every time
I go to the spirits I find their response to be a total surprise. I
guess if there were no surprises, they would be giving me
nothing new, and there would be no need for their coming.
When I try to set up expectations for them, they refuse to
come at all.

Father Stolzman's books are evidence of a new openness I never saw
in the many missionary priests I knew as a child. His participation in ceremony helped to develop his intuition by attuning his senses to Nature
and learning to take meaning from winds, eagle cries, lightning, and
spending a calm night out in the open on a hilltop surrounded on all sides
with thunderstorms and hail. All of these entities are created and obedient
to Creator alone.

Before we leave Father Stolzman, I would like to recommend his
book, *The Pipe and Christ,* for those readers who are not ready or able to
embrace completely the Natural Way. His book is informative regarding
ceremony, culture, values, and beliefs on both sides of the coin. Many of
you are just too laden with too much fear, or is it faith from what I have
seen? Most of you are not that fearful but choose to simply blend both
Christianity and the Nature realm. Might be a smart move; you are covered on both bases. My mother seemed to manage that approach. (My
father preferred the Natural Way.) Unlike the fanatic Evangelicals of today, I abhor foolish statements of the opiated religious triumphalites,
"My Way Only." Or God is speaking through Me!" Those are historical
proven, dangerous attitudes that have consumed fatally, thousands of
innocents. We just could possibly be all beseeching to the same Great
Mystery. Who knows? I, for one, am not worried about it.

CHAPTER 12
BUDDHISM

Shintoism

I spent two years in the Orient, mostly in war torn Korea and later as a pilot in Japan and Vietnam. As mentioned, I was a conversational English teacher at Hiroshima University near my Marine airbase at Iwakuni, Japan. I came to know the enthusiastic Japanese students. It was a rewarding experience. Obviously, Hiroshima University has distanced itself from the old Samurai mentality that cruelly permeated as far as WWII. My Hiroshima students were obviously horrified by war and Samurai warrior-ism was a thing of the past. Years later I read Iris Chang's book- *The Rape of Nanking*. There was little difference between ISIS and the invading Japanese Army of that era when it came to unimaginable brutality toward one's fellow human except that the Japanese soldier was allowed to go free back to their homeland. Russia put their invading German soldiers in war damage repair bondage for several years before allowing repatriation. Oddly, only a few Nanking WWII duty Japanese generals were shot by China's investigative Military Crimes firing squads. The advocating 'Divine' Emperor and his colluding brother allowed by 'Shogun' MacArthur to continue completely free.

Supremacy based, Primal, Exclusive and Triumphalism Religion can come in varying forms. The Japanese were not Buddhists per se but mainly of the Shinto Religion which considered the Emperor of Japan as God-like and therefore, a blessing 'Divine' descendant of all that the Army would do. They fanatically bore no guilt since their leader, the 'Divine Emperor' came from heaven and placed no humanitarian restriction upon them. It is a horrifying book to read and to this day Japan will not admit its guilt nor pay compensation to millions of victims. At least Germany has paid millions and the Nuremburg War Crimes Commission sent far more guilty military fanatic culprits to the gallows.

The following is an excerpt from Iris Chang's *The Rape of Nanking*:

> Tominaga Shozo, veteran Japanese Army Officer: - An instructor pointed toward a thin emaciated Chinese in a detention center and told the officers: "These are the raw materials for your trial of courage." Day after day the instructor taught them how to cut off heads and bayonet living prisoners.
> Twenty four prisoners were squatting there with their

hands tied behind their backs. They were blindfolded. The regimental, battalion and company commanders all took their seats. Second Lieutenant Tanaka bowed to the regimental commander and reported. We shall now begin." He ordered a soldier to haul one of the prisoners to the edge of the pit, the prisoner was kicked when he resisted. The soldiers finally dragged him over and forced him to his knees. Tanaka turned toward us and looked into each of our faces in turn. "Heads should be cut off like this," he said, unsheathing his Army sword. He scooped water from a bucket, then poured it over both sides of the blade. He raised his sword in a long arc. Standing behind the prisoner, Tanaka steadied himself, legs spread apart, and cut off the man's head with a shout. "Yo!" The head flew more than a meter away. Blood spurted up in two fountains from the body and sprayed into the hole.

The scene was so appalling that I felt I couldn't breathe. [65]

Nagatomi Hakudo spoke candidly about his emotions in the fallen capital.

I remember being driven in a truck along a path that had been cleared through piles of thousands and thousands of slaughtered bodies. Wild dogs were gnawing on the dead flesh as we stopped and pulled a group of Chinese prisoners out of the back. Then the Japanese officer proposed a test of my courage. He unsheathed his sword, spat on it, and with a sudden mighty swing he brought it down on the neck of a Chinese boy cowering before us. The head was cut clean off and tumbled away on the group as the body slumped forward, blood spurting in two great gushing fountains from the neck. The officer suggested I take the head home as a souvenir. I remember smiling proudly as I took his sword and began killing people.

After almost sixty years of soul searching, Nagatomi is a changed man. A doctor in Japan, he has built shrine of remorse in his waiting room. Patients can watch videotapes of his trial in Nanking and a full confession of his crimes. The gentle and hospitable demeanor of the doctor belies the horror of his past, making it almost impossible for one to imagine that he had once been a ruthless murderer.

"Few know that soldiers impaled babies on bayonets and

---

[65] Iris Chang , *The Rape of Nanking*, p.57.

tossed them still alive into pots of boiling water," Nagatomi said. "They gang raped women from the ages of twelve to eighty and then killed them when they could no longer satisfy sexual requirements. I beheaded people, starved them to death, burned them, and buried them alive, over two hundred in all. It is terrible that I could turn into an animal and do these things. There are really no words to explain what I was doing. I was truly a devil."[66]

Will this despicable result happen again once Over-population, Climate Change and Planetary Heating begins to hit its peak? Time will tell.

"Standing in marked contrast to the intolerant savagery of other religions, Buddhism is neither fanatical nor dogmatic--so say its adherents." M. Parenti

Across the U S A, Yoga and Buddhism flourish; among the younger generation mostly. Buddhism is highly regarded as no doubt the most peaceful religion among the major religions. I have made the statement that if I were not so enamored with Indigenous Spirituality, I would become Buddhist.

When China invaded Tibet, I sided with the 'poor Tibetans' – the loss of their 'Shangri-La, peaceful Way, their serene, nirvana Lahaska Monastery in mountainous, remote Tibet once tucked happily, prayerfully away and now under the rule of those bad Chinese Communists. Little did I realize that within the former serf state Tibet; its citizens would not adapt to a non-existent, communistic 'Nirvana' but at their worst still would be better off. They refused to back the CIA attempts to stir up an uprising which Michael Parenti's following article will reveal. The nobility's sons, vainly imagining/expecting zealous peasant support, were parachuted in with caches of small arms; 90% disappeared. Killed no doubt by angry and revengeful, scarred serf slaves instead of the Chinese army. After reading from Michael Parenti's exposing article, I have to wonder how National Geographic, after several Tibetan coverings down through the years could totally miss the brutality of the once landed 'Nobility' in league with the Yellow Hat monks and the Dalai Lama. Like other visiting western writers they too painted the 'Shangri-La' fiction. Not so, Michael Parenti. Buddhism, not unlike Islam and Christianity, has its dark side too.

---

[66] Ibid p.59

Empty Friendly Feudalism: The Tibet Myth[67]

"Michael John Parenti (born 1933) is an "American political scientist, historian, and cultural critic who writes on scholarly and popular subjects. He has taught at American and international universities and has been a guest lecturer before campus and community audiences."[68]

For Lords and Lamas

Along with the blood drenched landscape of religious conflict there is the experience of inner peace and solace that every religion promises, none more so than Buddhism. Standing in marked contrast to the intolerant savagery of other religions, Buddhism is neither fanatical nor dogmatic--so say its adherents. For many of them Buddhism is less a theology and more a meditative and investigative discipline intended to promote an inner harmony and enlightenment while directing us to a path of right living. Generally, the spiritual focus is not only on oneself but on the welfare of others. One tries to put aside egoistic pursuits and gain a deeper understanding of one's connection to all people and things. "Socially engaged Buddhism" tries to blend individual liberation with responsible social action in order to build an enlightened society.

A glance at history, however, reveals that not all the many and widely varying forms of Buddhism have been free of doctrinal fanaticism, nor free of the violent and exploitative pursuits so characteristic of other religions. In Sri Lanka there is a legendary and almost sacred recorded history about the triumphant battles waged by Buddhist kings of yore. During the twentieth century, Buddhists clashed violently with each other and with non-Buddhists in Thailand, Burma, Korea, Japan, India, and elsewhere. In Sri Lanka, armed battles between Buddhist Sinhalese and Hindu Tamils have taken many lives on both sides. In 1998 the U.S. State Department listed thirty of the world's most violent and dangerous extremist groups. Over half of them were religious, specifically Muslim, Jewish, and Buddhist.

In South Korea, in 1998, thousands of monks of the

---

[67] Updated and expanded version, *Atlantic Monthly* - January 2007) (also http://www.michaelparenti.org/Tibet.html)

[68] "Michael Parenti," *Wikipedia,* accessed April 8, 2017. https://en.wikipedia.org/wiki/Michael_Parenti.

Chogye Buddhist order fought each other with fists, rocks, fire-bombs, and clubs, in pitched battles that went on for weeks. They were vying for control of the order, the largest in South Korea, with its annual budget of $9.2 million, its millions of dollars' worth of property, and the privilege of appointing 1,700 monks to various offices. The brawls damaged the main Buddhist sanctuaries and left dozens of monks injured, some seriously. The Korean public appeared to disdain both factions, feeling that no matter what side took control, "it would use worshippers' donations for luxurious houses and expensive cars."

As with any religion, squabbles between or within Buddhist sects are often fueled by the material corruption and personal deficiencies of the leadership. For example, in Nagano, Japan, at Zenkoji, the prestigious complex of temples that has hosted Buddhist sects for more than 1,400 years, "a nasty battle" arose between Komatsu the chief priest and the Tacchu, a group of temples nominally under the chief priest's sway. The Tacchu monks accused Komatsu of selling writings and drawings under the temple's name for his own gain. They also were appalled by the frequency with which he was seen in the company of women. Komatsu in turn sought to isolate and punish monks who were critical of his leadership. The conflict lasted some five years and made it into the courts.

But what of Tibetan Buddhism? Is it not an exception to this sort of strife? And what of the society it helped to create? Many Buddhists maintain that, before the Chinese crackdown in 1959, old Tibet was a spiritually oriented kingdom free from the egotistical lifestyles, empty materialism, and corrupting vices that beset modern industrialized society. Western news media, travel books, novels, and Hollywood films have portrayed the Tibetan theocracy as a veritable Shangri-La. The Dalai Lama himself stated that "the pervasive influence of Buddhism" in Tibet, "amid the wide open spaces of an unspoiled environment resulted in a society dedicated to peace and harmony. We enjoyed freedom and contentment."

A reading of Tibet's history suggests a somewhat different picture. "Religious conflict was commonplace in old Tibet," writes one western Buddhist practitioner. "History belies the Shangri-La image of Tibetan lamas and their followers living together in mutual tolerance and nonviolent goodwill. Indeed, the situation was quite different. Old Tibet was much more like Europe during the religious wars of the Counterreformation." In the thirteenth century, Emperor Kublai Khan created the first Grand Lama, who was to preside over all the other lamas as might a pope over his bishops. Several centuries later, the Emperor of China sent an army into Tibet to support the Grand Lama, an ambitious 25-year-old man, who then gave himself the title of Dalai (Ocean) Lama, ruler of all Tibet.

His two previous lama "incarnations" were then retroactively recognized as his predecessors, thereby transforming the 1st Dalai Lama into the 3rd Dalai Lama. This 1st (or 3rd) Dalai Lama seized monasteries that did not belong to his sect, and is believed to have destroyed Buddhist writings that conflicted with his claim to divinity. The Dalai Lama who succeeded him pursued a sybaritic life, enjoying many mistresses, partying with friends, and acting in other ways deemed unfitting for an incarnate deity. For these transgressions he was murdered by his priests. Within 170 years, despite their recognized divine status, five Dalai Lamas were killed by their high priests or other courtiers.

For hundreds of years competing Tibetan Buddhist sects engaged in bitterly violent clashes and summary executions. In 1660, the 5th Dalai Lama was faced with a rebellion in Tsang province, the stronghold of the rival Kagyu sect with its high lama known as the Karmapa. The 5th Dalai Lama called for harsh retribution against the rebels, directing the Mongol army to obliterate the male and female lines, and the offspring too "like eggs smashed against rocks.... In short, annihilate any traces of them, even their names."

In 1792, many Kagyu monasteries were confiscated and their monks were forcibly converted to the Gelug sect (the Dalai Lama's denomination). The Gelug school, known also as the "Yellow Hats," showed little tolerance or willingness to mix their teachings with other Buddhist sects. In the words of one of their traditional prayers: "Praise to you, violent god of the Yellow Hat teachings/who reduces to particles of dust/ great beings, high officials and ordinary people/ who pollute and corrupt the Gelug doctrine." 8 An eighteenth-century memoir of a Tibetan general depicts sectarian strife among Buddhists that is as brutal and bloody as any religious conflict might be. This grim history remains largely unvisited by present-day followers of Tibetan Buddhism in the West.

Religions have had a close relationship not only with violence but with economic exploitation. Indeed, it is often the economic exploitation that necessitates the violence. Such was the case with the Tibetan theocracy. Until 1959, when the Dalai Lama last presided over Tibet, most of the arable land was still organized into manorial estates worked by serfs. These estates were owned by two social groups: the rich secular landlords and the rich theocratic lamas. Even a writer sympathetic to the old order allows that "a great deal of real estate belonged to the monasteries, and most of them amassed great riches." Much of the wealth was accumulated "through active participation in trade, commerce, and money lending."

Drepung monastery was one of the biggest landowners in the world, with its 185 manors, 25,000 serfs, 300 great pastures, and 16,000 herdsmen. The wealth of the monasteries rested in the hands of small numbers of high-ranking lamas. Most ordinary monks lived modestly and had no direct access to great wealth. The Dalai Lama himself "lived richly in the 1000-room, 14-story Potala Palace."

Secular leaders also did well. A notable example was the commander-in-chief of the Tibetan army, a member of the Dalai Lama's lay Cabinet, who owned 4,000 square kilometers of land and 3,500 serfs. Old Tibet has been misrepresented by some Western admirers as "a nation that required no police force because its people voluntarily observed the laws of karma." In fact. it had a professional army, albeit a small one, that served mainly as a gendarmerie for the landlords to keep order, protect their property, and hunt down runaway serfs.

Young Tibetan boys were regularly taken from their peasant families and brought into the monasteries to be trained as monks. Once there, they were bonded for life. Tashi-Tsering, a monk, reports that it was common for peasant children to be sexually mistreated in the monasteries. He himself was a victim of repeated rape, beginning at age nine. The monastic estates also conscripted children for lifelong servitude as domestics, dance performers, and soldiers.

In old Tibet there were small numbers of farmers who subsisted as a kind of free peasantry, and perhaps an additional 10,000 people who composed the "middle-class" families of merchants, shopkeepers, and small traders. Thousands of others were beggars. There also were slaves, usually domestic servants, who owned nothing. Their offspring were born into slavery. The majority of the rural population were serfs. Treated little better than slaves, the serfs went without schooling or medical care, They were under a lifetime bond to work the lord's land--or the monastery's land--without pay, to repair the lord's houses, transport his crops, and collect his firewood. They were also expected to provide carrying animals and transportation on demand. Their masters told them what crops to grow and what animals to raise. They could not get married without the consent of their lord or lama. And they might easily be separated from their families should their owners lease them out to work in a distant location.

As in a free labor system and unlike slavery, the overlords had no responsibility for the serf's maintenance and no direct interest in his or her survival as an expensive piece of property. The serfs had to support themselves. Yet as in a slave system, they were bound to their masters, guaranteeing a fixed and permanent workforce that could neither organize nor strike nor freely depart as might laborers in a market context. The overlords had the best of both worlds.

One 22-year old woman, herself a runaway serf, reports: "Pretty serf girls were usually taken by the owner as house servants and used as he wished"; they "were just slaves without rights." Serfs needed permission to go anywhere. Landowners had legal authority to capture those who tried to flee. One 24-year old runaway welcomed the Chinese intervention as a "liberation." He testified that under serfdom he was subjected to incessant toil, hunger, and cold. After his third failed escape, he was merciless beaten by the landlord's men until blood poured from his nose and mouth. They then poured alcohol and caustic soda on his wounds to increase the pain, he claimed.

The serfs were taxed upon getting married, taxed for the birth of each child and for every death in the family. They were taxed for planting a tree in their yard and for keeping animals. They were taxed for religious festivals and for public dancing and drumming, for being sent to prison and upon being released. Those who could not find work were taxed for being unemployed, and if they traveled to another village in search of work, they paid a passage tax. When people could not pay, the monasteries lent them money at 20 to 50 percent interest. Some debts were handed down from father to son to grandson. Debtors who could not meet their obligations risked being cast into slavery.

The theocracy's religious teachings buttressed its class order. The poor and afflicted were taught that they had brought their troubles upon themselves because of their wicked ways in previous lives. Hence they had to accept the misery of their present existence as a karmic atonement and in anticipation that their lot would improve in their next lifetime. The rich and powerful treated their good fortune as a reward for, and tangible evidence of, virtue in past and present lives.

The Tibetan serfs were something more than superstitious victims, blind to their own oppression. As we have seen, some ran away; others openly resisted, sometimes suffering dire consequences. In feudal Tibet, torture and mutilation--including eye gouging, the pulling out of tongues, hamstringing, and amputation--were favored punishments inflicted upon thieves, and runaway or resistant serfs. Journeying through Tibet in the 1960s, Stuart and Roma Gelder interviewed a former serf, Tsereh Wang Tuei, who had stolen two sheep belonging to a monastery. For this he had both his eyes gouged out and his hand mutilated beyond use. He explains that he no longer is a Buddhist: "When a holy lama told them to blind me I thought there was no good in religion." Since it was against Buddhist teachings to take human life, some offenders were severely lashed and then "left to God" in the freezing night to die. "The parallels between Tibet and medieval Europe are striking," concludes Tom Grunfeld in his book on Tibet.

In 1959, Anna Louise Strong visited an exhibition of torture equipment that had been used by the Tibetan overlords. There were handcuffs of all sizes, including small ones for children, and instruments for cutting off noses and ears, gouging out eyes, breaking off hands, and hamstringing legs. There were hot brands, whips, and special implements for disemboweling. The exhibition presented photographs and testimonies of victims who had been blinded or crippled or suffered amputations for thievery. There was the shepherd whose master owed him a reimbursement in yuan and wheat but refused to pay. So he took one of the master's cows; for this he had his hands severed. Another herdsman, who opposed having his wife taken from him by his lord, had his hands broken off. There were pictures of Communist activists with noses and upper lips cut off, and a woman who was raped and then had her nose sliced away.

Earlier visitors to Tibet commented on the theocratic despotism. In 1895, an Englishman, Dr. A. L. Waddell, wrote that the populace was under the "intolerable tyranny of monks" and the devil superstitions they had fashioned to terrorize the people. In 1904 Perceval Landon described the Dalai Lama's rule as "an engine of oppression." At about that time, another English traveler, Captain W.F.T. O'Connor, observed that "the great landowners and the priests... exercise each in their own dominion a despotic power from which there is no appeal," while the people are "oppressed by the most monstrous growth of monasticism and priest-craft." Tibetan rulers "invented degrading legends and stimulated a spirit of superstition" among the common people. In 1937, another visitor, Spencer Chapman, wrote, "The Lamaist monk does not spend his time in ministering to the people or educating them. . . . The beggar beside the road is nothing to the monk. Knowledge is the jealously guarded prerogative of the monasteries and is used to increase their influence and wealth." As much as we might wish otherwise, feudal theocratic Tibet was a far cry from the romanticized Shangri La so enthusiastically nurtured by Buddhism's western proselytes.

II. Secularization vs. Spirituality

What happened to Tibet after the Chinese Communists moved into the country in 1951? The treaty of that year provided for ostensible self-governance under the Dalai Lama's rule but gave China military control and exclusive right to conduct foreign relations. The Chinese were also granted a direct role in internal administration "to promote social reforms." Among the earliest changes they wrought was to reduce usurious interest rates, and build a few hospitals and roads. At first, they moved slowly, relying mostly on persuasion in an attempt to effect reconstruction. No aristocratic or monastic property was confiscated, and feudal lords continued to reign over their hereditarily bound peasants. "Contrary to popular belief in the West," claims one observer, the Chinese "took care to show respect for Tibetan culture and religion."

Over the centuries the Tibetan lords and lamas had seen Chinese come and go, and had enjoyed good relations with Generalissimo Chiang Kaishek and his reactionary Kuomintang rule in China. The approval of the Kuomintang government was needed to validate the choice of the Dalai Lama and Panchen Lama. When the current 14th Dalai Lama was first installed in Lhasa, it was with an armed escort of Chinese troops and an attending Chinese minister, in accordance with centuries-old tradition. What upset the Tibetan lords and lamas in the early 1950s was that these latest Chinese were Communists. It would be only a matter of time, they feared, before the Communists started imposing their collectivist egalitarian schemes upon Tibet.

The issue was joined in 1956-57, when armed Tibetan bands ambushed convoys of the Chinese Peoples Liberation Army. The uprising received extensive assistance from the U.S. Central Intelligence Agency (CIA), including military training, support camps in Nepal, and numerous airlifts. Meanwhile in the United States, the American Society for a Free Asia, a CIA-financed front, energetically publicized the cause of Tibetan resistance, with the Dalai Lama's eldest brother, Thubtan Norbu, playing an active role in that organization. The Dalai Lama's second-eldest brother, Gyalo Thondup, established an intelligence operation with the CIA as early as 1951. He later upgraded it into a CIA-trained guerrilla unit whose recruits parachuted back into Tibet.

Many Tibetan commandos and agents whom the CIA dropped into the country were chiefs of aristocratic clans or the sons of chiefs. Ninety percent of them were never heard from again, according to a report from the CIA itself, meaning they were most likely captured and killed. "Many lamas and lay members of the elite and much of the Tibetan army joined the uprising, but in the main the populace did not, assuring its failure," writes Hugh Deane. In their book on Tibet, Ginsburg and Mathos reach a similar conclusion: "As far as can be ascertained, the great bulk of the common people of Lhasa and of the adjoining countryside failed to join in the fighting against the Chinese both when it first began and as it progressed." Eventually, the resistance crumbled.

Whatever wrongs and new oppressions introduced by the Chinese after 1959, they did abolish slavery and the Tibetan serfdom system of unpaid labor. They eliminated the many crushing taxes, started work projects, and greatly reduced unemployment and beggary. They established secular schools, thereby breaking the educational monopoly of the monasteries. And they constructed running water and electrical systems in Lhasa.

Heinrich Harrer (later revealed to have been a sergeant in Hitler's SS) wrote a bestseller about his experiences in Tibet that was made into a popular Hollywood movie. He reported that the Tibetans who resisted the Chinese "were predominantly nobles, semi-nobles and lamas; they were punished by being made to perform the lowliest tasks, such as laboring on roads and bridges. They were further humiliated by being made to clean up the city before the tourists arrived." They also had to live in a camp originally reserved for beggars and vagrants--all of which Harrer treats as sure evidence of the dreadful nature of the Chinese occupation.

By 1961, Chinese occupation authorities expropriated the landed estates owned by lords and lamas. They distributed many thousands of acres to tenant farmers and landless peasants, reorganizing them into hundreds of communes. Herds once owned by nobility were turned over to collectives of poor shepherds. Improvements were made in the breeding of livestock, and new varieties of vegetables and new strains of wheat and barley were introduced, along with irrigation improvements, all of which reportedly led to an increase in agrarian production.

Many peasants remained as religious as ever, giving alms to the clergy. But monks who had been conscripted as children into the religious orders were now free to renounce the monastic life, and thousands did, especially the younger ones. The remaining clergy lived on modest government stipends and extra income earned by officiating at prayer services, weddings, and funerals.

Both the Dalai Lama and his advisor and youngest brother, Tendzin Choegyal, claimed that "more than 1.2 million Tibetans are dead as a result of the Chinese occupation." The official 1953 census--six years before the Chinese crackdown--recorded the entire population residing in Tibet at 1,274,000. Other census counts put the population within Tibet at about two million. If the Chinese killed 1.2 million in the early 1960s then almost all of Tibet, would have been depopulated, transformed into a killing field dotted with death camps and mass graves--of which we have no evidence. The thinly distributed Chinese force in Tibet could not have rounded up, hunted down, and exterminated that many people even if it had spent all its time doing nothing else.

Chinese authorities claim to have put an end to floggings, mutilations, and amputations as a form of criminal punishment. They themselves, however, have been charged with acts of brutality by exile Tibetans. The authorities do admit to "mistakes," particularly during the 1966-76 Cultural Revolution when the persecution of religious beliefs reached a high tide in both China and Tibet. After the uprising in the late 1950s, thousands of Tibetans were incarcerated. During the Great Leap Forward, forced collectivization and grain farming were imposed on the Tibetan peasantry, sometimes with disastrous effect on production. In the late 1970s, China began relaxing controls "and tried to undo some of the damage wrought during the previous two decades."

In 1980, the Chinese government initiated reforms reportedly designed to grant Tibet a greater degree of self-rule and self-administration. Tibetans would now be allowed to cultivate private plots, sell their harvest surpluses, decide for themselves what crops to grow, and keep yaks and sheep. Communication with the outside world was again permitted, and frontier controls were eased to permit some Tibetans to visit exiled relatives in India and Nepal. By the 1980s many of the principal lamas had begun to shuttle back and forth between China and the exile communities abroad, "restoring their monasteries in Tibet and helping to revitalize Buddhism there."

As of 2007 Tibetan Buddhism was still practiced widely and tolerated by officialdom. Religious pilgrimages and other standard forms of worship were allowed but within limits. All monks and nuns had to sign a loyalty pledge that they would not use their religious position to foment secession or dissent. And displaying photos of the Dalai Lama was declared illegal.

In the 1990s, the Han, the ethnic group comprising over 95 percent of China's immense population, began moving in substantial numbers into Tibet. On the streets of Lhasa and Shigatse, signs of Han colonization are readily visible. Chinese run the factories and many of the shops and vending stalls. Tall office buildings and large shopping centers have been built with funds that might have been better spent on water treatment plants and housing. Chinese cadres in Tibet too often view their Tibetan neighbors as backward and lazy, in need of economic development and "patriotic education." During the 1990s Tibetan government employees suspected of harboring nationalist sympathies were purged from office, and campaigns were once again launched to discredit the Dalai Lama. Individual Tibetans reportedly were subjected to arrest, imprisonment, and forced labor for carrying out separatist activities and engaging in "political subversion." Some were held in administrative detention without adequate food, water, and blankets, subjected to threats, beatings, and other mistreatment.

Tibetan history, culture, and certainly religion are slighted in schools. Teaching materials, though translated into Tibetan, focus mainly on Chinese history and culture. Chinese family planning regulations allow a three-child limit for Tibetan families. (There is only a one-child limit for Han families throughout China, and a two-child limit for rural Han families whose first child is a girl.) If a Tibetan couple goes over the three-child limit, the excess children can be denied subsidized daycare, health care, housing, and education. These penalties have been enforced irregularly and vary by district. None of these child services, it should be noted, were available to Tibetans before the Chinese takeover.

For the rich lamas and secular lords, the Communist intervention was an unmitigated calamity. Most of them fled abroad, as did the Dalai Lama himself, who was assisted in his flight by the CIA. Some discovered to their horror that they would have to work for a living. Many, however, escaped that fate. Throughout the 1960s, the Tibetan exile community was secretly pocketing $1.7 million a year from the CIA, according to documents released by the State Department in 1998. Once this fact was publicized, the Dalai Lama's organization itself issued a statement admitting that it had received millions of dollars from the CIA during the 1960s to send armed squads of exiles into Tibet to undermine the Maoist revolution. The Dalai Lama's annual payment from the CIA was $186,000. Indian intelligence also financed both him and other Tibetan exiles. He has refused to say whether he or his brothers worked for the CIA. The agency has also declined to comment.

In 1995, the News & Observer of Raleigh, North Carolina, carried a frontpage color photograph of the Dalai Lama being embraced by the reactionary Republican senator Jesse Helms, under the headline "Buddhist Captivates Hero of Religious Right." In April 1999, along with Margaret Thatcher, Pope John Paul II, and the first George Bush, the Dalai Lama called upon the British government to release Augusto Pinochet, the former fascist dictator of Chile and a longtime CIA client who was visiting England. The Dalai Lama urged that Pinochet not be forced to go to Spain where he was wanted to stand trial for crimes against humanity.

Into the twenty-first century, via the National Endowment for Democracy and other conduits that are more respectable sounding than the CIA, the U.S. Congress continued to allocate an annual $2 million to Tibetans in India, with additional millions for "democracy activities" within the Tibetan exile community. In addition to these funds, the Dalai Lama received money from financier George Soros.

Whatever the Dalai Lama's associations with the CIA and various reactionaries, he did speak often of peace, love, and nonviolence. He himself really cannot be blamed for the abuses of Tibet's ancient régime, having been but 25 years old when he fled into exile. In a 1994 interview, he went on record as favoring the building of schools and roads in his country. He said the corvée (forced unpaid serf labor) and certain taxes imposed on the peasants were "extremely bad." And he disliked the way people were saddled with old debts sometimes passed down from generation to generation. During the half century of living in the western world, he had embraced concepts such as human rights and religious freedom, ideas largely unknown in old Tibet. He even proposed democracy for Tibet, featuring a written constitution and a representative assembly.

In 1996, the Dalai Lama issued a statement that must have had an unsettling effect on the exile community. It read in part: "Marxism is founded on moral principles, while capitalism is concerned only with gain and profitability." Marxism fosters "the equitable utilization of the means of production" and cares about "the fate of the working classes" and "the victims of . . . exploitation. For those reasons the system appeals to me, and . . . I think of myself as half-Marxist, half-Buddhist.

But he also sent a reassuring message to "those who live in abundance": "It is a good thing to be rich. Those are the fruits for deserving actions, the proof that they have been generous in the past." And to the poor he offers this admonition: "There is no good reason to become bitter and rebel against those who have property and fortune. It is better to develop a positive attitude."

In 2005 the Dalai Lama signed a widely advertised statement along with ten other Nobel Laureates supporting the "inalienable and fundamental human right" of working people throughout the world to form labor unions to protect their interests, in accordance with the United Nations' Universal Declaration of Human Rights. In many countries "this fundamental right is poorly protected and in some it is explicitly banned or brutally suppressed," the statement read. Burma, China, Colombia, Bosnia, and a few other countries were singled out as among the worst offenders. Even the United States "fails to adequately protect workers' rights to form unions and bargain collectively. Millions of U.S. workers lack any legal protection to form unions. . . ."

The Dalai Lama also gave full support to removing the ingrained traditional obstacles that have kept Tibetan nuns from receiving an education. Upon arriving in exile, few nuns could read or write. In Tibet their activities had been devoted to daylong periods of prayer and chants. But in northern India they now began reading Buddhist philosophy and engaging in theological study and debate, activities that in old Tibet had been open only to monks.

In November 2005 the Dalai Lama spoke at Stanford University on "The Heart of Nonviolence," but stopped short of a blanket condemnation of all violence. Violent actions that are committed in order to reduce future suffering are not to be condemned, he said, citing World War II as an example of a worthy effort to protect democracy. What of the four years of carnage and mass destruction in Iraq, a war condemned by most of the world—even by a conservative pope--as a blatant violation of international law and a crime against humanity? The Dalai Lama was undecided: "The Iraq war—it's too early to say, right or wrong." Earlier he had voiced support for the U.S. military intervention against Yugoslavia and, later on, the U.S. military intervention into Afghanistan.

III. Exit Feudal Theocracy

As the Shangri-La myth would have it, in old Tibet the people lived in contented and tranquil symbiosis with their monastic and secular lords. Rich lamas and poor monks, wealthy landlords and impoverished serfs were all bonded together, mutually sustained by the comforting balm of a deeply spiritual and pacific culture.

One is reminded of the idealized image of feudal Europe presented by latter-day conservative Catholics such as G. K. Chesterton and Hilaire Belloc. For them, medieval Christendom was a world of contented peasants living in the secure embrace of their Church, under the more or less benign protection of their lords. Again we are invited to accept a particular culture in its idealized form divorced from its murky material history. This means accepting it as presented by its favored class, by those who profited most from it. The Shangri-La image of Tibet bears no more resemblance to historic actuality than does the pastoral image of medieval Europe.

Seen in all its grim realities, old Tibet confirms the view I expressed in an earlier book, namely that culture is anything but neutral. Culture can operate as a legitimating cover for a host of grave injustices, benefiting a privileged portion of society at great cost to the rest. In theocratic feudal Tibet, ruling interests manipulated the traditional culture to fortify their own wealth and power. The theocracy equated rebellious thought and action with satanic influence. It propagated the general presumption of landlord superiority and peasant unworthiness. The rich were represented as deserving their good life, and the lowly poor as deserving their mean existence, all codified in teachings about the karmic residue of virtue and vice accumulated from past lives, presented as part of God's will.

Were the more affluent lamas just hypocrites who

preached one thing and secretly believed another? More likely they were genuinely attached to those beliefs that brought such good results for them. That their theology so perfectly supported their material privileges only strengthened the sincerity with which it was embraced.

It might be said that we denizens of the modern secular world cannot grasp the equations of happiness and pain, contentment and custom, which characterize more traditionally spiritual societies. This is probably true, and it may explain why some of us idealize such societies. But still, a gouged eye is a gouged eye; a flogging is a flogging; and the grinding exploitation of serfs and slaves is a brutal class injustice whatever its cultural wrapping. There is a difference between a spiritual bond and human bondage, even when both exist side by side

Many ordinary Tibetans want the Dalai Lama back in their country, but it appears that relatively few want a return to the social order he represented. A 1999 story in the Washington Post notes that the Dalai Lama continues to be revered in Tibet, but

. . . few Tibetans would welcome a return of the corrupt aristocratic clans that fled with him in 1959 and that comprise the bulk of his advisers. Many Tibetan farmers, for example, have no interest in surrendering the land they gained during China's land reform to the clans. Tibet's former slaves say they, too, don't want their former masters to return to power. "I've already lived that life once before," said Wangchuk, a 67-year-old former slave who was wearing his best clothes for his yearly pilgrimage to Shigatse, one of the holiest sites of Tibetan Buddhism. He said he worshipped the Dalai Lama, but added, "I may not be free under Chinese communism, but I am better off than when I was a slave."

It should be noted that the Dalai Lama is not the only highly placed lama chosen in childhood as a reincarnation. One or another reincarnate lama or tulku--a spiritual teacher of special purity elected to be reborn again and again--can be found presiding over most major monasteries. The tulku system is unique to Tibetan Buddhism. Scores of Tibetan lamas claim to be reincarnate tulkus.

The very first tulku was a lama known as the Karmapa who appeared nearly three centuries before the first Dalai Lama. The Karmapa is leader of a Tibetan Buddhist tradition known as the Karma Kagyu. The rise of the Gelugpa sect headed by the Dalai Lama led to a politico-religious rivalry with the Kagyu that has lasted five hundred years and continues to play itself out within the Tibetan exile community to-day. That the Kagyu sect has grown famously, opening some six hundred new centers around the world in the last thirty-five years, has not helped the situation.

The search for a tulku, Erik Curren reminds us, has not always been conducted in that purely spiritual mode portrayed in certain Hollywood films. "Sometimes monastic officials wanted a child from a powerful local noble family to give the cloister more political clout. Other times they wanted a child from a lower-class family who would have little leverage to influence the child's upbringing." On other occasions "a local warlord, the Chinese emperor or even the Dalai Lama's government in Lhasa might [have tried] to impose its choice of tulku on a monastery for political reasons."

Such may have been the case in the selection of the 17th Karmapa, whose monastery-in-exile is situated in Rumtek, in the Indian state of Sikkim. In 1993 the monks of the Karma Kagyu tradition had a candidate of their own choice. The Dalai Lama, along with several dissenting Karma Kagyu leaders (and with the support of the Chinese government!) backed a different boy. The Kagyu monks charged that the Dalai Lama had overstepped his authority in attempting to select a leader for their sect. "Neither his political role nor his position as a lama in his own Gelugpa tradition entitled him to choose the Karmapa, who is a leader of a different tradition..." As one of the Kagyu leaders insisted, "Dharma is about thinking for yourself. It is not about automatically following a teacher in all things, no matter how respected that teacher may be. More than anyone else, Buddhists should respect other people's rights—their human rights and their religious freedom."

What followed was a dozen years of conflict in the Tibetan exile community, punctuated by intermittent riots, intimidation, physical attacks, blacklisting, police harassment, litigation, official corruption, and the looting and undermining of the Karmapa's monastery in Rumtek by supporters of the Gelugpa faction. All this has caused at least one western devotee to wonder if the years of exile were not hastening the moral corrosion of Tibetan Buddhism.

What is clear is that not all Tibetan Buddhists accept the Dalai Lama as their theological and spiritual mentor. Though he is referred to as the "spiritual leader of Tibet," many see this title as little more than a formality. It does not give him authority over the four religious schools of Tibet other than his own, "just as calling the U.S. president the 'leader of the free world' gives him no role in governing France or Germany."

Not all Tibetan exiles are enamoured of the old Shangri-La theocracy. Kim Lewis, who studied healing methods with a Buddhist monk in Berkeley, California, had occasion to talk at length with more than a dozen Tibetan women who lived in the monk's building. When she asked how they felt about returning to their homeland, the sentiment was unanimously negative. At first, Lewis assumed that their reluctance had to do with the Chinese occupation, but they quickly informed her otherwise. They said they were extremely grateful "not to have to marry 4 or 5 men, be pregnant almost all the time," or deal with sexually transmitted diseases contacted from a straying husband. The younger women "were delighted to be getting an education, wanted absolutely nothing to do with any religion, and wondered why Americans were so naïve [about Tibet]."

The women interviewed by Lewis recounted stories of their grandmothers' ordeals with monks who used them as "wisdom consorts." By sleeping with the monks, the grandmothers were told, they gained "the means to enlightenment" -- after all, the Buddha himself had to be with a woman to reach enlightenment.

The women also mentioned the "rampant" sex that the supposedly spiritual and abstemious monks practiced with each other in the Gelugpa sect. The women who were mothers spoke bitterly about the monastery's confiscation of their young boys in Tibet. They claimed that when a boy cried for his mother, he would be told "Why do you cry for her, she gave you up--she's just a woman."

The monks who were granted political asylum in California applied for public assistance. Lewis, herself a devotee for a time, assisted with the paperwork. She observes that they continue to receive government checks amounting to $550 to $700 per month along with Medicare. In addition, the monks reside rent free in nicely furnished apartments. "They pay no utilities, have free access to the Internet on computers provided for them, along with fax machines, free cell and home phones and cable TV."

They also receive a monthly payment from their order, along with contributions and dues from their American followers. Some devotees eagerly carry out chores for the monks, including grocery shopping and cleaning their apartments and toilets. These same holy men, Lewis remarks, "have no problem criticizing Americans for their 'obsession with material things.'"

To welcome the end of the old feudal theocracy in Tibet is not to applaud everything about Chinese rule in that country. This point is seldom understood by today's Shangri-La believers in the West. The converse is also true: To denounce the Chinese occupation does not mean we have to romanticize the former feudal régime. Tibetans deserve to be perceived as actual people, not perfected spiritualists or innocent political symbols. "To idealize them," notes Ma Jian, a dissident Chinese traveler to Tibet (now living in Britain), "is to deny them their humanity."

One common complaint among Buddhist followers in the West is that Tibet's religious culture is being undermined by the Chinese occupation. To some extent this seems to be the case. Many of the monasteries are closed, and much of the theocracy seems to have passed into history. Whether Chinese rule has brought betterment or disaster is not the central issue here. The question is what kind of country was old Tibet. What I am disputing is the supposedly pristine spiritual nature of that pre-invasion culture. We can advocate religious freedom and independence for a new Tibet without having to embrace the mythology about old Tibet. Tibetan feudalism was cloaked in Buddhism, but the two are not to be equated. In reality, old Tibet was not a Paradise Lost. It was a retrograde repressive theocracy of extreme privilege and poverty, a long way from Shangri-La.

Finally, let it be said that if Tibet's future is to be positioned somewhere within China's emerging free-market paradise, then this does not bode well for the Tibetans. China boasts a dazzling 8 percent economic growth rate and is emerging as one of the world's greatest industrial powers. But with economic growth has come an ever deepening gulf between rich and poor. Most Chinese live close to the poverty level or well under it, while a small group of newly brooded capitalists profit hugely in collusion with shady officials. Regional bureaucrats milk the country dry, extorting graft from the populace and looting local treasuries. Land grabbing in cities and countryside by avaricious developers and corrupt officials at the expense of the populace are almost everyday occurrences. Tens of thousands of grassroot protests and disturbances have erupted across the country, usually to be met with unforgiving police force. Corruption is so prevalent, reaching into so many places, that even the normally complacent national leadership was forced to take notice and began moving against it in late 2006.

Workers in China who try to organize labor unions in the corporate dominated "business zones" risk losing their jobs or getting beaten and imprisoned. Millions of business zone workers toil twelve-hour days at subsistence wages. With the health care system now being privatized, free or affordable medical treatment is no longer available for millions. Men have tramped into the cities in search of work, leaving an increasingly impoverished countryside populated by women, children, and the elderly. The suicide rate has increased dramatically, especially among women.

China's natural environment is sadly polluted. Most of its fabled rivers and many lakes are dead, producing massive fish die-offs from the billions of tons of industrial emissions and untreated human waste dumped into them. Toxic effluents, including pesticides and herbicides, seep into ground water or directly into irrigation canals. Cancer rates in villages situated along waterways have skyrocketed a thousand-fold. Hundreds of millions of urban residents breathe air rated as dangerously unhealthy, contaminated by industrial growth and the recent addition of millions of automobiles. An estimated 400,000 die prematurely every year from air pollution. Government environmental agencies have no enforcement power to stop polluters, and generally the government ignores or denies such problems, concentrating instead on industrial growth.

China's own scientific establishment reports that unless greenhouse gases are curbed, the nation will face massive crop failures along with catastrophic food and water shortages in the years ahead. In 2006-2007 severe drought was already afflicting southwest China.

If China is the great success story of speedy free market development, and is to be the model and inspiration for Tibet's future, then old feudal Tibet indeed may start looking a lot better than it actually was.

For human; Myth is difficult to give up. For an intelligent human; what should be the truthful, unbiased, non-distorted observation of history? Just another example of dangerously groomed false promises. Organized Religion: Superstition, Ignorance – Power and Control. It starts with superstitious Myth, then,... perpetuated Ignorance. Those who do the manipulating, wreak their new found Power over the unquestioning Ignorant. Lo! – we have complete control.

CHAPTER 13
FIGHTING TERRORISM

War Department – Indians - Pre- Civil War

The British blew their chances to defeat the Colonists. Colonists learned to fight ' Indian style' ambushes in protective wooded areas covering trails Brit' Redcoats had to pass through. Red does not camouflage too well.

Next, the War Department mid-1850s turned down the 12 shot Winchester repeater for Springfield Arms single shot. Springfield Arms made the military musket and therefore were in on the bottom floor with the War Department (Aptly named back then.) when they started designing the rolling block single shot, copper cased cartridge firing 45.70 that jammed on a hot day after the second shot. Copper cartridge casing swelled; not so the brassy .44/.45 caliber pistol cartridge. Winchester had spent their limited funds manufacturing several hundred repeating rifles and were headed for bankruptcy after their disappointing rebuff from the corrupt War Department. Springfield Arms paid under the table to forego the highly advanced repeater despite realizing a civil war was brewing. The War Department had to come up with some excuse and chose "It would use up too much ammunition." Had the repeater been purchased and the Union Army so armed: the Civil War would have lasted, maybe a year. Had the Southern Confederacy had it they may have won the war. Ambitious traders however bought enough rifles to head west destined for the Sioux, who would become Winchester's major customer. Chief Red Cloud initially purchased enough to realize how devastating they were against Indian enemies and later the U. S. Cavalry. Had Chief Red Cloud, whom was the 'Decider' never purchased them then how did the rifles get into the hands of the Indians? Did the business minded Traders offer up hundreds of free sample? How did less than 700 of Crazy Horses chosen warriors readily defeat 1440 of General Crook's troops in less than two days fighting just a bit over a week before the Big Horn Battle? Certainly they were not limited to bows and spears as the gullible, foolish writers attempt to proclaim. Likewise they errantly make the same false assumptions regarding the latter Custer defeat. That battle lasted less than a half hour. A repeating rifle was the only weapon, and plenty of them that could end it so quickly. The white writers and even a couple of our own Indian ones never interviewed the Sioux and Cheyenne warriors who were there! Such is Dominant Society history. The Treaty of 1868 would have never been won were it not for the Winchester and Red Cloud's logistic wisdom, yet writers, Indian and White continue to vilify him nor mention his wise decision to deal with the Gun Traders.

Sioux hostilities with the Army began with the Lieutenant Grattan fight. My tribe was referred to as Sioux back in that time span; 1856, wherein Grattan and his men were wiped out mostly with pistol fire. A young Red Cloud figured in that brisk event and some historians give him credit for killing an intoxicated Lt. Grattan. It wasn't long before gun traders courted Red Cloud and Spotted Tail of the Sichangu Sioux, Red Cloud's close allies. The traders kept Winchester from bankruptcy through the Sioux; mainly paid for in furs and later, abundant Black Hills Gold that could initially be picked by hand flashing from the stream beds. Winchester won for the Sioux under Chief Red Cloud -the Treaty of 1868 – as mentioned, wherein my tribe has a billion dollars in the bank drawing interest as compensation for U S breaking this treaty won by the Sioux in fair combat. Red Cloud couldn't help but win his many battles with such an advanced fire arm compared to the Cavalry's jamming single shot. Sherman accurately estimated he needed 20,000 soldiers to defeat the estimated 2,000 Sioux, fire armed warriors enjoying an 8 to 1 kill ratio in the Sioux's favor. Except for WWII, America's warfare modus operandi has little changed up to the present conflicts, forever handicapped by the meddling politicians.

President Grant invited Red Cloud to Washington after the Treaty was signed and told the Chief that he had changed his mind and was now planning to dispatch the Sioux to Indian territory, Oklahoma. This was one year after the U. S. put the Treaty of 1868 in front of the Sioux, captioned "In God We Trust." He was reminded by a defiant Red Cloud that they still had their Winchesters and plenty of the Cavalry's captured (And their pistols too.) pistol ammunition for which Grant's troops would suffer dearly. ("You do not have the Winchester. We do. We will fight and probably lose in the end but not after you pay a great price in men...and now settlers." Then Red Cloud went across the street and advised the Senate, many of whom had little love for Grant. The Senate wisely overruled Grant as settlers were now in Sioux Territory. We Sioux still are in the Dakotas, thanks to Winchester Arms and a capable non-attempting 'politically correct' military leadership. The pistol ammo conveniently supplied Sioux Winchesters as most soldiers in the field realized they had to depend on more than a jamming 'two shot' to stay alive. Their saddle bags were loaded with more pistol ammunition than 45.70 ammo. Our warriors went for the supply immediately when dispatching a soldier while just out of the soldier's return fire pistol range. A few fantasizing white writers, are finally realizing the Sioux used such 'Repeaters' and captured ('two-shots'- Nupa peytah) as the Sioux referred to the jamming Sharps. Sioux also rode Mongolian style both arms free. Makes a lot of difference for aiming while on the move. Try it with reins on the run and still keeping control of your horse. You won't be very accurate.

Characteristically, superiority driven Army generals refused to adopt such an advancement to their 'Bit and Reins' mode. This ignoring ability to adapt thus resulted in suffering numerous battle loses which began back in Genghis Khan's days. His archers were effectively mounted. 'Bit and Reins' prevented the European archers from being horse borne, combat engagement mounted on the move as were the deadly Mongol archer troops. Ego and that destructive false sense of disastrous producing witless Superiority has cost many a European battle down through time. The European descendants brought that ego with them to America. Guess who lost the most engagements with the horse borne Sioux?

Foolish, egotistical spawned 'Superiority' too often results in needless casualties regarding your own troops. Accurate, American military history needs a thorough review as we go on to engagements in the Mid-east.

First Vietnam - How not to fight ISIS.

I am opportune to have many veterans yet alive and some from the Korean and Vietnam conflicts loaded with direct experience and who now have offspring or friends of Mid-east combat vets some stationed there now, so hence the following information, I consider as quite accurate and revealing.

The same old government 'political handicapping', hold back is POTUS's S. O. P. (President of the United States Standard Operating Procedure) -customary of all POTUS operandi since Korean War - still in operation and now within the Desert Wars combat theatres despite the blatant danger of ISIS (Dayesh) who naturally reap enduring advantage. We veterans, especially us combat baptized ones now await to see where our new president, Donald Trump will act as CIC especially regarding Afghanistan and present ISIS holdings in Iraq. But first let me present from personal, repeatedly front line experience how and why politicians need to stay the hell out of handcuffing our military when we fight a war.

Logistics fights wars, without supply you lose. The Haiphong logistic receiving docks were off limits to us pilots. 'Cannot endanger non-combatants unloading ships at the docks', was some insane reasoning. You could see the long line of ships waiting at the Haiphong port waiting to unload. A merchant's heaven. Yet our snake eye bombs dropped at masthead level could have surgically taken out the docks with unloading ships docked alongside receiving negligible blast damage. A smaller bomb with less blast yet capable to destroy the docks would have done the job and or the bridge/shore work leading up to the docks. The world cartel didn't want to lose the business and hence DOD followed their 'hands off' protocol. Such is the way modern wars are fought – commerce influenced restrictions.

Likewise when a SAM (Surface to Air) missile was fired at us, they usually came up in pairs or more, we could not return fire unless we contacted Air Force Command and would have a half hour required wait to allow the Russian mentors training the NVA below to get away safely. Typical meddling damned civilians, politicians and DOD bureaucrats messing with our military lives. There is always this 'concern' for civilian lives yet the results most often develop that more civilians on our side get put away or displaced not to mention increased casualties for our own troops. Look at the long lines of refugees strung across Europe at present due mainly because POTUS and his advisors are so overly concerned about 'Civilian casualties' which ISIS wisely sprinkles among their troops and logistic bases.

Radar, which tracked us in those days, was still glitch filled - technology wise and also the airworthiness of the SAMs coming up at us had to be a bit tricky for the control operators. Often they would be overcorrected tracking us and would tumble wildly or fail to explode at the proper time. This happened once to me earlier on a mission and on the same mission that I got hit by one, my section leader had one go right by his F-4 and fail to fire. No shrapnel miraculously penetrated my plane but the blast suffocated my port engine and it flamed out while I was inverted doing a split S maneuver trying to escape. Inverting your aircraft and pulling your control stick changes your altitude and forward movement rather quickly. (Hence avoiding where the SAM is programmed to intercept you.). I relit my engine over the South China Sea and we went back in on the tell-tale SAM smoke trail pointing to the SAM's firing base. We destroyed it with two passes each- napalm and 500 pounders. We were both so pissed (Close calls have that effect) that we didn't bother to contact Air Force and wait their prescribed half hour. Fritz was getting out to fly for the airlines and I was going to law school in the matter of a few months. We considered our own non-beholding terms as exoneration for taking out the Sam Site. Political interference, subterfuge and intrigue hasn't changed regarding the way we are continuing to apply today to handcuff our military. Whatever, do not fight in the Mid-east the way we had to in Vietnam.

> From: Richard Peinert [mailto:hontasman@gmail.com]
> Sent: Monday, January 11, 2016 4:16 PM
> Subject: Fwd: Vietnam - Why were so many planes shot down? Interesting revelation from Dean Rusk.
>
> You are the one on the list most likely to know if this is true. Sadly, I cannot just dismiss it out of hand because of justifiable lack of faith in our political leadership.
>
> -----Original Message-----
> From: Randy Thornton <randythornton885@gmail.com>
> Sent: Mon, Jan 11, 2016 2:50 pm
> Subject: Vietnam - Why were so many planes shot down? Interesting revelation from Dean Rusk.
>
> Don't know if this is true, never heard it before. If true, disgustingly unbelievable. Flat out treasonous. That is the result of a mixture of the military and politicians trying to "fight a war". The problem is, politicians are too damn P. C. [Politically Correct] whereas the military enters a conflict to win, at any cost.
>
> Randy Thornton

The following tracks very closely an Amazon review of the following book. The quote shown below appears to be accurately reproduced from the original.

"The Secret War and Other Conflicts" [69]

> Ever wondered why so many of our aviators in Vietnam got shot down? Hard to believe. Even after all these years this is still disgusting to hear. No wonder so many people despise our political leadership. Vietnam - Why were so many planes shot

---

[69] Charles P. Slaton, Amazon review of General Pete Piotrowski, *Basic Airman to General: The Secret War & Other Conflicts: Lessons in Leadership & Life* (Xlibris, 2014), https://www.amazon.com/gp/customer-reviews/R2QD1OC8KRJI96/ref=cm_cr_dp_d_rvw_ttl?ie=UTF8&ASIN=1493161873

down? Following is a quote from the book I found to be of much interest, from pages 246/247: "Nearly twenty years later, former Secretary of State Dean Rusk being interviewed by Peter Arnett on a CBC documentary called, "The Ten Thousand Day War". Mr. Arnett asked, "It has been rumored that the United States provided the North Vietnamese government the names of the targets that would be bombed the following day. Is there any truth to that allegation?" To everyone's astonishment and absolute disgust, the former Secretary responded, "Yes. We didn't want to harm the North Vietnamese people, so we passed the targets to the Swiss embassy in Washington with instructions to pass them to the NVN government through their embassy in Hanoi." As we watched in horror, Secretary Rusk went on to say, "All we wanted to do is demonstrate to the North Vietnamese leadership that we could strike targets at will, but we didn't want to kill innocent people. By giving the North Vietnamese advanced warning of the targets to be attacked, we thought they would tell the workers to stay home."

No wonder all the targets were so heavily defended day after day! The NVN obviously moved as many guns as they could overnight to better defend each target they knew was going to be attacked. Clearly, many brave American Air Force and Navy fliers died or spent years in NVN prison camps as a direct result of being intentionally betrayed by Secretary Rusk and Secretary McNamara, and perhaps, President Johnson himself. I cannot think of a more duplicitous and treacherous act of American government officials. Dean Rusk served as Secretary of State from January 21, 1961, through to January 20, 1969, under President John F. Kennedy and Lyndon B. Johnson. Mr. Peter Arnett opined that "this would be a treasonous act by anyone else.

A very sad revelation.

Let us go back to WW II. Congressman Lyndon Johnson wore a Navy Cross for sitting bravely back in a Navy Transport as a passenger. An alleged Jap zero made a strafing run and LBJ sat in back displaying "unfearing bravery with calm" - so the commendation reads. The only non-combatant that was awarded the medal which is next to the Medal of Honor. Worse! Such an Ego had Johnson that he wore it all during his presidency on his suit lapel!

Vietnam- Marine Close Air Support (CAS) vs Air Force TAS (U S Air Force Mig Chasing.)

Air Force strategy vs Marine Minimum Close Air.

The U. S. Air Force allowed the NVA to infiltrate into the South. This tattle tale bombing warning to the enemy by Former Sec. of State Dean Rusk explains why and how the immense B-52 Arc Lights did so little damage. They bombed mostly nothing and not - well camouflaged jungle located, civilian manned factories if any. Let's now add that 5,000 Phantoms were manufactured by McDonnell Aircraft. 1,000 F4Cs were made after the mostly Marine Corps and Navy F4Bs were received. These services traded in their Korean War Vintage Douglass ADs for the F4B contract. Close Air (Dropping ordnance at close proximity) was the Marines Combat 'Bread and Butter' ticket. The less efficient ADs, if survivability of the aircraft from NVA 37s and 51 millimeter anti-aircraft fire was considered, propeller driven and slower, were termed Spads and later nick named by AF- Sandys. Why most of the F4s were winding up in Turkey, Egypt, UK, Germany while a hot war was going on besides other places is not puzzling when we consider political meddling. Each F4 could combat carry twelve -500 lb bombs but few were utilized for close air support and most never used 'down and dirty', beginning the bombing run at tree top level like we Marines conducted and were far more accurate than the A F - 'Too High and too Many' attempts with what few squadrons they designated for Close Air despite flying from much farther away airbases. Yah! Thailand? Our base at Chu Lai was right in the heart of the major battle area which allowed us to return to base, reload and refuel after touch down from a mission and back out again to save troops in 12 minutes. Ask any 'snuff' ground pounder who has experienced real Close Air beneath providing Marine F-4s. His life is on the line. He wants you back as soon as you can get back rearmed and refueled. Life hadn't changed much regarding the White Man's military I.Q. from the War Department mistake of the Civil War turning down the Winchester repeater.

Likewise the Navy CAS. It takes too long to operate effectively from an aircraft carrier for repeated return missions on the same target area wherein our troop's lives are at stake. Tail hook trapping, towing to an elevator and waiting for a second landing aircraft, refueling and re-arming below decks and returning for catapult is a bit longer than 12 minutes – four to five times longer at least. How far out at sea the carrier is located has to be considered as well. F-4 aircraft from USAF bases out of Thailand is more than a bit longer yet.

Two of us F-4s were flying cover for two H-46s downed up on a mountainous Highlands ridge. One chopper was closest to a closing in enemy NVA battalion and were captured after my third mission when darkness came. They were all shot- no POW roles. Just outright murdered after capture. Had we had a division of F-4s (4 aircraft) I believe we would have saved that chopper but instead they were scattered (over 5,000 in all) somewhere out far away from the combat theater. We fought on into the night, we two Phantoms on hot pad duty coming back and back. An A-4, Sky Hawk, an AD Sky Raider and two Huey gun ships were downed yet all crashed safely on a short Helio Courier airstrip carved on the ridge. Their crews got out too when we finally outlasted, severely damaging the NVA battalion despite nightfall.

The Army Airborne command didn't want AF around after too many high drop casualties inflicted upon them. So they called on us- Marines. A 500 pounder is one helluva lethal weapon. You don't need six or even a preposterous 12 dropped down in front of you where the enemy is at when you call for help from above. That AF pilot too often drops his load and runs. Marines come in for one at a time or damn well none if they don't like what they see below- mainly where your own troops just might be too close to the target zone. We Do <u>Not</u> kill our own troops. One at a time was a common virtue for Marine F4 pilots. We usually dropped one or two only- hell, a single 500 pounder is lethal- Napalm worse. You come back and drop another 1 or 2 at most and again and again. You stay longer in the pattern to protect those beleaguered snuffs below and that big flying fuel farm, the F-4, could do it and get back so much faster for reload than a 200 knot, propeller driven Spad (Sandys). One mission doesn't stop a battle or an all-day beleaguered insert running from a higher force. The F4 comes in at 500 knots- drops or even a no drop fully loaded, it could pull up and ACCELERATE! Busting Mach and ten grand altitude safely in damn few seconds. 37s AA can't get turned quick enough to take you on when you are zipping over at 500 knots. Plain common grunt Marine damn sense- "I live!" Beleaguered Grunts below. "They Live." Flying technique. We touched down hot back at Chu Lai, "50 out, hot pad," you tell the tower. ("I am 50 miles out and hot pad priority over all other incoming aircraft.") All incoming birds orbit. You taxied hot and were reloaded, refueled. 12 minutes later and back out again. Saved lives. What the hell we were there for.

AF Spads, A-1's, had to be disbanded because their slower pull out- sitting duck, barely- above -Helo speed that the 37s and 51s feasted on. Oh there were lots of AF F4s in and around Nam but never based in the heart of the major fighting like Marine base Chu Lai. A few were out of Da Nang admittedly but DaNang was too crowded to efficiently allow priority to hot pads. Get out fast. Get back fast. Get back out! Pretty difficult to do whilst' based out of Thailand or Thon Son Nut. But the Chinese baited those AF F4s with their MIG s. They tantalized hell outta' the AF who egotistically took the bait. Don't ever think the Chinese are as dumb, military-wise as we are. AF squadrons went aloft and stayed all day refueling. Round and Round they went chasing their tails- nary a bomb underneath them. Reason why we Marines did 2 to 3 real, shot - at missions by 37s, 51s and ground fire. I see Vets all summer at my book selling: They verify and would disdain working for some over ruling 'Think Tank'. The above is a bit of repetition but I want to get my points across because we are doing the same in the Mid-east at present. If repetition to strongly make military non-Think Tank points to save our troops and demolish our enemy then- so-be-it!

Come Winters, away from my book selling, I learned from Chinese millionaire dairy entrepreneurs who told me the Chinese baiting success in Vietnam. (their success not ours.). A cooperating state university and a certain professor who saw value in my services put us together. At first, the NVA was worried by the F4C AF contract with McDonnell, but was allayed, relieved by the Chinese AF wiser operations. The NVA successfully went on to plan and infiltrate South Vietnam with their ground troops untouched by the awesome arc lights. Guess what? They eventually won the war. Not enough of those 5,000 F4s utilized for what they were highly efficient at. Go on Amazon/Kindle- order *Warrior's Odyssey* if you want to learn more.

My Bio [70]

For Marine Close Air, Close Air Support (CAS) is Down, Deep and Dangerous. I guess you can describe it as such, but oh so highly effective as thousands of visiting Vietnam combat veterans eventually have attested almost daily over the years when I am selling my books from my table at Crazy Horse Mountain Museum in the Black Hills of South Dakota. Such high praise every one of them had for that effective F-4 Phantom that flew so close over them attacking and protecting. "So damn close you could see the pilot, feel the heat of the napalm or his bomb blast,"

---

[70] An excerpt from my Bio. A bit repetitive admittedly from the above.

was and yet is a common expression. Actually a lot more dangerous and death defying overall than the glamorized TAS—Tactical Air Support; the AF MIG chasers who go aloft to orbit round and round for hours, plug into a KC-135 tanker and orbit in complete boredom some more time punching holes in the sky, often plugging in a second time; even a third. I didn't plug in that much; as CAS you get back to base as quickly as you can- another F4 advantage over every other CAS model including the A-4. The A-6 carried 20 some 500 pounders but came in much slower and up and out slower yet. It also was blind on one side for the controlling pilot who sat side by side. You do not do effective CAS by being half blinded. If you look at the statistics, there were damn few MIGs shot down or engaged compared to the daily encounters we Marine CAS pilots experienced against ground fire, 37mm/51mm AA fire (dubbed by pilots as Jane Fondas, Fonda Janes.) and occasional SAM missiles enroute to our targets. Black mountains at night and worse, under flares cannot be downplayed. You do not drop your load—'Air Force Style' either. Besieged, often desperate troops are down there. You drop one or a couple and have to go back in repeatedly as this chapter illustrates. More lives than yours are at stake and that is what you are getting paid and were trained for. None of this, 'Drop High and too Many' as most every one of the many combat Vets I have had the privilege to meet complained about regarding their opinions of Air Force Close Air. The Airborne eventually banned the Air Force attempts at Close Air after losing troops and called on us Marines to support them. I dropped many a load, one at a time, tree top level just beyond beleaguered or attacking Airborne who were highly professional with their communication and position marking to us.

Once a fellow pilot and I went into a grunt Airborne O'club that offered actual frozen slush margaritas and damn near got beat up. Some big stud Lieutenants. and Captains didn't like us, taking us for AF and we mistakenly walking in with our flight suits on and one of us bore a F4 patch. Curtains and our double order of margaritas almost didn't make it until they found out who we really were. We couldn't pay for our drinks all evening and had to stay over. Our squadron had recently covered successfully for a big operation they were involved in. We had all the free margaritas we wanted.

The Chinese controlled the other side of Nam' Air Power. The NVA lost a lot of troops to our Marine Close Air which is our 'Bread and Butter' as far as ground support is considered. In Vietnam, it all began with the A-1 Sky Raider (Spad, Sandy) trade. It was a single radial engine, min-iature attack bomber compared to the twin and four motored types. Pre-Vietnam it was carrier borne toward end of the Korean War by the Ma-rines and Navy. Some Air Force higher-ups were mesmerized by the plane's ability to 'Carry its own weight in Bombs.' Unfortunately for the Air Force they traded their McDonnell F-4B contract to the Navy for all the Navy's A Ds which included the Marine's birds as well since we are part of the Navy. Our CAS experienced Generals readily complied and with glee I might add. I may never have been here writing books had not that trade been made and if I had flown a Spad instead. The Air Force designated 'Air Commando' squadrons with much fanfare and sent them off to Vietnam. Unfortunately, drastically inferior to the F-4, the A D could not pull off safely above the enemy 37 millimeter AA guns and often, even their small arms fire.

The numerous 37s (Fonda Janes) we encountered were light, detach-able, easily transportable, and highly effective against 'slow movers' such as the Spad and helicopters. As I said, the Spad with a full load of fuel and bombs would slow to 145 knots (If not all ordnance expended or still heavy with fuel) on pull up against gravity out of the enemy zone. (Not too difficult to figure out regarding CAS that the Air Force made a huge mistake.) Eventually, due to the high aircraft and pilot loss, the 'Carries its own weight in bombs' infatuation had to be disbanded. The highly touted 'Warthog'—A-10, I mentioned would have gone a similar route had it made the Vietnam scene for it too had no afterburners to get it out, up and away rather swiftly as the Phantom could perform. Within seconds from tree top, we F-4 pilots already doing 500, were breaking 5, 6 thou-sand feet on up to ten thousand for our turn around and back in again out of small arms fire and the 37s. Worse, for the enemy, they never led us enough when they were firing. Once in a while they did have tracers and you could see that they were not leading us enough. These tracers, always coming up and falling behind, were no doubt our captured weap-ons and ammunition. The Wart Hog coming in at 350 and no burners would be a sitting duck when it had to go full power to get the hell out of the enemy troops return fire - but yes- too often fatally slowing down. Non-acceleration is considered lethally dangerous after drop by experi-enced Marine CAS pilots.

The Phantom was near perfect for close air. It had the pilot in front within a fishbowl cockpit with the best visibility platform and not half blind on one side as in the A-6 Intruder that had the two pilots side by side. The much smaller A-4 had equal visibility but could not carry a Phantom's load nor stay on station nearly as long and most importantly come in as fast as the F-4 nor exit as quickly. Also, it could not get back as fast to reload and re-fuel to return back to the battle area. Those beleaguered troops below want you back as soon as possible. That is why the Marines always want a (Close to combat) land base so you can get turned around quickly. On a carrier, out farther at sea, you go below after being trapped by your tail hook. The Navy did try to effect reloading and refueling topside carriers, but land bases were more practical and most often closer to combat operations involving ground troops. Marines practice CAS, although in my time we wasted more time with those RIOs (Radar Intercept Officers) and not dropping practice bombs while in training stateside. Our few remaining F-4s are now being wasted as target drones. D.O.D. stupidity.

The NVA realized the deadly effectiveness of the F-4 and obviously were quite worried when the Air Force began receiving F4s to replace their less effective single engine F-100s especially when it came to CAS. As mentioned, the Chinese figured out how to save the war. They baited the Air Force with MIGs, some older models even. It was a too tantalizing bait for the Air Force to refuse. Squadrons of F-4s went airborne after MIGs, refueling several times; hence disregarding CAS against the NVA which was shelved too often. Grandeur Ego over common sense prevailed. The Focus of War became remote. It was MacArthur all over again—his failure to inspect the ill equipped 8th Army in Korea and disregard of the intelligence on the North Korean military buildup. The 'Shogun of Japan— Imperial Palace' grandeur was too overwhelming. Distraction! Not much difference than that Marine Commander John R. Allen in Afghanistan texting that attractive 'Chick' 20 times a day, Jill Kelley, who wiggled her hind end into some kind of title, Honorary Ambassador to U S Central Command Coalition Forces, instead of focusing on his troops getting blown away. Allen was investigated by Sec. DOD Panetta and retired in 2013. Good riddance. Let's not leave out General Petraeus and his jogging honey/mistress/biographer in the Mideast- Paula Broadwell. He got stung but not enough over Honey Paula's top-secret look see. In China—both of these married deviates would be hauled to Beijing and sent out to the rice paddies if the jury felt lenient.

I learn a lot from my vantage point at Crazy Horse Museum where a million tourists a summer pass by my book selling table there. Thousands of combat veterans stop by to chat and relive old memories. Recently an

AF F-4 pilot who did two tours told me it was not uncommon to have 100 AF F4s in the sky at one time coming from various bases outside of Hanoi and Haiphong for MIG Cap operations. The Marines were left to do effective CAS but there were not enough F-4 Marine squadrons to carry out the needed missions to subdue the NVA, especially when they became offensive with their operations. Who won the war?

Number one requirement in CAS is that you have to get away to return again and again.

1. Your machine, fully loaded and fully fueled, has to accelerate against gravity. Gravity slows down your ascent unless you have 'serious' afterburners, yes, real 'serious' when you take on fire from 37 and 51 millimeter anti-aircraft. That first pass, you need to know exactly where your troops are before you drop. The Air Liaison below or spotter bird is talking to you to make sure you do. Drones cannot do that. Civilian casualties? Drones don't distinguish either compared to the CAS pilot.

2. Be big enough to carry enough fuel to stay on station to drop one at a time, preferably tree top level where you can see where your own troops are.

3. Get back to base after your last drop rather quickly and back again fully loaded and refueled. 7, 800 knots is rather quick.

4. Carry enough Ordinance. F-4 carried 12—500 pounders. F-100 only 4 and A-4—6. Both slowed on pull up fully loaded (Not enough serious' after burner.). A-6 carried 22 but blind on one side for the pilot and like the A-4, no after-burner for get away. Relegated to higher altitude, non-CAS missions.

Getting blown away on a velocity slowing pull up due to inadequate power does not do that combat infantryman below much of a favor, does it? He needs you and will tell you so in years to come as I often hear from them speaking from near-death experience as I autograph my books to this day. Every military ground pounder experiencing lifesaving Phantoms and Douglas Sky Hawks, so far is critical of Air Force technique and commend highly the 'Tree-Top' single bomb, down and dirty pattern the Marines use. The dead from inadequate CAS can't talk. The misuse of the majority of available F-4s in 'Nam' along with the politicians was a major reason why we lost that war; my opinion. Put me back on duty in the Corps. TAD (Temporary Duty) me to the Air Force. Save our remaining F-4s. I have some experienced advice. Such fantasy I can still hold.

Note: W.E.B. Griffin was a famous writer, dearly loved by the military. Although described as fictional, he based his books on historical fact. President Roosevelt did take a civilian shipping magnate who possessed a maritime shipping, unlimited tonnage captain's credentials based on experience and gave him naval captain's rank to be his eyes and ears in the Pacific theatre. He could go anywhere and see anywhere. He later was appointed with a Marine general's star which insured and enhanced his status and ability to ferret out misleading information back to POTUS. FDR was pretty serious about winning that War. Obama had 8 years to take out ISIS but attacked Syria instead. The new POTUS needs to do the same as FDR in the Mid-east. We wait and see.

Afghanistan – Contribution from a Former military pilot friend.

A very interesting read, a Marine's View of what is really going on. This young man is articulate and has a flare for colorful language, and descriptive prose; Scorpions, Chiggers & Sand Fleas. It's a great letter, a must read for every American citizen.

From a Recon Marine in Afghanistan: From the Sand Pit.

It's freezing here. I'm sitting on hard cold dirt between rocks and shrubs at the base of the Hindu Kush Mountains, along the Dar'yoi Pamir River, watching a hole that leads to a tunnel that leads to a cave. Stake out, my friend, and no pizza delivery for thousands of miles.

I also glance at the area around my ass every ten to fifteen seconds to avoid another scorpion sting. I've actually given up battling the chiggers and sand fleas, but the scorpions give a jolt like a cattle prod. Hurts like a bastard. The antidote tastes like transmission fluid, but God bless the Marine Corps for the five vials of it in my pack. The one truth the Taliban cannot escape is that, believe it or not, they are human beings, which means they have to eat food and drink water. That requires couriers and that's where an old bounty hunter like me comes in handy.

I track the couriers, locate the tunnel entrances and storage facilities, type the info into the hand held, and shoot the coordinates up to the satellite link that tells the air commanders where to drop the hardware. We bash some heads for a while, and then I track and record the new movement. It's all about intelligence. We haven't even brought in the snipers yet. These scurrying rats have no idea what they're in for. We are but days away from cutting off supply lines and allowing the eradication to begin. But you know me;

I'm a romantic. I've said it before and I'll say it again: This country blows, man. It's not even a country. There are no roads, there's no infrastructure, there's no government.

This is an inhospitable, rock-pit shit-hole ruled by eleventh century warring tribes. There are no jobs here like we know jobs. Afghanistan offers only two ways for a man to support his family, join the opium trade or join the army. That's it. Those are your options. Oh, I forgot, you can also live in a refugee camp and eat plum-sweetened, crushed beetle paste and squirt mud like a goose with stomach flu, if that's your idea of a party. But the smell alone of those 'tent cities of the walking dead' is enough to hurl you into the poppy fields to cheerfully scrape bulbs for eighteen hours a day.

I've been living with these Tajiks and Uzbeks, and Turkmen and even a couple of Pashtu's, for over a month-and-a-half now, and this much I can say for sure: These guys, are Huns, actual, living Huns. They LIVE to fight. It's what they do. It's ALL they do. They have no respect for anything; not for themselves, their families, or for each other. They claw at one another as a way of life. They play polo with dead calves and force their five-year-old sons into human cockfights to defend the family honor. Just Huns, roaming packs of savage, heartless beasts who feed on each other's barbarism. Cavemen with AK-47's. Then again, maybe I'm just a cranky young bastard.

I'm freezing my ass off on this stupid hill because my lap warmer is running out of juice, and I can't recharge it until the sun comes up in a few hours. Oh yeah! You like to write letters, right? Do me a favor, Bizarre. Write a letter to CNN and tell Wolf and Anderson and that awful, sneering, pompous Aaron Brown to stop calling the Taliban "smart". They are not smart. I suggest CNN invest in a dictionary because the word they are looking for is "cunning". The Taliban are cunning, like jackals, hyenas, and wolverines. They are sneaky and ruthless, and when confronted, they are cowardly. They are hateful, malevolent parasites who create nothing and destroy everything else. Smart? Bullshit! Yeah, they're real smart, Most can't read, but they've spent their entire lives listening to Imams telling them about only one book (and not a very good one, as books go). They consider hygiene and indoor plumbing to be products of the devil. They're still trying to figuring out how to work a Bic lighter. Talking to a Taliban warrior about improving his quality of life is like trying to teach an ape how to hold a pen. Eventually he just gets frustrated and sticks you in the eye with it.

OK, enough. Snuffle will be up soon, so I have to get back to my hole. Covering my tracks in the snow takes a lot of practice, but I'm good at it. Please, I tell you and my fellow Americans to turn off the TV sets and move on with your lives. The story line you are getting from CNN, ABC, CBS, NBC and other liberal news agencies is utter bullshit and designed not to deliver truth but rather to keep you glued to the screen so you will watch the next commercial. We've got this one under control. The worst thing you guys can do right now is sit around analyzing what we're doing over here. You have no idea what we're doing, and you really don't want to know. We are your military, and we are only doing what you sent us here to do.

From a Jack Recon Marine in Afghanistan.

A Look See into ISIS

He runs his terror group like a CEO -- with spreadsheets on missions, assassinations and captured assets. Reports from Iraq's government suggest ISIS leader Abu Bakr al-Baghdadi may have been hit in airstrikes over the weekend -- though it's not clear whether he was wounded, whose strikes he may have been hit by and in what part of the country he may have been struck. But if al-Baghdadi is dead, what would happen to the radical Sunni militant group?

Don't expect ISIS to just crumble.

"It will morph, and new leaders will emerge," retired U.S. Maj. Gen. James "Spider" Marks said. Odds are al-Baghdadi or the Shura Council, which handles the group's religious and military affairs, has planned this scenario in advance. "ISIS likely has a clear line of succession," said Lauren Squires of the Institute for the Study of War. "This is a bureaucratic organization with a deep bench ... either Baghdadi has signed off on the line of succession himself or the Shura Council has agreed to a line of succession."

Top two deputies

Al-Baghdadi has a Cabinet of advisers as well as two top deputies -- Abu Muslim al-Turkmani, who oversees ISIS' mission in Iraq, and Abu Ali al-Anbari, who is in charge of operations in

Syria, according to the Terrorism Research and Analysis Consortium. Beneath each deputy are 12 governors for both Iraq and Syria. Those governors handle financial, military, legal, media and intelligence councils, among others. What's interesting about the bureaucratic hierarchy of ISIS is that it looks a lot like those of some Western countries whose values it rejects -- except there's no democracy involved and there's a council tasked with considering who to behead.[71]

Shades of the Haiphong Docks- Logistics, one way or the other. Black market tanker trucks or incoming merchant ships fueling the wars. All the same result.- 'Business prioritized over human lives, maimed and wanton destruction. Author.

How to fight ISIS + Ground Troops.

ISIS has yet no Surface to Air missiles- yes, not yet. So therefore A-10s are effective barring the G D-limiting politicians. No 37s or 51s (Anti-aircraft). If they do then put away your A-10s. As stated earlier but worth repeating, they come in too slow and out slower on the vulnerable pull out with no afterburner but effective against limited small arms return fire. In Vietnam, as mentioned, what remained of the Spad squadrons were disbanded. Granted the propeller driven Spad came in a bit slower than the A-10 but not much. (200 + mph range. Their pull out slower- vulnerable 175 mph). Phantom F4 came in at 500 knots with ordinance, usually 500 pounders or Nape and left accelerating even with ordinance remaining. Percentage wise, far, far fewer knocked down or hit from ground fire. Now, far more accurate laser guided missiles and Tow are available. F4 went up and out faster yet with its two afterburners. At 10 grand in a matter of seconds (with full fuel and full bomb load after first pass look see for safety of our own troops). 10 Grand and you are out of reach even of 37s.

---

[71] Holly Yan and Brian Todd, "ISIS after al-Baghdadi: What happens if the terror leader is killed?", CNN, December 22, 2014, http://www.cnn.com/2014/11/11/world/meast/al-baghdadi-replacement/

Boeing's Phantom Eye prototype autonomous unmanned aircraft system climbs into the morning sky after takeoff on its first flight June 1, 2012 at NASA's Dryden Flight Research Center at Edwards, Calif.

Boeing's Phantom Eye.

This all new unmanned drone has incredible capability. It currently can stay aloft for 4 days but soon will soon stay up 10 days.

While designed as a surveillance platform, it carries a 5 ton payload that includes Hellfire missiles. F4 Phantom carried a 3 ton payload and at most stayed up without refuelling, ideal conditions (Bombing close to base) - maybe 3 hrs.

Flying at 65,000 feet - the very edge of space, it was out of range of missiles. Phantom Eye- is also loaded with laser guided ISIS blasting weaponry.

However, the TV screen the operator is dependent upon cannot offer the 360 degree view the CAS pilot has available. The drone cannot make split second, battle field expected decisions nor discern accurately where every one of your own troops are located on an ever changing battlefield let alone a near-by settlement or occupied dwelling out beyond the operator's TV screen purview. Lest not forget the life and death requirements besieging our ground troops which the drone is incapable of contemplating before we rush it upon a contested battlefield.

General Characteristics

Wingspan :	150 ft. (46 m)
Takeoff gross weight :	9,800 lbs. (4,445 kg)
Cruise speed :	150 kts.
Maximum speed :	200 kts.
Altitude :	65,000 ft.
Engines :	(2) 2.3L 150 horsepower
Endurance :	4 days at 65,000 ft.

Wingspan is equal to the width of a good size building lot.

It's relatively light (at 5 ton), slow, flies at twice the altitude of commercial transport.

It's powered by 2 truck engines and stays aloft for 4 days. The new drawing board version is an unbelievable 10 days. Should become an ultimate terror weapon.

ISIS History

al-Baghdadi (aka Abu Du'a) - 2010 – 2015

As leader of al-Qaeda in Iraq.

The Islamic State of Iraq (ISI), also known as al-Qaeda in Iraq (AQI), was the Iraqi division of al-Qaeda. Al-Baghdadi was announced as leader of the ISI on 16 May 2010, following the death of his predecessor Abu Omar al-Baghdadi.[72]

As leader of the ISI, al-Baghdadi was responsible for masterminding large-scale operations such as the 28 August 2011 suicide bombing at the Umm al-Qura Mosque in Baghdad, which killed prominent Sunni lawmaker Khalid al-Fahdawi. Between March and April 2011, the ISI claimed 23 attacks south of Baghdad, all allegedly carried out under al-Baghdadi's command.

Following the death of founder and head of al-Qaida, Osama bin Laden, on 2 May 2011, in Abbottabad, Pakistan, al-Baghdadi released a statement praising bin Laden and

---

[72]"Abu Bakr al-Baghdadi," *Wikipedia,* accessed on April 8, 2017, https://en.wikipedia.org/wiki/Abu_Bakr_al-Baghdadi

threatening violent retaliation for his death. On 5 May 2011, al-Baghdadi claimed responsibility for an attack in Hilla, 100 kilometres (62 mi) south of Baghdad, that killed 24 policemen and wounded 72 others.

On 15 August 2011, a wave of ISI suicide attacks beginning in Mosul resulted in 70 deaths. Shortly thereafter, in retaliation for bin Laden's death, the ISI pledged on its website to carry out 100 attacks across Iraq featuring various methods of attack, including raids, suicide attacks, roadside bombs and small arms attacks, in all cities and rural areas across the country.

On 22 December 2011, a series of coordinated car bombings and IED (improvised explosive device) attacks struck over a dozen neighborhoods across Baghdad, killing at least 63 people and wounding 180. The assault came just days after the US completed its troop withdrawal from the country. On 26 December, the ISI released a statement on jihadist internet forums claiming credit for the operation, stating that the targets of the Baghdad attack were "accurately surveyed and explored" and that the "operations were distributed between targeting security headquarters, military patrols and gatherings of the filthy ones of the al-Dajjal Army", referring to the Mahdi Army of Shia warlord Muqtada al-Sadr.

On 2 December 2012, Iraqi officials claimed that they had captured al-Baghdadi in Baghdad, following a two-month tracking operation. Officials claimed that they had also seized a list containing the names and locations of other al-Qaeda operatives. However, this claim was rejected by the ISI. In an interview with Al Jazeera on 7 December 2012, Iraq's Acting Interior Minister said that the arrested man was not al-Baghdadi, but rather a sectional commander in charge of an area stretching from the northern outskirts of Baghdad to Taji.

Leader of Islamic State in Iraq and the Levant (ISIL)

Expansion into Syria and break with al-Qaeda

Al-Baghdadi remained leader of the ISI until its formal expansion into Syria in 2013 when, in a statement on 8 April 2013, he announced the formation of the Islamic State of Iraq and the Levant (ISIL)—alternatively translated from the Arabic as the Islamic State in Iraq and Syria (ISIS).

When announcing the formation of ISIL, al-Baghdadi stated that the Syrian Civil War jihadist faction, Jabhat al-Nusra—also known as al-Nusra Front—had been an extension of the ISI in Syria and was now to be merged with ISIL. The leader of Jabhat al-Nusra, Abu Mohammad al-

Julani, disputed this merging of the two groups and appealed to al-Qaeda emir Ayman al-Zawahiri, who issued a statement that ISIL should be abolished and that al-Baghdadi should confine his group's activities to Iraq. Al-Baghdadi, however, dismissed al-Zawahiri's ruling and took control of a reported 80% of Jabhat al-Nusra's foreign fighters. In January 2014, ISIL expelled Jabhat al-Nusra from the Syrian city of Ar-Raqqah, and in the same month clashes between the two in Syria's Deir ez-Zor Governorate killed hundreds of fighters and displaced tens of thousands of civilians. In February 2014, al-Qaeda disavowed any relations with ISIL.

According to several Western sources, al-Baghdadi and ISIL have received private financing from citizens in Saudi Arabia and Qatar and enlisted fighters through recruitment drives in Saudi Arabia in particular.

Declaration of a Caliphate

On 29 June 2014, ISIL announced the establishment of a worldwide caliphate. Al-Baghdadi was named its caliph, to be known as "Caliph Ibrahim", and the Islamic State of Iraq and the Levant was renamed the Islamic State (IS). There has been much debate, especially across the Muslim world, about the legitimacy of these moves.

The declaration of a caliphate has been heavily criticized by Middle Eastern governments, other jihadist groups, and Sunni Muslim theologians and historians. Qatar-based TV broadcaster and theologian Yusuf al-Qaradawi stated: "[The] declaration issued by the Islamic State is void under sharia and has dangerous consequences for the Sunnis in Iraq and for the revolt in Syria", adding that the title of caliph can "only be given by the entire Muslim nation", not by a single group.

As a caliph, al-Baghdadi is required to hold to each dictate of the sunnah, whose precedence is set and recorded in the sahih hadiths. According to tradition, if a caliph fails to meet any of these obligations at any period, he is legally required to abdicate his position and the community has to appoint a new caliph, theoretically selected from throughout the caliphdom as being the most religiously and spiritually pious individual among them. Due to the widespread rejection of his caliphhood, al-Baghdadi's status as caliph has been compared to that of other caliphs whose caliphship has been questioned.

In an audio-taped message, al-Baghdadi announced that ISIL would march on "Rome"—generally interpreted to mean the West—in its quest to establish an Islamic State from the Middle East across Europe. He said that he would conquer both Rome and Spain in this endeavor and urged Muslims across the world to immigrate to the new Islamic State.

On 5 July 2014, a video was released apparently showing al-Baghdadi making a speech at the Great Mosque of al-Nuri in Mosul, northern Iraq. A representative of the Iraqi government denied that the video was of al-Baghdadi, calling it a "farce". However, both the BBC and the Associated Press quoted unnamed Iraqi officials as saying that the man in the video was believed to be al-Baghdadi. In the video, al-Baghdadi declared himself the world leader of Muslims and called on Muslims everywhere to support him.

On 8 July 2014, ISIL launched its online magazine *Dabiq*. The title appears to have been selected for its eschatological connections with the Islamic version of the *End times*, or *Malahim*.

According to a report in October 2014, after suffering serious injuries, al-Baghdadi fled ISIL's capital city Ar-Raqqah due to the intense bombing campaign launched by Coalition forces, and sought refuge in the Iraqi city of Mosul, the largest city under ISIL control.

On 5 November 2014, al-Baghdadi sent a message to al-Qaeda Emir Ayman al-Zawahiri requesting him to swear allegiance to him as caliph, in return for a position in the Islamic State of Iraq and the Levant. The source of this information was a senior Taliban intelligence officer. Al-Zawahiri did not reply, and instead reassured the Taliban of his loyalty to Mullah Omar.

On 7 November 2014, there were unconfirmed reports of al-Baghdadi's death after an airstrike in Mosul, while other reports said that he was only wounded.

On 13 November 2014, ISIL released an audio-taped message, claiming it to be in the voice of al-Baghdadi. In the 17-minute recording, released via social media, the speaker said that ISIL fighters would never cease fighting "even if only one soldier remains". The speaker urged supporters of the Islamic State to "erupt volcanoes of jihad" across the world. He called for attacks to be mounted in Saudi Arabia—describing Saudi leaders as "the head of the snake" and said that the US-led military campaign in Syria and Iraq was failing. He also said that ISIL would keep on marching and would "break the borders" of Jordan and Lebanon and "free Palestine." Al-Baghdadi also claimed in 2014 that Islamic jihadists would never hesitate to eliminate Israel just because it has the United States support.

On 20 January 2015, the Syrian Observatory for Human Rights reported that al-Baghdadi had been wounded in an airstrike in Al-Qa'im, an Iraqi border town held by ISIL, and as a result, withdrew to Syria.

On 8 February 2015, after Jordan had conducted 56 airstrikes, which had reportedly killed 7,000 ISIL militants from 5–7 February, Abu Bakr al-Bagdadi was said to have fled from Ar-Raqqah to Mosul, out of fear for his life. However, after a Peshmerga source informed the US-led Coalition that al-Baghdadi was in Mosul, Coalition warplanes continuously bombed the locations where ISIL leaders were known to meet at for 2 hours.

On 14 August 2015, it was reported that he had allegedly taken American hostage Kayla Mueller as his wife and raped her repeatedly. Mueller was later alleged to have been killed in an airstrike by anti-ISIL forces. However, other reports cite that Mueller was murdered by ISIL.

Sectarianism and theocracy

Through his forename, al-Baghdadi is rumored to be styling himself after the first caliph, Abu Bakr, who led the "Rightly Guided" or Rashidun. According to Sunni tradition, Abu Bakr replaced Muhammad as prayer leader when he was suffering from illnesses. Another feature of the original Rashidun was what some historians dub as the first Sunnist Shiist discord during the Battle of Siffin. Some publishers have drawn a correlation between those ancient events and modern Salafizing and caliphizing aims under al-Baghdadi's rule.

Due to the relatively stationary nature of ISIL control, the elevation of religious clergy who engage in theocratization, and the group's scripture-themed legal system, some analysts have declared al-Baghdadi a theocrat and ISIL a theocracy. Other indications of the decline of secularism are the evisceration of secular institutions and its replacement with strict sharia law, and the gradual caliphization and Sunnification of regions under the group's control. In July 2015, al-Baghdadi was described by a reporter as exhibiting a kinder and gentler side after he banned videos showing slaughter and execution.....

Suspected location

al-Baghdadi is the top target in the war against ISIL, but his location is not known. U.S. Intelligence believes he is based in Raqqa and that he keeps a low profile, hiding among the civilian population. ISIL is believed to be headquartered in a series of buildings in Raqqa, but the proximity of civilians makes targeting the headquarters off limits under U.S. rules of engagement. [73]

However, as of December 2015, reports by the Fars News Agency and the Libyan government placed him in Libya.

ISIS Rule

According to Newsweek, there is a widening gap in living standards for those under ISIS rule. Members of the organization have access to food, free medical care, and desirable housing. In contrast, people who aren't ISIS members suffer under a barely functioning economy with rapidly increasing prices.

ISIS can afford to pay people seeking to join its ranks through four main sources of income: oil, the sale of looted antiquities, taxation, and kidnapping ransoms.

The militant group either controls or has an operational presence around a number of oil wells in Iraq and in the majority of oil-producing areas in Syria. This allows the group to earn a steady income from oil production and smuggling that helps it to continue its daily operations.

The New York Times estimates that ISIS can make upward of $40 million a month through oil-related activities. TIME magazine on ISIS ruler, al Baghdadi, 2015 Man of Year articles states 70 million. In a bid to cut the group's income, the US conducted its first airstrikes against ISIS oil trucks on November 16. [2015]. Why did they wait so long?

Amwal al Ghad, ISIS's main source of income is significantly more difficult for the US and other coalition partners to target by air. According to Foreign Policy, ISIS makes the majority of its money through extortion and taxation of people living under the group's rule.

ISIS taxes nearly every possible economic activity, with the revenue ultimately covering the expenses of waging continuous war along multiple fronts. Foreign Policy notes that taxes are put in place for militants who loot archaeological sites. Non-Muslims must pay religious taxes, and all ISIS subjects pay a base welfare and salary tax in support of the fighters. All vehicles passing through ISIS territory — which may carry the only food available to those living under ISIS

[73] Ibid.

control — must pay taxes often totaling hundreds of dollars.

This ad hoc war economy means that ISIS has little money to spend on improving the lives of those who are forced to live under its rule. But as Abu Khaled's account confirms, it still finds the money for conducting military operations and incentivizing militants to join the group.

That money and the other benefits that ISIS fighters receive means that Syrians join ISIS out of desperation — and not necessarily out of religious or ideological conviction.

Pamela Engel contributed to this report.[74]

Family

Little is known about al-Baghdadi's family and sources provide conflicting information. "Reuters, quoting tribal sources in Iraq, reports Baghdadi has three wives, two Iraqis and one Syrian.... The Iraqi Interior Ministry has said, 'There is no wife named Saja al-Dulaimi' " and that al-Baghdadi has two wives, Asma Fawzi Mohammed al-Dulaimi and Israa Rajab Mahal A-Qaisi.[75]

---

[74] Jeremy Bender, "An ISIS defector explained a key reason people continue joining the group," *Business Insider,* last modified November 18, 2015,
http://www.businessinsider.com/isis-defector-explains-why-people-continue-joining-group-2015-11
[75] "Abu Bakr al-Baghdadi," *Wikipedia,* accessed on April 8, 2017,
https://en.wikipedia.org/wiki/Abu_Bakr_al-Baghdadi

CHAPTER 14
MILITARY RELIGIOUS FREEDOM FOUNDATION

"Congress shall make no law respecting an establishment of religion, or prohibiting the free exercise thereof..."
- FIRST AMENDMENT TO THE UNITED STATES CONSTITUTION

Separation of Church/State First Amendment Clause- U. S. Constitution

The Military Religious Freedom Foundation (MRFF) is the sole non-profit civil rights organization dedicated to ensuring that all members of the United States Armed Forces fully receive the Constitutional guarantee of both freedom of religion and freedom from religion, to which they and all Americans are entitled. Fighting for our servicemembers' rights, so they can fight for ours.

> Over 50,000 active duty, veteran, and civilian personnel of the United States Armed Forces have come to this foundation for redress and assistance in resolving or alerting the public to their civil rights grievances, with hundreds more contacting MRFF each day. 96% of them are Christians themselves. MRFF is technically in our 12th year now. 96% of MRFF's clients are practicing Protestants or Roman Catholics themselves who are oppressed for not being "Christian enough". Currently, 954 members of the LGBTQ community in the military are MRFF's clients. MRFF also represents about 18% of all Muslim-Americans in the US military.

> Michael L. "Mikey" Weinstein – Founder and President
> Our Mission
> Religious Freedom and the Military: A Short History
> The concept and practice of religious freedom in the United States Armed Forces date back to the earliest days of this nation. The United States Constitution outlines the basic

concept of religious freedom as understood by Americans in the Bill of Rights. More specifically, the First Amendment to the Constitution specifies that "Congress shall make no law respecting an establishment of religion. [76]

In this time of world destructive weaponry, such danger could eventually lead to a nuclear unleashing far more disastrous than Hiroshima and Nagasaki most likely by none other than religious fanatics as by now ample evidence within this work has been provided. Already, if certain dictatorial controlled countries or religious based rebellions such as ISIS had such weaponry, the larger American cities would be their major targets, no question. Hate filled Kim Il Sung (Little Kim, Kim Il) of North Korea and Sunni sect Al Baghdadi wouldn't hesitate. In our own country, the American military, especially the U. S. Air Force is undergoing a severe shift toward promoting Religious Evangelicalism especially in their officer corps beginning with the officer generating Air Force Academy. Hundreds of complaints emanating from within the Air Force ranks in particular and lately the U. S. Army, have been sent to the protective Military Religious Freedom Foundation (MRFF) seeking intervention based on the Church/State separation constitutional backed First Amendment clause.

Mainly the enlisted ranks are being forced to adhere to one religion only- Christianity if they want to remain promotable. In my military days it was unheard of for a superior commanding officer to question a Marine's religious beliefs or whether he had any or not. We had wars to fight and that alone was our major focus. An aircraft technician has the pilot's life in his hands and it would be unthinkable to promote only the church attending ones over others. Such unconstitutional religious fervor within a military organization has caused thousands of trained and valuable technicians, to leave in angry disgust, the services for willing jobs in the civilian sector. A far more dangerous scenario can and possibly will happen when the sordid combination of likeminded military fanatics ("God is speaking to me!") are gathered together to 'go forth and 'save' the world from an imagined religious degeneration. How many Air Force personnel of such fervor would it take to start WWIII? But a bare handful. The Twin Towers destruction was carefully planned and orchestrated by but a few fanatics, bankrolled by the Saudis. It happened. An atomic

[76] https://www.militaryreligiousfreedom.org/about/

weapon carrier with a limited, brain washed crew could be gathered together, far fewer would be required for a missile launch. Preposterous?
Simply review - 9/11. I repeat. Religious fervor along with forced proselytization such as the Air Force presently employs, has no sane place
within any countries military especially those that harbor atomic weaponry.

Below is a typical letter to MRFF calling on their aid to contact
higher commanding officers to redress fanatic military personnel who go
to the extreme with religious proselytization.

> From: Active Duty U.S. Army Enlisted Soldier's E-Mail
> Address Withheld
> Subject: Army priority to come to Jesus.[77]

In Korea as a Marine corporal, I never was subjected to such
unconstitutional proselytizing as illustrated below. 'Nam' either. W.E. B.
Griffin, a favorite and quite famous military author, mostly on Marines
beginning with the olde China Marines starting out in Shanghai, latter
30's, pre-WWIl. This highly accurate work even though portrayed in
fiction form begins. Many Series he wrote and eagerly read by Marines
and Army combatants. A Marine buck Sergeant (Ken McCoy) begins his
long hitch in the Corps spying on the Japanese garrison, winding up as a
Major always gathering intelligence on various enemies and oft behind
the lines. Not one bit of pushing Religion is within the many Series WEB
weaves.

> Date: February 24, 2017 at 9:34:42 AM MST
> To: Information Weinstein
> <mikey@militaryreligiousfreedom.org>
> To Mr. Weinstein,
> Me and my 4 fellow soldiers here at Fort (name withheld)
> wanted to thank you for talking to our (superior unit's name
> withheld) commander about our (subordinate unit's name
> withheld) commander's statements about Jesus.
> (Subordinate commander's name withheld) talked to me
> and my battle buddies and our whole (unit name withheld)
> about the Christian faith which he made at a mandatory
> attendance formation on Feb. (date withheld), 2017.
> He said that as far as he "(subordinate commander's name

withheld) was concerned it was an Army priority to come to the Lord Jesus Christ." He even went on for another 5 minutes about this same thing. What are we supposed to do? How messed up is that to say to your soldiers? We have plenty of non- Christian soldiers in our (unit's name withheld) include some of my battle buddies. We all were pissed. He don't have the right to hit us with that Jesus shit.

Nobody said nothing because he's our commander. If you call him out your just done and he knows that. But even though I am Christian even I know that what he said to us is wrong. So we call you Mr. Weinstein and you handle it for us all. You talked to higher command and our (enlisted position rank withheld) Sergeant (name withheld) told some of us that our commander had been 'counseled" by the (superior unit's name withheld) commander to stop doing for what he said. Don't know exactly what that means for our commander but we think it is good for us soldiers. And not for our commander.

If he tries to do this Christian talk again to us we will call you again too. But we don't think he will because we already had another mandatory (subordinate unit's name withheld) formation yesterday and he didn't do it then. And didn't even do a prayer to Jesus to start the meeting as he always did before. He said nothing about Jesus.

Thank you all at the MR Freedom Foundation for fixing this shit for us.

Please do not use my name or any other stuff that could get us in trouble for seeking help outside of the Army to stop what (name, rank and unit's name withheld) was saying to us about Jesus. Thank you all again so much. From me and my homies here at Fort (name withheld).

(Active Duty U.S. Army enlisted soldier's name, rank, MOS, unit and assigned installation all withheld).[78]

A Colorado Christian college held a debate with the head of MRFF, Mikey Weinstein, former Air Force lawyer and an associate. The following is part of the discussion. I am not an Atheist however and had a similar experience at the University of Oklahoma although they attempted to hold me back and restrict my spiritual views even though I was invited by the Indian students there for their Indian Week celebration. The positive

<hr>

[78] Ibid.

commentary following this posting on my Facebook page was appreciated.

It is evident that you are strongly opposed to any form of Christian evangelization.

This is absolutely untrue. Both Mikey and I have lifelong friends and family who are Christians--even many evangelical Christians--whom we love and respect, even if we disagree with them on some fundamental subjects. I have no problem with Christian evangelizing, either, so long as it is conducted in the proper venue and under the proper conditions. In the civilian world that's almost anywhere that isn't part of a government operation (like a public school). Even there, it's all about the relationship. A high school sophomore can "recruit" a classmate to go to church with him or her through a conversation in the hallways, but a teacher at a government-funded public or charter school can't recruit their students for their Christian church any more than they should for a Madrassah. Likewise, they should never denigrate a student for the student's beliefs if the teacher happens to be an atheist or of a different religious bent. I have been "evangelized" by many. When they are my peers and it's a social situation, I have no problem with that.

Within the military, though, the issues get MUCH more complex. A military officer, such as yourself, can put on civilian clothes and evangelize on a street corner or go door-to-door handing out pamphlets or even deliver a sermon at Sunday service, so long as they're doing so on their own time and in no way referring to or using their military position and rank in a coercive manner. On the job, they may THINK that their subordinates would be better off if they accepted Christ as their lord and savior, but (n the interest of morale, unit cohesion and good order and discipline) the guidance is quite clear that they cannot evangelize in the workplace nor should they create an environment in which their subordinates feel like their religious beliefs MIGHT be a basis for performance evaluations (good or bad), promotion recommendations, or follow-on jobs. My brother-in-law is a naval officer and commander. He told me long ago that the rule in the officers' mess is that they NEVER discuss religion, politics, or sex. I think that's a good rule. At the Academy, at the end of the semester, a cadet should have no more idea what their instructor's religion is than whom they voted for or with him they spend their Saturday nights.

Out of curiosity, are you an atheist or is it just that you are against the divinity-idea of Jesus?

I, personally, am an atheist. I won't speak for Mikey. I was raised Lutheran, but was a doubter from a very early age and never really "bought it." My wife is the same--raised in the church, but never accepted the mythology. My children were happily allowed to go to church with friends, never dissuaded from investigating religion, but are both atheists. I've read the bible cover-to-cover. It contains great examples of moral behavior and standards that any human should strive to emulate-- but it also has an enormous number of silly, demonstrably false, illogical, and misogynistic passages that are absolutely irrelevant (if not anathema) to modern life. I do not believe it is divinely inspired, but rather a compilation of tribal legend, poetry, historical fiction, allegory, moral guidance, incoherent prophecy, and tools used by generations to subjugate a wide variety of victims and justify power for a few. To me, the idea that Jesus was the Son of God (if he even existed and wasn't just a moral construct/allegory made up almost a Century later) is laughable. Where's the sacrifice in dying if you know you're the son of God and will rise again to live forever? That's just a bad weekend IMHO.

In other words, do you hold to the belief that life arose by chance, or was there a Designer/designer, however labeled?

I can come up with no better explanation on how life arose on Earth than by chance and physics. I can't PROVE that it wasn't designed by someone or something any more than you can prove that it was. In all of my reading, though, I have not heard any convincing evidence to suggest that, billions of years ago, someone planted the amino acids that became simple life that became cells that became animals that became us and that this development was guided along the way by some unseen force or loving hand. Biblical creation is, to me, an explanation created to make sense to simple illiterate shepherds by a few slightly more intelligent priests or village mystics who needed some sort of power over the locals (magic) to control them. That there are similarly bizarre and ludicrous creation accounts in almost all other religions (though unrelated) tells me that that's how the ignorant powerful explain things to the ignorant powerless. I see no Hand of God in the Platypus, the Man, or the Paramecium. If that makes us a hunk of meat that will disappear upon death, then that also tells me that I'd better squeeze every bit out of the life I have and not waste any of it a church on Sunday, a Mosque on Saturday, or trying to determine if there's life after death--I don't think there is.

As a biologist, let me share one of the strongest pieces of evidence that persuades me there had to be a designer:

Life, of any kind, is composed of cells (as you recall from your Life Science classes).

Humans are composed of 50 to 100 trillion cells (So reports Google).

These cells all originated from one completed cell (an egg cell from your mother and a sperm cell from your father).

Now here's the remarkable fact: That single completed-cell has within it the design for all the other trillions of cells (organized into the myriad different bodily systems)!

For all of that to occur against what we know about entropy is, to me, pretty miraculous!

So, regardless of what you might call "Him" (God, Son, Holy Spirit, or Whatever), wouldn't you say that's more than reasonable?

That's a nice story, but it's unrelated completely to Christianity and evangelism. Even if I granted you the point that something created life on Earth, and I can't absolutely PROVE that evolution and natural selection shaped the development of the species over the last few billion years, that's still no justification for believing the specifically CHRISTIAN story told in the Bible any more than I should believe the scribblings of those that followed the Prophet Mohammed, The Buddha, Confucius, Janism, Zoroastrianism, Ba'hai, or any of the other thousands of religions that were created by tribes and peoples over the millennia to explain things they had no ability to understand. The preponderance of the scientific evidence available to us TODAY supports evolution and directly contradicts whole biblical tracts. If more evidence is found to contradict evolution and come up with a better theory that more closely conforms to the evidence--even if it's biblical--then I'll reconsider. Your argument, though, is certainly no reason to try to pressure the people that work for me to believe as I do just so that I can bask in the warmth of I'm knowing that I've saved their immortal souls based upon the legends taught me as a child.

Now, let me ask you a question: If the only way to eternal life is through acceptance of Jesus, then why does your Creator allow people to live out their whole lives without any chance of ever hearing about Jesus--in the jungles of the Amazon, highest Tibet, and most of the world outside of Europe until well past the 1500s? Only to die and not have the chance at Salvation because someone didn't come to their door and hand them a pamphlet or a Bible and offer to save them? Also, it sure seems to me that the religion to which most of the world adheres is the one that was available when they were raised. Children of Muslims become Muslims, same with Buddhists and Christians. There really isn't much conversion going on out there relative to the raw numbers of adherents that just stay with what they've always found comfortable--and the only evangelizing done, in reality, is to spread their religion so that there are really just more people in the world around which the evangelizer will feel more comfortable (less threatened).

Anyway, I've enjoyed this little exercise. Thanks again for attending last night. I'm sure I'll see you again before too long.

A Senior Active-Duty Air Force Officer
(And I don't give you my name because I've already been 'targeted' by Christians in the military for my atheist perspective--it's cost me jobs and promotions, hurt my family, and made me hesitant to EVER reveal my identity. Without Mikey, I'd really have no hope--nor would thousands of others in our military)

As mentioned, regarding Facebook commentary, here is an example.
Michael F. So true. I lost a good position with a school district because I was opened up about what I believe in. I had worked for that district ever since I graduated from college, except for 2 years when I moved because of marriage, for 13 years. It was one of those things done in hushed whispers or behind closed doors. Now I don't tell anyone where I work what I believe in. Not because I am ashamed, but because I fear I would suffer the same fate again. I have two "Christian" friends, my mom and a lady I use to work with, who know what I believe in, but no one else. [Endless travail, victimization takes place against innocent folk because of the narrow minded zeal from those who lie to themselves and foolishly claim to 'Know exactly Who, Whom and What' Great Mystery actually is!] Author.

CHAPTER 15
PLANETARY PERIL

E-Mail from World Population Balance Organization of which I am a Board Member.

We're now at about 7.4 billion. 7 billion was 2011. 6 billion— 1999. 5 billion — 1987

As you've probably noticed in our material, we're no longer focusing/framing the issue as "population growth."

Since human numbers are way above true sustainability, we're focusing/framing it for what it really, more truthfully, is: OVERpopulation.

Thinking of it another way, in 1960s (when there were 3+ billion) the main "population" problem *was* "population growth." But . . . since we did not then stop the (population) growth (at, say, 3.5 to 4 billion) . . . *now* the primary problem is, really, OVERpopulation.

And, the only *humane* way to get human numbers back down to 1-3 billion is to dramatically reduce birth rates — everyone's birth rates — well below an average of two per family. And, the closer we can get it to, say 1.5 (or even one, but that's highly unlikely, I realize), the better!

David Paxson, President
World Population Balance
   612-869-1640
   paxson@worldpopulationbalance.org
   P.O. Box 23472
   Minneapolis, MN 55423
   http://www.WorldPopulationBalance.org/
   One child families can save humanity.

Over Population Facts

Religious controlled countries throughout the world are too fearful to address this most destructive issue facing humanity. Overpopulation's exponential increase now let loose worldwide, only worsens with each passing year but governments are too fearful to take successful action, especially democracies and worse those countries, democratic or not, who are controlled by Organized Religion. Their leaders depend upon popular vote to remain in office.

The article talks about certain interesting facts related to overpopulation. Also stated are interesting facts regarding the countries of China and India and how they handle the over-population problem. One country suffers no control or ma-nipulation by Organized Religion.

Fact 1. India, while only having 170 million hectares of land for farming, has a population of more than 1 billion. This is why millions of people in the country suffer from hunger and food problems.

Fact 2. India, while it is suffering from overpopulation, still produces the most number of people on the planet every day. The consensus (Litke) says that 12 million are born every year in India; while (ENN) says that it is not 12 million every year but 18 million every year.

Fact 3. Prime Minister Indira Gandhi of India once used coercive [but practical] methods to solve overpopulation prob-lems. People were forced to have vasectomies and were steri-lized without personal consent. The religious populace foolish-ly rose up and under threat of losing her position, the Ghandi political party backed off from attempting practical methods to attempt reasonable population control solutions.

Fact 4. A solution to lowering the overpopulation crisis is usually managed by its death rate. While there are many people born every year, there are also plenty who die every year.

Fact 5. Overpopulation is not a problem if people can provide enough food and goods for everybody.[79]

This statement neglects the raw fact that each citizen regardless of country contributes to planetary heating. It is quite obvious that the wealthier citizen, the ultra-consumer, puts up more pollution than the less affluent ones.

Fact 6. The temperature increase in our planet is due to overpopulation. Global temperatures have risen six degrees centigrade [because of the fact there are too many people re-gardless of what a nation's per capita rating is.]

Fact 7. The more overpopulated our world is, the hotter it will become. [Simply stated: More people- More Planetary Heating.]

Fact 8. In China there is a population control method against overpopulation called the 'One child per family policy.' If you do not comply with these regulations, then you will not

[79] http://infomory.com/facts/facts-about-overpopulation/

get any special benefits from the government.[80]

China is not a democracy yet they are one of the few that is taking positive action. Eventually, world governments will have to follow China's lead- IF they wish to survive. Nature can care less whether a nation or the entire planet is democratic. She also totally ignores what religious soothsayers pretend that Planetary Heating will eventually go away. Nature reacts to how much pollution is thrust into her atmosphere.

> **Fact 9.** If you have more than one child in China, your taxes will go up by 50 percent of your total income, or you will be terminated from your job. [The rest of the world needs such discipline. Definitely India and Bangladesh.]
>
> **Fact 10.** Mothers with unplanned pregnancies in China need to have abortions to control the issues of overpopulation. [81]

Amniocentesis (fetal image diagnosis) is also needed to be available, in case where alcoholic and narcotic drug syndrome pregnancies occur, unless parents or grandparents desire to care take several decades for severely retarded or deformed offspring. A hard fact that often changes the most severe opponents of abortion.

> **Fact 11.** Overpopulation in certain regions can lead to a ruinous degradation of the land and its resources.[82]

Correct, accurate estimate of world population could well be errant. Possibly 8 billion by now if exponential speeding math is considered. Maybe, it is edging upward toward 9 billion?

* * * *

Researchers at the University of Wisconsin-Madison.

Thanks to satellite data, scientists have finally figured out why Greenland's ice sheet is melting.

Greenland's vast ice sheet continues to melt, and thanks to two recently-launched satellites we're beginning to understand why it's happening so quickly. Researchers at the University of Wisconsin-Madison be-

---

80 Ibid.
81 Ibid.
82 Ibid

lieve increased cloud cover over the ice sheet itself may be to blame for up to a third of the ice melt that is occurring, a new study indicates.

Clouds are like nature's blanket, and their effect on temperature is one of the first things you learn in introductory meteorology courses. For an example, think of temperatures at night when skies are clear versus when it's cloudy. On that clear night, the temperature falls quicker than on a night where skies are overcast. Clouds, by nature, trap heat in the atmosphere below them, causing temperatures to stay higher.

Professor Tristan L'Ecuyer says that his study found surface temperatures were up to three degrees higher as a result of increased cloud cover over the Greenland Ice Sheet. It does seem like the melt itself may be causing a feedback loop of its own: moisture in the air is a key component for cloud formation, which in turn traps heat in, which causes more melting, which puts more moisture in the air and allows more clouds to form.

Related: Oregon State University wants to use your computer to solve climate issues.

How did L'Ecuyer and his team come to their conclusions? It's thanks to two new high tech NASA satellites launched over the past decade, CloudSat and CALIPSO. The researchers took X-ray images of clouds between 2007 and 2010 over the ice sheet to study cloud composition and structure. From there, a team at the University of Leuven in Belgium led by graduate student Kristof Van Tricht combined the satellite data with ground observations and climate and snow model simulations to understand the effects of these clouds on ice melt.

"Once you know what the clouds look like, you know how much sunlight they're going to reflect and how much heat from Earth's surface they're going to keep in," L'Ecuyer explains.

What they found is that the normal daytime ice melt was not refreezing at night, and was running off instead. That process also fed on itself, accelerating the ice melt overall. This may start to explain Greenland's rapid ice loss in a more tangible form.

L'Ecuyer and Van Tricht's work is important. One issue with present-day climate models is their inability to properly resolve cloud cover. Most models have far underestimated the amount of ice-sheet loss, in something meteorologists and climatologists studying climate change attribute to "cloud-climate feedback."

Birth control

My view on the world population explosion favors birth control as a practical approach toward solving the population crisis. China has had to take effective birth control measures to stem their population problem. The following article, captioned, "Doomsday Coming?" appeared in the *Minneapolis Star Tribune.*

> In 1960, Dr. Heinz von Foerster predicted that the human race would breed itself into infinity by November 13, 2026. We're halfway there and guess what? We're not on schedule, we're ahead of it!
>
> The prediction was the conclusion of a scientific study on population growth and now, new evidence, according to a physicist for the Harvard-Smithsonian Center for Astrophysics, Owen Gingerich, states that we are 18 months ahead of schedule.
>
> "Setting a specific date for "doomsday" is not part of my thinking, but we can certainly wreck the world systems and make them by present standards quite unlivable," says Nobel laureate Henry Kendall, MIT physicist and founder and chairman of the Union of Concerned Scientists (UCS). "We can do irreversible damage to the biosphere as well as to parts of the geophysical systems—the atmosphere, the oceans and the fresh water supply—which would stimulate enormous widespread and permanent misery everywhere in the world," says Kendall.
>
> The proof of such contentions, in fact, is already starting to appear. "We have begun to see scientific evidence that our injury to the atmosphere, the ozone layer, is beginning to affect biological systems," says Kendall.
>
> Overpopulation and the issues of population pressure on food production will replace war as the greatest menace to survival on the planet.
>
> The bulk of misery will be visited first upon the Third World, where it will occur "brutally," Kendall says, and then it will spread to the United States. "If we wait until we see the damage here, it will be too late. If we don't act now, Nature will curb the human population with mass starvation."
>
> According to a study sponsored by the World Bank and United Nations, one in five people in the world today does not get enough to eat and one in ten suffers from serious malnutrition. Unfortunately it is not the Hungry, the 'With-outs' who control Society's Law Making. Instead the 'Well- feds' decide.

One of the earliest scientists in modern history to hypothesize about the threat of overpopulation was British political economist Thomas Robert Malthus (1766-1834), who theorized that global population tends to increase geometrically while food supply expands linearly. At some point, Malthus projected, population will outbreed the food supply. In scientific circles, that point is known as the "Malthusian limit."

In November 1992, the UCS published a "World Scientists Warning to Humanity," which Kendall called "the most authoritative document" that the world scientific community has published on the issues of global population, pressure on environmental systems and environmental damage.

Signed by more than 100 Nobel laureates and other senior scientists from around the world, the warning states, "No more than one or a few decades remain before the chance to avert the threats we now confront will be lost and the prospects for humanity immeasurably diminished."

The following information is relative to this issue of Birth Control and population control.

1.2 billion people live in absolute poverty, more than the population of the entire planet only 150 years ago.

In recent years no other species of God's blessed creatures has increased like we have, while thousands of others have dramatically decreased or become extinct.

World population will grow by 3 billion people in the next 30 years, a number equal to the entire population in 1960.

Reducing birth rates to balance with deaths—population stabilization—will help preserve the planet's resources and environmental quality.

Reducing birth rates will reduce the number of people needing food, which means there will be more food for the thousands of children who now die each day because of poor nutrition—another good way of feeding the hungry.

If high U.S. growth rates continue for the next few decades, by the time your younger sister or brother becomes a grandparent there will be an additional 128 million people here, a gain of 50%—adding to pollution and resource depletion problems.

The United States population is growing by about 3 million people each year, with about 2 million from births and the other million from immigrants.

Because the average American consumes about 30 times more resources than the average person from a developing country, these additional 3 million people will have more impact upon the Earth than all of the millions added in China, India and Africa combined.

In terms of global resource depletion and pollution impact, the United States has the world's greatest population growth problem.[15]

What did Natural Way people do about Birth Control? The old time Sioux did not have the large families that the missionaries would come along later and urge them to have. The Sioux were nomads upon the Great Plains and it was a handicap to be burdened down with large groups of small children. The men married at a much later age in comparison to the dominant society. They wanted to prove themselves first, in hunting skills, adventure and upon the warrior road. Young men, the Dog Soldiers, lived together in separate, bachelor lodges to be the first line of defense. They looked down on anyone their age who would forsake the opportunity to seek honor and provide for the camp. Also, there was little preoccupation with premarital sex. In other words, no "Play Boy magazines" or related works would be found in their lodges or upon their war parties. Their stories and discussions focused on a much higher plane.

Women nursed their children for a much later time period and therefore kept themselves from ovulating. This method imparted a closer relationship between mother and child. Grandparents, aunts and uncles helped raise the children. The lifestyle took its toll as well, in regard to the newborn. The strongest survived. The proof is: Native Americans were on this continent for thousands of years and did not bring about overpopulation. The European has been here but a few centuries.

Removing Oneself

The Northern Indian was not remiss to 'Take themselves out' or 'Remove themselves' so as not to be a burden, especially among the Elder who were making it difficult for the tribe to travel. My parents had many reservation Indians visit summers and stayed for several days as we had two spare houses available. They would shop at the stores in Rapid City. Many a story was told of Indians before them when the tribe was nomads on the plains. When an older person got sick or injured and could not travel, the tribal members would offer food to be put way and shelter erected usually near water, usually a small tent and the sick person would be left behind in the hope that they would recuperate and rejoin the tribe at a designated meeting place estimate. My mother told of a woman, the 'Wolf Woman' who had to be left behind. She had hurt her leg which would not allow her to keep up with the tribe. She was placed in a shelter and did recover to catch up with the tribe but to exist a pack of wolves helped feed her when they brought back game. After she had rejoined her people, she claimed she could estimate approaching severe weather by the way the prairie wolves howled at night. My Mother stated she saw this woman who was quite older when my Mom was a small girl. In buffalo hunting days the tribe had to be on the move to follow the herds to harvest enough meat for the long winter and could not stay back for the injured or the ill. In the winter if an elder felt they were a burden to their adult children who were now raising their own, the elders would often 'Remove themselves' by 'Taking a Walk' in a blizzard late at night and preferably during a snowstorm. Thus, they would simply disappear and often not be found. Their belief in an understanding Creator feared no punishment in an afterlife.

Ice Shelfs and Icebergs

Observed evidence worldwide cannot be truthfully denied. If a writer declares that Creator is believed to be 'All Truth' which he declares through his direct observation of Creator's Nature, then it would be hypercritical would it not for him to omit such obvious evidentiary evidence? Just to be politically obsequious or avoid offending a narrower-minded readership (while the planet plunges into obvious glacier melting Climate Change—I may add)? Observed evidence worldwide cannot be truthfully denied. No less than a United Nations declaration, a National Federal Assessment and even the Retired Generals and Admirals association including two Department of Defense heads have declared Planetary Heating as an extreme issue regarding world civilization.

Regardless, even the most overzealous religious fanatic has to look down from a ship's rail cruising the now open Arctic sea lanes at a floating, starved to death polar bear with a vanishing Greenland glacier for a background and must have to wonder: 'This planet. Is it, really, truly heating?'

Huge ice shelves, not just some mere icebergs, float constantly by Nova Scotia. 'We no longer see the ice bergs. They are pushed further out to sea on their southward journey. Instead we see, mass floating ice shelves.' It is hard to convince those 'Direct Observation' folks that Planetary Heating is just some Al Gore invention.

CHAPTER 16
THE LOST SIX

I was going to omit this Lost Six chapter. What? It could easily discredit my writing as if I have not reached literary havoc already innocently attempting to relate how at least one Indian academic brazenly thinks based often on Direct Observation which I just cannot denounce or deny. I had an abundance of experiences, I guess, in that Native Indigenous Spiritual Past. Non-Indian writers familiar somewhat with our culture were only at the periphery and no doubt held back by their own deeply ingrained too often paralyzing concepts. Although this ceremony has appeared in most of my previous works I realized I was writing earlier for a more captive, sincere and sympathetic related audience who no doubt were more open-minded. Not surprisingly, the majority of my readership is not Native American folk but rank and file non-Indian due mainly to overwhelming population numbers. Simply go up on Facebook. Many, many appreciated and encouraging accolades come from them. Indeed many, are searching for new spiritual avenues, thought and practices much like so many American younger generations are embracing yoga.

I came to realize that I would not be truthful to myself if I omitted the Lost Six happening at the University of South Dakota way back when I was in law school. I state many times that I believe Creator is All Truth and All Knowledge. I simply must remain truthful as to what I have observed. It happened!

In several of my books I mention a very similar ceremony (the Yuwipi spirit ceremony) experienced by explorer Jonathan Carver way back in the 1700s. Wisconsin was referred to as Ouisconsin Territory back then. Carver's Lake and cave within St. Paul, MN is named after him. I often stay at my son's home which borders those shores. Thankfully Carver wrote respectfully about that ceremony conducted by a tribal medicine man particularly for his benefit. Carver was apprehensive about the whereabouts of his winter's supplies which were overdue. The medicine man accurately predicted their critical arrival through Spirit communication via a highly similar ceremony. A numerous following of people seem not to be ridiculed for believing Sasquatch lives. A Television show even thrives on what to me is pure fantasy and fiction. I personally think such is far more preposterous than a simple Native beseechment.

Yuwipi Spirit Calling

Black Elk called into the Spirits when he conducted successful healing communication into that Spirit World beyond. Spirits, messengers of
Great Ultimate would hear the calling songs to the beat of a special drum
separately toned than that of the Sweat Lodge or Sun Dance. Creator
utilizes song within the animal world, would it not similarly employ the
same method for two -legged to call into its spirits? (Most of us believe
they are simply former humans who have advanced into that world of
knowledge and are who are now capable of returning to help us. With the
allowance/blessing of Creator of course.) Christians have angels that re-
semble humans with wings attached; Indians have Spirits. Highly ethical
and moral Humans while here, obviously move on if Creator is All
Knowledge. I speak of them as having actually observed them via form
or voices. I have! Check with me in the Spirit World when you arrive
there. Time also appears to be frozen, therefore we can have a look see.

I will include the following – an actual Spirit Calling ceremony. This
beseechment calling to Creator's forces of knowledge actually happened
before a smaller audience whom can verify its happening. I have often
wondered, 'For what inducing reason would the Sioux, up and leave what
appeared to be a lush paradise (Carolinas) and finally arrive at a hostile,
harsh Great Plains?' My answer would be the very same Spirit Ceremony
that you are about to witness.

Prediction from undoubtedly former moral and ethical humans of
the indigenous past is my supposition as to whom are these Spirit Guides
cultivated by our spiritual leaders termed holy men or holy women. Medicine men or women are other terms. Black Elk's Blue Man of Corruption,
Greed, Control and Planetary Disaster is the most widely known spiritual
prediction. Another powerful prediction is of a long black snake that
would be cast upon native tribal folk. It would endanger many lives and
not just Indians alone. No doubt the Spirit World or Creator is issuing a
warning of the dangerous pipeline that is being attempted to come across
reservation lands.

I primarily offer the following as an attempt to help those to understand more fully, not only Black Elk but the mind of the two spiritual
leaders, Fools Crow and Chief Eagle Feather, my mentors so similar to
Black Elk. Fools Crow was a protégé of Black Elk and in turn, Eagle
Feather of Fools Crow. There were no 'Tricks are hidden gun powder';
no conjuring whatever anthropologist Raymond DeMallie's intentions

appear in the latter versions of the book *Black Elk Speaks*. The original version of this well-known book is absent from any of DeMallies allowed meddling by the now book controlling grandchildren of author John Neihardt (deceased). With that type of attitude, a dubious DeMallie would have to leave the ceremony at its very beginning for the incoming Spirits would call him out and the conductor would read his thoughts as Bill Eagle Feather did so to one scoffing, attending University professor, Joe Cash. These discipline prone spirits allow no distraction and will not 'Come in.' so to speak until the distractor leaves or made to promise he will behave himself. The following ceremony speaks for itself.

In America, this ceremony is probably considered an impossible ceremony by many, the majority actually, especially such is the influence of the overzealous and narrow minded despite the extreme fabrication, myth, fiction and fantasy so obvious in their Bible. I am not a student of the Koran but I suspect equivalent fantasy exists also starting with the 72 promised virgins for the jihadists. All that I can offer for verification is that many such ceremonies are held and have been held down through time at least by members of my tribe and other plains tribes of related ceremony and of course, as previous, such ceremony conducted by another tribe in the 18th century, the 1700s; as narrated by Captain Carver, early American explorer.[83]

Dr. Wm. K. Powers, a noted anthropologist has written several books on the subject Powers - *Oglala Religion* and *Yuwipi* (Lincoln, NE: University of Nebraska Press, 1977 & 1982).

This happening was another of my mystery projecting experiences and was certainly observed with a host of other interested people. The participants in this particular situation, the following, were all University of South Dakota related and some sporting some rather high degrees academically along with accomplished Track Records from an academic point of view. Unfortunately, Dr. Bryde whom I have depended considerably upon for much of my Sioux historical material has recently passed away. He was present at this happening. The years have gone by but Lula Red Cloud, who was but 20 years at the time, she is the great, great granddaughter of Chief Red Cloud and was also present. Lula can verify what took place back in 1970. Without further distraction let us continue.

---

[83] See Spirit Ceremony- Chapter 5, Ed McGaa, *Black Elk Speaks IV* (Rapid City, SD, Dakota West Books, 2004).

University of South Dakota

At the request of the University Administration, Chief Eagle Feather came to the University of South Dakota to conduct a revealing Yuwipi (Spirit Calling) ceremony.

At this ceremony, in the late 60's, many so-called 'credible' people from the white man's view attended, as previously mentioned. These were university professors with graduate degrees. (Therefore, I guess, a detractor would almost have to assume that they were maybe more 'credible' than most ordinary folks.) This ceremony was for the benefit of non-Indian people and was held to find five students and their pilot/professor who crashed a light, single engine airplane somewhere in the cold, remote, snow-covered region called the Nebraska Sand Hills whose terrain is akin to parts of Mongolia and Northern China. This area also receives a heavy winter snow fall. They were returning from Denver, Colorado to Sioux Falls, South Dakota, and encountered a blizzard. The pilot developed vertigo and it was presumed the plane had crashed on the windswept Nebraska Sand Hills and was covered by snow. An all-out search began -- even the Nebraska National Guard was used -- but after a while it was too expensive and futile to continue. The search was called off. At that point the University of South Dakota Indian Studies program, where I worked part time since my major occupation was a law student; Indian Studies had connections with Sioux holy men and none other than the President of the school called upon them for help. At the ceremony, I sat next to his beautiful blonde wife, Connie Bowen.

Bill Eagle Feather asked for a map. He specified that he wanted; "the airplane kind of map (WAC chart) and not the ordinary road map." A line was drawn from Denver to Sioux Falls, the light passenger plane's intended destination and Eagle Feather proceeded to study it before the scheduled evening's ceremony in the basement of the school's museum. The aircraft, a Cherokee Six, held a maximum capacity of 5 passengers plus the pilot.

The ceremony began with Eagle Feather's ceremonial peace pipe being offered to the Ultimate Powers under one Benevolent and All Providing Creator. Each of the Four Directions was included, then to Father Sky in a circular, angular motion and down to Mother Earth- the Sixth Power.[43] Last, the Pipe was held straight up to Creator- Wakan Tanka. "Ho! Wakan Tanka. We are going to ask you to find those who have passed on in the airplane." Bill stated. After this opening acknowledgment, Lula Red Cloud, a university student held the pipe just outside a rectangle made of small tobacco offerings enclosed in black cloths tied to a continuous string after the opening.[44] At each corner a singular Red, Yellow, Black or White cloth, three to four inches in size, mounted on a choke cherry stick about twice the length of the gallon coffee can container, stood upright. Dirt from a prairie dog or moles mound filled the container. Within these several hundred rectangular tobacco offerings to the Spirits, Chief Eagle Feather was bound and covered with a lightly wrapped blanket. Before the blanket was placed over him to be tied, he was bound first with a light rope, his hands tied behind his back. We then lowered the huge man face first to the rug provided for some comfort for him over the hard granite floor. After the rooms lights turned off, the ceremony began in pitch black darkness.

The major ceremonies always open with a beseechment to the Six Powers and on up to Creator.

Sweat lodge, Vision Quest, Sun Dance, Pipe Offering and Yuwipi all begin by acknowledging these six Entities and of course ending to the Maker of them- Ultimate Creator.

After the ceremony, the tobacco offerings would be burned, sending up their ingredients to the on looking Spirits.

The singer boomed out the calling song, an eerie loud, high pitched, staccato wail that sounded so ancient that one's genes knew that it was ancient and told you so. After a few minutes of this calling and drumming there was nothing but black silence. Finally Bill's muffled voice spoke up. "Ho! There is someone in here who thinks this ceremony is nothing but a bag of tricks. He thinks I am an old man who will untie myself and jump around with a cigarette lighter waving sparks and shaking those two rattles on the floor." Silence. "Ho! You just moved your hand up to your knee. Now you moved it again." There was a startled man's gasp. "Unnhh, Unnnh" It was Professor Joe Cash known for his skeptical and overly critical classroom attitude toward Indians despite his position as anthropology head. Eagle Feather spoke sternly. "We are going to begin again. We all must be of one mind to begin this ceremony. You must be reminded, Professor. This ceremony is for you white folks' benefit. If the Spirits do not come in, you will have to leave." Eagle Feather paused. "Hupo Chan gleska." he instructed his singer to commence his drumming. Connie Bowen, the beautiful University President's wife, touched my wrist and whispered to me. "I am going to tell my husband about this." The singer hit his drum and the Spirits came in.

The Spirit People (or Spirit Forces) entered, flourishing in the form of blue-green lights. Around and around before us, above us and in close to us at times they flourished seeming in tune to the mesmerizing drum beat. The calling song to the spirits finally finished as all who sat there were placed into a spiritual void totally separating them from all that was earthly. Such a power that was before us that had one asked another what their own name was- maybe they would not have been able to answer or care to.

A brief discussion now seemed to occur between Eagle Feather's muffled voice and some other entity. This entity which was called upon was simply Spirit (Wahnahgi) although later, Bill informed us it was Grey Weasel. The conversation did not last long. A moment of silence between the two: A song was called for and once it began, the electrical-appearing lights reappeared and seemed to exit through the wall. Eagle Feather called for the song of Chief Gall of the Hunkpapas. Whatever it was that had communicated to Eagle Feather, it had now left the room. The singer sang out, and at the conclusion of a special song, Grey Weasel, the entity, Eagle Feather's spirit helper, came back again. Possibly ten to fifteen minutes had elapsed but the effects were so startling that time seemed to be shortened.

A purring sound filled the room. The patter of small feet was accompanied by the excited chattering of a weasel. A weasel in America is very much like a ferret or an ermine or mink. Ferrets are kept as pets by a few people and allowed to roam freely in their dwellings. Eagle Feather began to talk in Sioux to the animal, and the visitor chattered (spoke) back and purred as the holy man spoke. They continued to converse for a period until finally the animal no longer chattered but purred slowly.

Then Eagle Feather called for the same song. A woman sang.

I was not going to include this part of the ceremony. It is too preposterous to expect many to believe it. This ceremony alone will be too much for probably most readers, my opinion, such is their indoctrination. I am confident that the Spirit World will eventually verify for all, however, as we will all be going there eventually. But earlier before the ceremony, that morning we took Eagle Feather from his motel room to see the place the ceremony would be held at the bottom floor of the University's museum. Eagle Feather approved and queried the door adjacent to the designated ceremony room. The Museum Director nervously opened the door and Eagle Feather walked in to where a number of long wooden military ammunition boxes were stacked. They contained bones of several tribes found by anthropologists and probably their students. Eagle Feather reached down and picked up a skull, holding it in the palm of his large hand. 'Mandan Woman' with numbered co-ordinates was written on the forehead. He looked at me and said, "Hmmmh Nephew, Wahsteah wahneech. Sheechah. (This is not good.) He looked at Dr. Howard and said. "Tomorow, we should talk about this." He put the skull down and we left the room. "Wahsteah Waneech," he repeated with muffled breath.

Later during the ceremony, the woman's skull appeared up on a ledge within the room. It was lit up enough that one could discern a skull like form. I never bothered to look for a ledge attached to the room's wall after the ceremony. It was too awesome an event to even think about verifying factors. When her song finished, a loud crack came from the center of the floor and something slid toward the keeper of the pipe. I felt it impact into my feet with a sharp jab. I actually leaped sideways and into the lap of Connie Bowen. Sheepishly, I remarked to her that something had hit me. You must remember that all of this was taking place in the darkened room within the bottom of the university museum building.

Predictions

Once the song ended, Eagle Feather called out: "Ho, Grey Weasel has made seven predictions:

1. The airplane crashed in a storm not far from a town that has two creeks with almost the same name. We should send an airplane out to look for it. A man and woman will fly that airplane.

2. The animals will point to where we should go.

3. If we fly where the animals point and head past the town with two creeks, we will fly over the plane, but it is pretty well covered with snow.

4. The plane sent out will have to land but everyone will walk away from it. Do not worry, the pilots will be smiling as they look back.

5. In the next day or two some people who are not looking for the plane will be led to it by an animal.

6. Only five will be found. One of the six will be missing within the airplane. She landed away from the others, but she will not be too far away.

7. Her face will be upon an ice colored rock. She has a Chinese (pageboy) hairdo and wore big glasses.

"Those are the seven predictions. Now also, a rock that looks like ice has entered the room. It will have these signs I spoke of." Eagle Feather took a deep breath. "Ho, Nephew (meaning me). Reach out in front of you and pick up the rock. Hold it until the final song. You are of the rock clan, and you should welcome your rock brother, not be afraid of it." Somewhat skeptical, or else still in a degree of remaining fear from the encounter, I readily handed the rock to Connie Bowen, who asked for it.

Before the final song and the lights turned on, Eagle Feather said, "The two who fly like the winged ones," meaning my companion and I (Carol D.) – "both pilots will hopefully find the crashed plane by flying and using the stone as a map."

The next morning, we flew a Cessna 180, single engine plane from the University town's airport which was close to the Missouri River. As we lifted, I looked down and saw that the deer in the meadows were grazing, and they all were pointing downstream. We banked the airplane downstream. It must be noted that deer usually graze (feed) towards evening and seldom are seen in the morning hours. In a short while we came to another stream, a creek which emptied into the river. Deer were standing close to its mouth and all were pointing upstream. We followed the deer's indications which seemed to be foretold on the stone because deer images were inscribed on it. We came to the two creeks with the same name and flew on to see a town in the distance. One creek was named South Wolf Creek and the other was Middle Loup Creek. Loup means Wolf in French. We passed over the small town of Arnold, Nebraska, a very isolated and remote cattle town. The surrounding land and landscape was very vast with few or no fences and no planted agriculture- only vast grassland for cattle feeding and some stunted trees and tall cottonwoods at springs and dry creek collection points. We figured out that the cloudy, unclear sign on the opaque, ice gray crystal stone represented fog, as we were starting to notice the clouds getting lower to the ground. Across and away from the town we passed over a ranch where cattle were all standing on one side of a soybean/cracked corn cake feeding trough and pointing us toward some deer pulling hay from a haystack and who also pointed us onward in the same direction that the feeding cattle were indicating. Cattle, when feeding, always stand on each side of a trough when they gather no different than when they are taking on water from an elongated container but not these particular cattle at that given moment. We circled for a while over a spot as the fog was pushing us downward, visibility wise we were beginning to get into flying trouble and soon we were homeward bound to avoid the descending fog. An eerie feeling came over both of us before we banked the airplane back to Vermillion, South Dakota and the University airfield as though those deceased down below us were telling us that we had arrived at their final destination.

Eventually, we landed back where we started from barely in time because the fog was settling on the runway as we put the airplane in its hangar. It could have been fatal for us had we not returned in time to find the runway because of the oncoming descending fog. Carol held a commercial flying license as I did also. She was a very pretty, blonde and a good ten years younger than I. My flying skills had been honed by the military especially my combat missions in Vietnam. She had flown many hours in civilian planes despite her youth, now in her twenties but she was a natural, gifted pilot and a welcome addition in the cockpit when adverse weather came in. In those days many pilots flying small aircraft eventually met their doom fatally due to weather conditions which could isolate you from direct visibility. We both were well aware of what we had escaped from. It was now dark and we promptly drove to Main Street and had several relaxing drinks as most typical pilots would have been prone to do. The modern instruments of today were not yet invented then. Even when I was flying the million dollar machine, the Phantom F4, navigational instrumentation was relatively crude when compared to the lifesaving (and aircraft saving) instruments now available to pilots.

Carol D. was above average in height, and likewise resembled Cheryl Teagues, a popular model of that era. We often flew together to take Dr. Bryde out to the Indian reservations and while we had to wait several hours or on into an evening, hence we often visited many of the Indian people. The Indian ladies were quite in awe when I would tell them that she was a pilot just like I was and would embarrass her when I would tell them that she was equally as good as I thought I was. We became close friends and even more so after this demanding mission. Years have gone by now and I have often wondered where she had gone onto after college graduation. Maybe she became an airline pilot.

Several of Dr. Bryde's lectures and research would be held on the Rosebud Reservation, (Sichangu Lakota). Those times, Carol and I would hail a ride to Chief Eagle Feather's dwelling, after depositing Dr. Bryde. The jovial medicine man of the Sichangu welcomed us and we would spend a few hours with him. He liked Carol, no doubt respecting her for being a pilot. When he came down to the University, she wanted to attend his ceremony to find the 'Lost Six.' Naturally she was readily granted permission by Eagle Feather.

The next day after we had had our narrow escape, close to where we had reversed the plane's course, two coyote hunters followed the tracks of a coyote. The animal's tracks led them to the wreckage of the Cherokee Six airplane. The tail of the doomed plane was exposed due to the rising temperature from the fog. They reported the position and soon rescue vehicles converged on the scene. All of Eagle Feather's (actually Grey Weasel's) predictions proved true.

Summary

Well, there you have a ceremony that the preachers, popes, cardinals, Joel Osteen, Oral Roberts, Jimmy Sweigert and mullahs, imams can never do. While other religions have their own ceremonies, there are a hundred clues as to the Beyond that lie within such a powerful ceremony. Nature's Path is truly the world's most powerful religion/spirituality if prediction and spiritual communication is the standard. It is also the result of the sheer truth and dedication of the intercessor (The conducting medicine person) and, of course, the sincerity of the audience that allows or makes a pleasing atmosphere for the spirits to come in or whatever what you wish to call these information giving, knowledge probing forces who come in or want to come in. I suspicion that various Chino/Mongol descended tribes that we 'Norte Americano Indios' came from long ago, may have had this ceremony as well but called it different names. I imagine the preparation and sincerity of the old Celtic bards that were once in Spain and most of Western Europe produced similar ceremony. It is all an allowance of the Ultimate Power, however; our point of view. It is not possible unless the Intercessor- the Holy Man or Holy Woman conductor or beseecher- has extreme Focus, yes an Ultimate Focus to cultivate an appearance; a bringing in of those Spirit Forces to come in to the ceremony. These men or women have cultivated themselves to arrive at what I term; Pure, Pure God-Truth! America's dominant Organized Religion does not have this ability and never will, is my predictive opinion. They have too much distracting outer focus coupled with outright Untruth, to put it bluntly. Having broken three Hundred and some supposed solemn treaties with the North American tribes, according to author Larry McMurtry, and declared under, "In God We trust," I can understand why.

Without respectful harmony and undiluted truth, however, nothing will happen. It is encouraging to believe that the Spirit World will truly be a truthful and sincere place where earthly lies and manipulation will not in the slightest be allowed or condoned. Nothing but pure truth will be the total mental (or thought-wise) atmosphere, possibly. Again, our observation of God's Nature readily displays, God's (Creator's) Nature is always truthful. Should not Creator's Spirit World be like wise? Makes one wonder why we long to stay here!

"Life is but a mere shadow on the wall compared to the complete reality that lies beyond." I reflect back upon Plato's meaning in his "Allegory of the Cave." What we experience here, observe here, can and no doubt will be reflected to a related degree in the Beyond.

It is obvious that the spirit is able to go back into time and discern what took place. The girl who was thrown out of the plane had her seat belt come unsnapped or the belt broke no doubt by flying debris from a high G force, or possibly her extreme increased weight due to the spinning airplane's centrifugal force. Extreme centrifugal force ejected her through the plane casting her out away from the others. This prediction would be impossible to conjure. The spirit guide obviously has the ability to revisit this happening back in time to be able to report specifically as to the findings. "One of the six will be missing. She landed out away from the others." I find that statement impossible to conjure and only come from an entity that had 'non-earthly' help. Can Time possibly be frozen? Such would be a possible supposition. A camera 'freezes' Time. God shows us, allows that.

Pure, Pure God Truth

Pure Truth extends much deeper than simply 'not telling a lie'. When a human being can develop themselves to shed all forms of 'un-truthful' habits, beliefs, as well as false superstitions, exaggeration, irresponsibility, non-appreciation, addiction, disregard for thanksgiving, non-observance and especially forego terroristic acts— especially of ignoring Nature's teachings immediately before you and all forms of disrespectful negativism; then that person is beginning to become in a position to extend oneself into a communicative mode to communicate to those Spirits that surround us. When one does arrive at such a positive state in regard to Pure Truth there is no Consecration, Anointment or related 'Recognition ceremony' conducted by mere man whom seems to love to insert various forms of hierarchy into his Organized Religions. Yes, mere Man, loves to elevate himself. Maybe he wants to be a 'Minny God' so to speak. This attitude does not work if one seeks to be able to call in the Spirits! Repeatedly, I will make the statement: Creator is All Truth and All Knowledge. It seems to be all very simple. Many virtues must be practiced, developed and put into action however, for one's lifetime. Sharing,

Generosity, Bravery, Courage, Observation, Perception, Recognition and more: all will lead one toward a higher state and a definite preparation for a Spirit World which lies beyond whether or not one will ever or care to communicate directly as the Indigenous Medicine persons so do. While one conducts oneself on such a positive Spiritual journey, one's body will harmonize with the surroundings of Nature and become a very helpful tool as well. Like a dancer at a pow wow whose heart beat synchronizes with the drumbeat and can dance effortlessly for hours such is the body of a human which can harmonize spiritually with Nature. The animal brothers and sisters exhibit this trait, this connection, every day.

Carolina Influence

This Spirit Calling ceremony, in my mind, could quite possibly have influenced the Carolina Dakota as to advise them what danger was about to cross over the Atlantic or the magnitude of the deadly danger (contagious disease) the Europeans had already brought. They up and left a lush existence rather suddenly. This would be highly unusual for an established society comfortably settled in to their surrounding environment. Later leaders (Red Cloud, Crazy Horse, Sitting Bull and Black Elk) in this writing undoubtedly knew of this ceremony and may possibly have depended upon it to some degree also when they so successfully fought the White Man's soldiers; who knows? Black Elk used this calling in the many healing ceremonies he admits to before the missionaries threw him in a wagon. I find that the Yuwipi ceremony has certainly influenced my journey.

Odd, that so many non-Indian readers (and some turn-coat Indians as well) will sincerely believe that the above innocent beseechment, the Yuwipi, intended to bring closure for the bereaved families of the crash victims, which was a direct observation, and even generously intended to help their own kind (Wahshichus), will be considered preposterous and thus they will have to invoke some sort of 'Evil' conjuration to it. Not long ago, a few centuries, we would have all been drawn and quartered or burned at a stake for simply wanting to find the six victims. Thankfully, we Americans at least, now have the protection of the clause: Separation of Church and State and so far no police have showed up to punish me although Texas Senator Ted Cruz and former Congresswoman Michele Bachmann have voiced their opposition to abolish it. No doubt they are joined by the political 'Court jester fool- Sarah Palin.

Lastly, Museum Curator, Dr. James Howard who had adopted two

Mandan orphans, agreed with Eagle Feather to take the Mandan Indian remains and bury them on the bluffs of the Missouri.

CHAPTER 17
DEVILS, SATAN'S AND FORGIVENESS

If God/Creator is 'The Great Spirit' – the All Controlling Great Spirit, then how can this 'Devil/Satan Entity' be allowed to function?

> Malleus Maleficarum - XII. "Whether the Permission of Almighty God is an Accompaniment of Witchcraft."
> XIII. "Herein is set forth the Question concerning the Two Divine Permissions which God justly allows, namely, that the Devil, the Author of all Evil, should Sin, and that our First Parents should Fall, from which Origins the Works of Witches are justly suffered to take place."[84]

Devils? Satans? - was no doubt the nagging question asked by any traditional Indian who was forced to inherit such belief from the White Man starting out with confinement in the Wahshichu's boarding schools at an early age. Traditionals who resisted, such as myself, were outnumbered. We are very fortunate that the protective constitutional separation of Church and State clause still exists but on shaky foundation according to too many of the GOP politically in power across the land especially in the Deep South or the Statue of Limitation shortening state of South Dakota. In that realm, one does not offer common sense questioning if one seeks to avoid conflict or get elected.

My God concept is viewed as totally good. It gave me life. That is where I would have to start. Is it a bad God? How could God be bad when it allows us so much harmonic freedom? And look at all it gave us. I live, I breathe, I think, I have flown through the sky at twice the speed of sound, I have seen many lands and I am allowed to be here. I just think that I should be thankful for my life. There is a beautiful song that I heard a woman sing. It is simply:

Wakan Tanka

Wakan Tanka. Pilamaya.

Pilamiyah. Wichoni heh.

Great Spirit. Thank you. I thank you for my life.

---

[84] Montague Summers, Malleus Malificarum, The Witches Hammer, of Heinrich Kramer and James Sprenger, (New York: Dover, 1971). p. i.

I live. I am here. I should not complain. If I enter the spirit world today or tomorrow, at least I have lived. I must be thankful for all that I
have been allowed to see, to hear and the continuance of my adventures.
I must also be thankful that a possibility exists that I may also get to live
on.

It is difficult for me to think of this Great Mystery as bad. Maybe I
will know more when I enter the spirit world. If there is bad in Nature
then it is possible there could be a bad God or at least some distinct entity whose focus or supernatural powers are strictly and totally 'evil', cruel,
wicked and totally intent on subjugating humankind totally. I do not see
such evidence, however.

Human has a tendency to think a snake or a spider could be considered bad because they can deliver a poisonous bite. Yet, it appears that
snakes catch rodents whose population could run amuck if they were not
kept in check. Then the grains that we rely upon would be consumed.
The spider catches bothersome insects, especially mosquitoes that come
in the night. Tigers, Lions and Eagles have to kill also to live. Some have
attacked humans. The Chowgarah man-eater tigress ate over one hundred
humans due to an incapacitating gun shot wound, yet cannot be considered bad or 'evil. [49]James Corbett, *Man-Eaters of Kumaon,* (London, Oxford
University Press, 1993 Reprint.)

I watched a spider build his web while I stayed in a jungle hut in Ha-
waii. What an architect! There were not that many mosquitoes to make
you too uncomfortable and after a certain time every evening, they
seemed to disappear as though Nature had programmed them to let everyone get some sleep. The spider had his web right up underneath the
lone light for the hut which was solar battery powered. I enjoyed lying
there and looking up at the spider with his net catching the mosquitoes
and assorted flies. His glistening web and its design had an elegant beauty.
Out on the window openings, other spiders were at work. I wished them
well and respected them. Was I afraid of this spider? No, even though I
knew that he had come down to the table the night before to anchor his
web to a vase that was on the table. I slept not far from this table but I
did not expect him to crawl further down the table to come over and
bother me. Why would he or she have need for that? I was not a part of
his own truth, which was to trap other insects, not humans. This bottom
anchoring had been consistently interfered with by humans who broke
this connection by reaching accidentally across the vase and thus severing
his anchoring, causing the web to hang loosely. I took a ball of string the

next day and strung it from one wall of the hut to the other and right below his web at about eight feet high out of the way of humans. That evening when we were asleep, the spider anchored firmly to several points along the string. Obviously he knew that the string was there to serve that purpose. I think that he or she was doing its own tiny part in the great circle of life and was made and programmed by the God who is good. The spider learned immediately to adapt also. It did not go back down to the vase to anchor. It is strange how an Indian would take a measly spider and attempt to answer whether or not God was good or bad. A learned and high degree carrying academic would never do such a thing. It would be too simple and certainly would not boost one's ego.

What is bad in Nature? It would have to be against Nature's harmony that has endured down through time. Ever since we humans were allowed to be here, Nature has provided for us. I cannot conceive of anything that is "bad" in Nature. Is death bad? I think that this world would be pretty crowded if there was no death. There would not be much room and the Generations Unborn would be cheated out of their space if we did not depart and make room for them. It is getting crowded as it is. Is pain bad? When you sprain or break a limb the pain is there to keep you from using it and it can become healed. Is a blizzard, a hurricane, a tidal wave bad? At the time of the happening one would think so, but new growth returns and more open space is usually accessible for the future generations. As in the case of my hometown, a major flood came through the town down a usually serene mountain stream that was becoming overcrowded by housing. Now quiet bike paths follow the stream bed for miles. Runners jog and Nature is allowed to be enjoyed by all of the residents. Maybe that flood was not so bad after all, at least, for the new generations who enjoy access to that beautiful mountain stream.

Is God all forgiving? Whether or not God is all forgiving is beyond my comprehension. It would be comforting to think so, yet a nagging question springs forth. Doesn't such a concept allow an absence of discipline? Creator's Nature is loaded with strict discipline however and appears not to be forgiving. Hollywood movies almost always have a happy ending and that is how most people in the dominant society are programmed. Life is not the movies, however. How does Nature handle real life situations? What clues can we gain from Nature, which the Great Spirit has created? Does the Eagle, the Hawk or the Osprey kick out the fledglings once they are able to fly on their own and provide?

A lazy son or daughter is influenced by overly doting parents. They might foolishly believe that their parents will care for them on into their adulthood. Tragedy could befall, however. The parents may pass on with little assets to bequeath and the drone offspring will have to fend for themselves and, of course, will have honed few skills for independent survival. Such could be a scenario for our spirit life. Creator's Nature does not <u>enable</u>, does it? Our moral, ethical, observant, concerned, responsible Track Record according to what Creator would desire from us, you establish or deny is my concept. Do those who have pleased Ultimate Provider move on to a higher realm of knowledge seeking opportunity? Is it possible those responsible ones move into deeper knowledge while the irresponsible and worse, the perpetrators of terroristic acts and harm to the planet such as the polluting corporate decision makers; will they receive their just punishments? If the memories of their victims who directly or indirectly suffered exists, I would think so. The harmful ones will no doubt have to exist for an eternity with their own kind, is another of my suppositions.

I know a pair, much older who still refuse to 'get on their own'. Their Mother, older than I am is now raising two twin great grandchildren (18 months) while a daughter of one of her sons, is in jail and pregnant from a different sire, a dead beat of course. What an enabling scenario. Grandmother and her retired from the military husband, their enabling has brought me to utilize them as examples how far one can go with Enabling. Her youngest son, is a self-proclaimed 'specialist', approaching 60 years, works in the summers only and draws unemployment winters. His brother, alcohol problems and over sixty, has lived for years rent free from his parents. You can suffer an extreme toll in your later years if you take up enabling your offspring such is their example. Beware of Enabling is my advice. I watch a pair of Ospreys who teach me every fall within view of my summer trout stream home that feeds the lake where they nest above. Some people are just beyond help and there comes a time when you have to think like the Eagle, the Osprey or the Hawk — Creator's indirect discipline offering advice. The white man's bible has not issued me any such practical passages.

How does Creator resolve life and death which is a constant factor across the planet at every tick of the clock of time? IT doesn't —does it? Life here on this journey you develop and prepare or you do not develop or care to prepare for that entity Beyond- if there is one. Free will allows you free choice.

There are extreme differences between the people of organized religion and those people of indigenous spiritual, earth based beliefs in regard to their actual conduct here on this earth. Historically, these differences were reflected and made visible in the values of truthfulness, generosity and consideration and also the vices of greed and prejudice. I believe that the root cause of much of this difference lies within the concept of ownership and possession. I also believe that the concept of forgiveness should be explored. For many of indigenous belief, there was an actual fear of going into the spirit world with the guilt of having done harmful acts to others, to society or to the animals that provided for you. There was no erasure of deeds done, good or bad. If they occurred, the result and the memory would be taken on into the spirit world. Suffering caused to victims would most certainly be well remembered on over into the Beyond World- would it not? Memory is memory and I highly doubt that one would obliterate what happened- good or bad, favorable or unfavorable. What happened, *happened*, and it could not be obliterated. The record of memory would be a significant portion of your spirit, and those who were affected, for better or for worse, would contribute to that memory. Old time Indians were very cautious about their conduct because they had a definite belief that the hereafter did exist and they would pay dearly in isolation and chastisement in the spirit world for offenses committed against others in this life. How could that be? The harmed victims all have a memory. This was an effective restraint towards harmful conduct while they walked upon this planet. Who gave us sheer memory, especially of the very important happenings, pleasant or very unpleasant which become attached to us? The most painful memories we seem to remember the most- do we not? ISIS may not hold to this concept but I will bet that their victims certainly will. What of the Japanese soldiers who ran rampant through the streets of Nanking- murdered, raped and tortured- over 300,000 Chinese in but a few weeks of horror? It happened and their victims have memories. Does the poor 'Comely Lass' depicted in the Jose Brito painting, depicted earlier, horribly suffering under the murderous hands of the two extreme pervert, miscreants, Sprenger and Kramer or their likes: does she abide in the Spirit World? These two Dominican warped misogynists who obviously, no doubt, did they not continue on within secure, comfortable enough lives to write their lengthy, praised by fellow hierarchy - Malleus Maleficarum? Did their Jesus truly have the 'power to 'forgive' their repeated atrocities because as part of medieval Church hierarchy, surely they died within the promises of the Church? Are they serenely floating about upon some spiritual cloud happily smugly strumming a rewarding harp? What of the poor victim?

I have observed that most Christians are not very fearful about their conduct in this present mortal life. Most Christians believe that they can be forgiven for any offense, even the most heinous. When brought to trial, they usually declare their innocence. Rarely do they admit, "I am guilty, or I did it." They have indicated to me little fear or worry about their perceived spirit life that lies beyond, in comparison to how many indigenous people contemplate this presumption. This attitude is a very key difference. (Forgiveness is a major consideration when I wonder why there is such a displayed difference in the track record between the dominant society and that of indigenous people.) Several Indian pedophiles or rapists have requested that they be castrated yet I have yet to discover a white rapist asking such. The Indian obviously admits truthfully as to what his problem is and at least seeks a sure correction.

I was teaching a class at the Omega Institute near Rhinebeck, NY. A British woman sat in the front row. It was a morning class and lunch was approaching. She raised her hand and in her English accent asked if I was going to cover what she understood was a differing view from dominant society, the Indigenous concept of Forgiveness. I answered that after lunch we would discuss it. She walked with me to the large dining building that catered to many students attending a wide variety of summer holistic classes by serving vegetarian meals only.

On the way she told me rather calmly and unemotionally as though she had done so repeatedly, her story about how she had been raped often as a young girl by a pair of uncles who employed her father. Her parents told her to remain quiet about the sordid affairs as they feared her father would lose his job. Naturally the dilemma bothered her to a high degree for a lifetime. She admitted to several divorces and considerable fees paid out to psychologists and counselors over the years including alcoholism. She said the predominant advice she ever received was 'to forgive' but such was to no avail nor resulted with positive results of healing. "Eagleman, I understand that you have a controversial view regarding 'Forgiveness,'" she queried as we stood in the cafeteria line to pick out our meal.

"Yah, controversial!" I answered. "Odd, I do not consider my view as 'Controversial.' We will talk about it this afternoon. It makes simple sense....my view. My adversaries...I admit that I am far out-numbered but in light of plain old common sense...they are a helluva lot more controversial than I am." I added. "Creator-Nature... is extremely pragmatic and practical. Man is too often not when he tries to insert some religious advice, prophecy or dictum he is usually loaded with. Reservation missionaries were the worst- my experience."

That afternoon began and she sat again in the front row eagerly anticipating. She was probably in her fifties but looked at least a decade older and bore a persistent, dejected look and accompanying frown hiding what was once a pretty face. "Forgiveness!" I began. I went on, borrowing considerably, quoting what I wrote in one of my books, since out of print.

The English woman raised her hand and asked to my nod of recognition. "Do you mean we can chastise or expose our victim makers once we reach the Spirit World, those who caused our lifetime of grief?"

"As I have repeated over and over." I answered. "My life is based principally on supposition. I refuse to lie to myself by falsely claiming that 'I Know' when in reality, I do not know for sure. To attempt a reply to your question, I have to admit that I do not know for sure as some learned psychiatric or psychology type would come back with some form of absolute answer. But given Creator's gifts to at least attempt a sound rationalization, I would supposition that our Memory plays the key part to our conceptualization of the afterlife. Your memory doesn't let go, does it?" I paused to ask, "Who designed, created and endowed us with such an encompassing memory?"

She nodded affirmatively and pointed to the sky.

"Most of us never will get our atonement in this present world, will we?" She lowered her eyes in dejection. "We can only hope some form of release in the hereafter. All religions and Spirituality as well tend to have a 'Heaven and Hell' concept, do they not?" The entire class of about 20 attendees was alertly listening. "I will have to go with my belief that all wrongs are to be righted if Truth is what Creator ultimately is. I firmly believe that my perpetrators of Untruth toward me will be able to be confronted in that world beyond at least. Justice or Supreme Truth- God's, Creator's All Truth- will be served. They will have no size or accomplices to physically harm me nor be able to exert control over me employment wise or over my family members — as they were able to in this world -will they?" Several in the class must have had similar experiences for around the classroom, a few heads and expressions indicated solemn interest. "There will be no politics to allow governmental control either." I spread out my hands. "I will be free to offer real Truth- if I care to and point out their guilt. Yes......" I spread my arms wider and turned in a circle. I placed my right arm down and pretended to pull an imaginary sword from its scabbard hanging from my waist. I drew the sword and held it upward to the sky. "Yes," I repeated. "And the whole world in this place of All Truth will know what you sons a bitches did to me un-truthfully, immorally, unethically and against what Creator would never condone." I could not help but feel a confident serenity as I 'lowered my imaginary sword,' placing it back in its scabbard and remaining in a long moment of silence before an equally silent class lost in their own moment of memory back upon some similar event in their past.

The English woman rose from her chair and clenched both fists, holding them high. "You mean I can finally get those sons a bitches in the Spirit World?" A serene smile came across her to add emphatically. "Those evil, controlling sons a bitches!" I have been to the United Kingdom almost annually in the last decade or two. At this point I have to state that United Kingdom citizens rarely swear or use the barrage of expletives most Americans, especially combat Marines that I have had the pleasure to associate with, generally use. She let out a few more expressive words not within the realm of the King or Queen's English. She ended with, "I am free. I am released! I can get those raping bastards in the Spirit World. What a relief."

Well, despite all the 'learned', professional doctorates of the mind who teach and preach 'Forgiveness,' this lady found her bliss. I had a few more class days to spend with her attendance at Omega Institute and she remained as exuberant as ever throughout the session. She even managed a humorous attempt in her morning greeting, "I am released!" Her fists clenched holding up high and a broad, exuberant grin.

If I wanted to "sell" a particular religion, or make one appealing in order to increase its membership, then I would offer some promises of forgiveness or attainment to the hereafter. I would promise that happy ending just like the movies. Such a promise would state that a person will come face to face with God after death if only they have exhibited a "faith" of course while they were yet upon the earth. It is also appealing to throw in a sudden retention of vast knowledge and of course be able to sit "at the right hand of God" for joining a particular church or belief system. This salesmanship has such an appeal, it is why the television evangelists are so popular, especially with the aging. The Church, no doubt, quickly attached a lucrative price tag and eventually the evangelicals did likewise.

Where does Nature convince us that such bliss may be attained and with so little effort expended? Go out and live in Nature for a few days or a week. Discover how non-forgiving Nature is. Harsh reality is quickly observed. I cannot find any clues that even hint that the Creator is all forgiving especially when I reflect upon a studied Nature- God's creation. I might want to wish it was so, and I suspect that this is what has happened for those who fervently believe that we can so easily attain a religion based nirvana regardless of the degree of suffering we have occasioned upon the memory of the victim. Some victims commit suicide. Others will go on and perpetuate the same crime against their own offspring. Such implantation is capable of spreading on and on to other victims. I cannot conceive of an all knowing Creator that creates a harsh, disciplined Nature and yet allows a condoning toleration, so to speak of forgiveness, especially such allowance for an exponential crime that is capable of spreading onward to generate numerous innocent victims. The non-allowance seems to be much more reflective of the Nature based concept of Creator's that my culture portrays. It is comforting to be able to formulate such Mystery with, "Oh well. We will find out in the Spirit World."

Sunday morning folks look considerably contented after they come out of those palatial 'Glass Cathedrals' or bask happily rubbing and filling their bellies at non –alcohol offering restaurants like Perkins afterwards. Incidentally, the larger and more cavernous the church it seems they have the least to offer the homeless downtrodden quite dissimilar from the Salvation Army types.

Fantasy is capable of circumventing or short circuiting the brain's memory. One may as well term it 'Fictional Magic' sort of like Superman being so effortlessly able to fly by simply wearing a magic cape. Creator's laws of a required aerodynamic propulsion source can be simply disregarded with such fantasized 'magic'. Nature's demands, her absolute laws are disregarded totally via human's fantasy but reality, will not be denied in this natural world we live in. Deny Nature's reality and a realistic answer from her will be projected sooner or later. Expect it. One's memory is what Creator has placed upon us, what happened has happened and one's retention is where we are all at. Pure and simple. Leap off a high bridge or a tower with a 'fantasy cape' and you will find out.

Now let us advance on into the Spirit World, that Beyond Entity where most of us believe we will all go to eventually when this life ends for us here. For those who do not believe in such, please allow our little venture. Hopefully, there is an afterlife. A few of we tribal Indigenous, the ones the missionaries failed to break totally, we do have a so-termed 'proof' that it exists if we can accept the previous chapter's Spirit Calling. Many of my tribe among others non-tribal have been fortunate to have experienced some convincing ceremonies that the 'Beyond' does exist. The Spirit messengers that came in to Fools Crow's or Chief Eagle Feather's calling to them left us with highly accurate predictions that all came true eventually. Such revelation was convincing enough for me. Of course, I have no 'Devil' to dissuade, deter me.

Judgement by Whom?

So let us go on into that Beyond. Does God come down and Judge us? Why did It gift us with a memory? We quite possibly then... possibly it is our Memory that will do the judging of one another...even ourselves. It is Creator's gifted tool. In the Spirit World it is my supposition that Our Memory without an elemental body needed here on this planet is what we obviously will evolve to. We won't need a body in the Beyond, will we? Without a dependency on others, we do not have to worry about the elements, do we? Food, shelter, clothing will not affect our conduct, will it? If we wronged another...caused Untruth to come to an innocent another- surely that individual will recall such; vice versa if we are the victim. You will be able to chastise forever how long you consider adequate for an eternity, if you will, - all those who wrongfully caused Untruth to happen to you. Is there a tendency for an aggrieved victim to want to seek some form of atonement for an alleged wrongful assault? Such is what most victims seek mainly through the courts of justice here in this planetary abode, do they not? Does a form of 'Freedom' evolve from at least a wished for 'Atonement' when we reach the Spirit World? A final release? Truth is the only 'Medicine' that bears the healing ingredient is my guess. An exposure of real Truth would seem to be rewarding. I certainly intend to expose some perpetrators that have caused me some troubling harm. I was no rape or pedophile victim, thank God or It's possibly protective Spirit Guides. I did suffer from a couple of harming perpetrators as mentioned that I definitely wish to expose and expect to do so. Like the English woman, It actually makes me feel better when I think that justice from the evidence in my prospective possibly awaits them.

What of the poor 'Comely Lass within the Brito painting? Hitler, Husseiin, his son, Stalin, al Baghadadi, Dick Cheney, 1930s collaborator with Adolph Hitler - Pius Pacelli, the medieval popes, slave profiteers et al. and General Tani Hisao, Commander of Japan's 6th Division who met his death by Nanking Military Trial gunfire- 1947? Let us also include the vicious, inhumane soldiers of Hiroshima 232nd Regiment, 39th Division. Although they were allowed safe passage back to Japan, they were met with the loss of 1/3rd of their civilian relatives and tasted some of the horror and sorrow they had inflicted at Nanking.

Tailored Marketing

Too much marketing has fallen into religion. Just turn on a television set on Sunday morning. By "marketing" I mean that a religion is tailored to appeal to an audience. The people are hearing what they want to hear and of course are encouraged to join with their pocket books. The religious leaders wind up living in lavish style like Joel Osteen who dupes thousands every Sunday. The depth and wisdom of spirituality becomes totally ignored. Spirituality is over-powered by the promises of tailored religion. The followers of this charade are left with an exuberant promise and most bask for a while with benevolent feelings afterwards clutching their black books, but the actual result is the society that we see now. It has become very greedy, selfish, distant and even dangerous. Huge churches are supported by well-dressed benefactors who drive up to these ornate monoliths for an hour's service of 'Worship' in late model vehicles that offer no homeless shelters or caretaking programs and incidentally are tax free. A spirituality or a religion should be able to encompass the entire society with its values as it actually did for the indigenous peoples of the past.

What was it that actually helped indigenous people fulfill and direct their life style toward a higher state of harmony? What power, what knowledge, what discovery or what mystery was it that could actually bring forth fruitful results from a people who had no jails, no homeless, no poor houses, no orphans, no rich and no poor and yet, had an elected leadership that was quite free from ruthless terror filled dictatorship?

Responsibility

Native peoples took responsibility for their own actions. They lived this life as if it had a high degree of significance for their life in the spirit world. They knew of the spirit world through their ceremonies. Their ceremonies allowed them to be quite convinced that a spirit world did exist and that they would someday become a very integral part of that mystery therefore one's conduct was a highly serious matter.

We used to have many old time Indians visit us and stay overnight or several days with us when I was a child. We had three houses on an area about 3/4th of a city block. My jovial, congenial 'Uncle Albert' built one and went off to help the World War II effort and never came back. We even had an orchard and chickens until the city got modern and banned farm animals. That did not keep my sister and me from attempting to raise a couple hundred pheasants. Because I played on the American Legion baseball team and was often hired by the Mayor to run some of his errands, he waived the chicken Ban and came up several times to our place to see how we were progressing. Even a police car would show up occasionally to gaze at our long tailed "chickens". Often on Sunday mornings they would give my Mom, sister and I a ride to church. Such was the hominess of our long time mayor's town. He even had my Indian Mom on his 'Mayor's Board' that met periodically. We had a big lawn and ran the chickens out of their chicken coop when the game birds got bigger. The mayor was quite a fan of our baseball team and I was probably one of the better players. I was never much of a home run or triples hitter but could often get on base with more than adequate reflexes to this day that still gift me for the fastest growing sport in the nation- www.pickleball.com. I won two gold medals in Minnesota Senior Games while in my seventies, no small accomplishment. If you wish to still remain physically fit for your approaching 70s or even 80s providing you still possess a pair of able legs- try it.

The reservation Indians who still retained their old values and knowledge came to Rapid City to shop and purchase essentials not sold on the reservations. Uncle Albert's furnished house was always empty except for when they came. Evening time, a fire would be built between the dwellings for the cool Black Hills summer nights and I heard many old time stories. It was better than television. They never mentioned the missionaries much. I do not believe that they integrated forgiveness into their spirituality, at least to the degree that Christians have integrated it. I doubt if many Christians will ever attempt to rationalize out what I have to say however. Like the boys in the pair of clashing pickup trucks, Forgiveness is too rigid a rule for them to attempt Nature based rationalization. Their resolve to always be right or correct will not allow many to be influenced by Nature- even though it is God's creation. The English woman was desperate so therefore she could understand and incorporate more fully our concepts and now especially what worked for her dilemma.

The more intelligent, the more aware, the more balanced a species, the higher their chance of survival is my guess. Where species did not adapt, then that species became extinct. Such was the harshness of God-designed nature down through eons. Humans who did not adapt or provide for themselves rarely survived. When humans lie to themselves over resources, land management or population control, we see their calamities unfold. Where human habitually lied throughout its society and great inequality and control ensued by an elite became the rule, these societies eventually decayed and fell from within. The recent fall of the ruthless, greed opiated, dictatorship controlled countries in the Mideast are recent examples.

Direct Observation or Fantasy

Should I follow Creator's exhibited Direct Observation or puny Man's fantasy? Odd how the vast majority of mankind choose the latter regardless of how error prone the countless examples are becoming exposed especially in this scientific age of direct revelation. Will human deserve punishment for perpetuating a religious mockery of those who seek spiritual solace as well as guidance from Nature observation– God's Creation? Will exponential Over-population become Nature's punishment? Such Ego human has, to place themselves as supreme over Creator. Responsibility for honing/fulfilling one's journey toward a more rewarding 'Beyond' is enhanced by a Nature respecting approach versus man based alone; my opinion.

I have also witnessed a history of lies upon lies told to us as Indian people by the dominant society and now in this age of communication many good and honest people from the dominant society hold similar viewpoints—that we all were lied to. Much suffering was caused by those who perpetuated those lies. Do you think that the victims are going to erase their memory of such suffering when they enter the spirit world? Have the Jewish people forgotten the Holocaust? I do not believe that this was the intention or purpose of the powerful movie, *Schindler's List*.

I must correct myself. Man will learn real truth eventually. Tragedy, extreme tragedy will finally do the teaching. Total Truth will ultimately evolve but it will be a painful teaching. The results of Overpopulation guarantees it is on its way.

Does a poor victim of incest or sexual abuse ever forget those grievous and heinous acts perpetrated upon them? The English woman attempted but finally accepted that her justice would come later and exhibited that she was quite satisfied. The rational psychologists that I have asked have told me that victims do not forget. I was so fortunate that I escaped some horrible crimes. As innocent children we knew very little about such conduct and as we grew older we thought there were only a few people who perpetrated such things and they had to be crazy in the first place to do such a thing. Eventually, we thought, they would all be discovered and placed in insane asylums. And all that time, church authorities were shuffling their own child molesting leaders around and were even protecting these clergymen. They lied. They were so intent on covering up that they ignored the degradation and violations committed upon the children of their very own followers. They did not care about the consequences. Period.

As an Indian in a white town, I was not good enough to be an altar boy, thankfully, even though I tried unsuccessfully several times to be one. I back that statement up with what happened to my aunt who wanted to be a nun. She was rejected from two religious orders because she was an Indian. This made my grandfather, who was a fairly wealthy cattleman, quite angry. Eventually, the Franciscan order accepted her and she remained a nun throughout her lifetime. She was quite healthy and retained her work ethic long into her aging. Times have changed, I know, but that was the prejudicial thinking even within most religious orders when I was young.

After I grew older and knew more about it, I asked my mom what happened in the old Indian way about this incest. She said that the Indians would kill anyone who did such a thing. My mom was no historical authority but when I read a book by Ohiyesa, a credible Sioux writer; he said that an Indian could be put to death for lying. If that was so, I believe that the old time Indians must have done the same to the child molester. Incest or rape- either one. There is very little record of this in our society. How can I back up this statement? Come to the reservations—at least to the Sioux reservations. I do not know that much about the other tribes. Come out and count all of the deformed, Mongoloids, (errant, prejudicial term for Down Syndrome) midgets, dwarfs and other people who are not of the average two legged. All of these categories or classifications are not a result of incest, I will admit, but it is worth noting, especially when a group of people do not display such characteristics or very few in their descendants. Then set up a graph and a chart like most academics do. I think that you will discover that maybe there was not much incest among those who had the least contact with the dominant society. (Unfortunately, there is alcoholic and drug syndrome that has come into our reservations. Those offspring are not the result of incest, however.)

I have received letters that bear a definite respect for so many of the concepts that indigenous people followed. The majority of these letters are from non-Indian people. I do not want to take a chance with the words of the "other" white man, this dominant society minister, priest or bishop or television evangelist, when it comes to my spiritual life beyond. What you do and how you wish to follow their guidance is your choice. I have my choice also as long as this is still a free country. Those who do not see Nature as reverently as the tribal people did, they have not exhibited enough of a positive track record to convince me to believe them. I think that the dominant culture's forgiveness concept has taken a lot of discipline and exemplary conduct out of present day society when I compare the two religious/spiritual ideologies.

Because of my belief that nothing is erased, I am going to try to be very truthful in my conduct. If I lie or do wrong then I believe I will be so charged in the spirit world. If I lie in my writings the spirit world will know. You will know when you enter because observing spirits will tell you so. Nothing will be erased. That is an effective deterrent toward harmful conduct that worked well upon this continent for a long time. What happened did in fact occur. If it caused a painful memory, the victim retains that memory. If good deeds were performed or risk was taken to save a life then the person saved or helped will always remember the good deed. We can meet a person and we either have a good memory or a disappointed or even a fearful memory of that person. We often burst out in admiration when we meet a certain person from our past. Obviously, that person has treated us with dignity and respect. Are there different degrees of lies? Are there different degrees of harm that you can do to a person with a lie or a series of lies? I think there are but you can answer that from your own experience. If I had to lie to save a person who was being terribly oppressed or was in a concentration camp of inhuman suffering and I could help them escape, I would have no problem telling a lie, but that does not justify one bit lying and harming an innocent person, especially for my own gain.

Sin?

Do I believe in sin and does my belief system have the concept of ultimate good and evil? I have never seen "sin." What does it look like? I do not think the Sioux had this concept and yet, they set a high example of being without it in more ways than one. Sin was not a word in their language prior to their exposure to the missionaries.

Is this another conjuration of dominant society? This "sin." Where is it evidenced in Nature? Is it something like this devil, which also I cannot see or comprehend? I know that the television evangelists make a big "to do" over it. I think it must be pretty useful to draw money out of people and it probably keeps them scared. If I can address some questions in this area, then maybe I can project some related viewpoints.

A few native medicine people possibly did dwell on "evil spirits" and yet the majority, at least in my tribe, were more intent on discovering or applying the healing medicine which they were familiar with. My teachers did not spend time on man designed entities such as "evil" but this does not rule out that some other medicine people might have tried to connect in this area. No one to my knowledge was ever successful at bringing in anything "evil" or had any power to bring such a superstition into a spirit calling ceremony. The main aspect of such an attempt is that no tribal member would go near them. Because of the nature of our spirituality, such thoughts are usually beyond even speculating. There is no need for it and I believe that most northern tribal practitioners of spiritual healing and communication would believe that an attempt to communicate with what is not harmonic would not be possible in the Creator's harmonic spirit world.

Medicine people and holy men had reputations for their curative or connecting power throughout the reservations. When you have been to a genuine spirit calling ceremony and have experienced the spirit helpers that come in to aid the holy man in prediction or healing, you just do not think of nor do you associate your tribal ceremonies with any type of "evil" connection. It is like looking at a mountain stream or a clear lake that is jumping with trout after evening flies. How could such a happening be evil? How could calling upon the Great Mystery, or through spirit helpers wherein this Great Mystery is always recognized, have any "evil" association? Any other way which does not perceive spiritual calling as good will not work.

Knowledge or Lack Thereof

My views on good and evil are not held by the dominant society from what I have observed. I do not know if there is evil. I tend to think that good is knowledge and bad is lack of knowledge. Bad is being loaded with ignorance and good is avoiding ignorance by striving to increase one's knowledge. Good is also what the Creator has created. Everything created, then, would be perceived as good, in some way or some design. Creator is All Knowledge and All Truth is how we want to view or believe. The third major aspect is Creator is obviously a Mystery. Nothing more. Nothing less. It is quite foolish to attempt to declare who, What, Why the Creator actually is.

Knowledge - Abatement of Hate

It seems that when some people attain knowledge, especially in the area of human relations or the humanities, they have less of a tendency to be prejudiced and hateful. Nature is not hateful, therefore I think that knowledge must move us closer to the higher good, closer to this all providing Nature. Knowledge about a society can certainly remove false fears, stereotypes, misconceptions and even harmful prejudice. That is proof alone that knowledge can cure so-called "evil" which is really ignorance in all appearances. It seems that those who are kept in a closed society, and also choose not to learn about other societies or the natural world around them, they are much easier led down a path of hatred, contempt and disrespect for differing cultures, religions or races. A broader person will couple his or her world knowledge with nature knowledge. One can then attain a higher degree of harmony and will function on a higher plane within society.

Prejudice against Indians in my state at least is slowly abating. There exists much intermarriage between my tribe and Dominant Society. We are basically a handsome people and seem to have little problem finding mates. Plus our cultural values can easily be appreciated. You can see this example at our sun dances that once was primarily only the full bloods as pledgers. Nowadays, quarter breeds on down are intermingled with the higher percentage breeds and full bloods, such is our intermarriage. Once prejudiced white ranchers have now overnight turned the other cheek once interracial grandchildren came along. Through this 'new knowledge' prejudice has been severely reduced.

I can see where this "sin" spoken about previously is identified with "evil." But I am more concerned with the prevention of it than I am its religious connotation. We are aware that ignorance can cause much suffering. Knowledge gives me hope that a wrongdoer can be changed by experiencing knowledge. Often, it is the lack of knowledge by society as a whole that can cause a wrong-doer to become so frustrated and angry that he will go out and "sin" or commit "evil." In another society he might have been a better citizen. Yes, society can actually enlighten itself and grow positively with affecting knowledge. I honestly believe that indigenous society had such a high regard for ethical and moral knowledge and spiritual harmony that it did "affect" its participants in a positive way.

I am sure that many of us know of, or have known a person, who was close to Nature and demonstrated to us that they truly had a profound respect for the ways of the natural world. I hear of a person's uncle who chose to spend most of his time in the woods or a person's friend who nursed a flower garden year upon year or watched many species of birds for a hobby. Rarely are these people unkind, cruel or devious. What is it that has them exhibit harmonic characteristics? The answer is simple. Their closeness to Nature has soothed them and empowered them to be harmonic. Nature has given them more variety to sharpen their intellect. Nature is much more dramatic than a city street or a soap opera. Go out into Nature, stay overnight and find a whole new dimension that changes several times during the night and can have added alteration because of the weather.

For some, a mere flower garden is adequate to follow one's bliss. Thoreau seemed to be well satisfied with his area of bliss. Japanese have aesthetic rock gardens sprinkled with a few plants and often dwarfed, miniature, decades old trees less than a foot tall. You do not have to travel to the ends of the earth to satisfy or find your bliss. Pet owners will adamantly verify this statement. But then again, life is allowed to be so diverse that for some, to travel and take in new knowledge may well be a means of satisfying one's bliss. Other forces will have their effect as well but immersion in Nature is strong medicine for the spirit.

What can bring about a positive change for humanitarian sharing and understanding? That is simply answered. Knowledge. Knowledge leads to wisdom, wisdom leads to understanding and understanding can bring peace. When you blend all of this with nature knowledge, it becomes a spiritual grace. I do not mean this statement to be merely poetic or flowery. It is a fact. People who are deeply knowledgeable and also immersed within Nature, actually do exhibit a spiritual grace. It is a pleasure to be around them. A handsome Golden Retriever loyally lying every night beside your bed or a purring cat in your lap will verify this provision of soothing, comforting 'Spiritual Grace'.

The depth of these questions which high school students had submitted are optimistic indicators of the availability of knowledge and its resultant influence. Modern students now have ready access to worldview knowledge and information, therefore they are asking probing questions which my age group would never have pondered when we were young. This age of communication places immense knowledge right at the fingertips of these new generations. I believe it is altering their lives so much earlier toward more open minded harmony than in our generations. Maybe knowledge gleaning Spirituality as reflective and similar to the ancient Celtic Bardship of olde when the Celts ruled Western Europe will blossom again. Honor, oaths, ethical, moral, selfless leadership is possible with this new tool of electronic communication most of the younger generations now possess. It gives me optimistic hope. It is now more difficult to lie and spread untruth. That elusive 'Holy Grail' that King Author's knights were always chasing; is that what our new communication tools are honing in on? Will future generations eventually find the Grail and go on to fully project honorable, undiluted, non-manipulated Truth closely equivalent to what we hope this Benevolent Creator projects through its Creation- Nature? Such would be the end of Terrorism.

I have observed that the more knowledgeable a people are, the happier they are. The more hateful and ignorant a people choose to be then the more despondent and pessimistic they show themselves. So-called "evil" and unhappiness seem to go together. In the later years of life, few people want to be around a person who has been notoriously "evil" or ignorant. These people lead lonely lives, nobody wants to have anything to do with them and their 'Disks of Life' (Memory, 'Organic USBs') are so blank that they cannot entertain or more fully satisfy themselves. In but a few decades past, it was "in" to be a spiteful and racist "good old boy" in many parts of the country. Celebrities could even hint that they espoused a racist and prejudiced way of thinking and that leaning did not endanger their social status. Professional sports teams were all one color. Even the Marine Corps and Navy excluded Negroes and Colored Troops (The terminology used in those days.) That attitude is not the popular case at present and I hope that such conduct will never be tolerated again. What has brought about this change? It has been the tremendous increase in communication throughout the globe. A Bull Connor from Selma, Alabama or a Shelton Grand Wizard of the KKK can no longer command a significant following. Even George Wallace had to change his political campaign practices. Political contestants have to couch their politically correct wordage. The Confederate flag over the South Carolina capitol no longer flies.

Medicine Story

Is humankind inherently good or evil? My friend, Manitonquat (Medicine Story), a Wampanoag tribal member, tells us, "The Creator made no evil. Every baby born is good, lovable, loving, intelligent, beautiful special and wonderful. That's who you really are."[85]

"Evil is an illusion. The illusion that there is really something fundamentally wrong in Creation. That sense of evil, of wrongness at the very heart of Creation, strikes terror in our souls." [86]

Could there be entities...Good and Evil? I would have to link them with humans and not with the spiritual. Yes, humans could be good and evil if the concept of knowledge and ignorance is too difficult to reason with. Whenever so-called "evil" is done by humans, I believe it is of their own choosing, their own manipulation and/or creation. I do not ascribe to the excuse, "The devil made me do it."

The system or the tribe can prevent a human from doing "evil" acts. Why is it that indigenous people were not inclined to do the 'evil' or ignorant acts that the dominant society did when they came to these shores? Why could early explorers and trappers simply leave their belongings in a pile in Indian Territory and identify them with a marking stick? This stick would bear a carved symbol to denote ownership. Indigenous people would leave these possessions alone and secure. Only among indigenous people did this happen. Back in the trapper's own society, his pile of goods would have been stolen. The dominant society allowed some very "evil" acts, such as not keeping one's word, making false treaties, capturing and selling slaves, coveting other people's lands and eventually the entire continent.

What practical reasoning could support such an intelligent power to have a need to create evil? Why would it have any need for creating a devil? I was told by missionaries that this entity actually projected evil? This devil seems to be a strong force in Christianity and among Islamic thought. Most of these followers believe that it exists, yet I have never met a person that could tell me truthfully that they have actually seen a so-called devil nor communicated with it as we see forces in Nature such

---

[85] Manitonquat (Medicine Story) - *Return to Creation*, (Spokane, WA, Bear Tribe Publishing, 1991) p. 28
[86] Ibid p. 28

as a storm, lightning, tornado, a waterfall, the waves of the ocean, etc.

'Reverend' Tilton

I once heard and watched a television preacher state that the Devil had appeared to him in his hotel room. I do not make it a practice of listening to television preachers but this happened by accident. I was in a television store when I was exposed to Reverend Robert Tilton. He was investigated by the Attorney General of Texas soon afterwards. He said that the Devil spoke to him stating that he, the Devil, was very unhappy and his demons were unhappy because of all the work for good which the television preacher was doing. Then Reverend Tilton made a pitch for more donations to keep the Devil unhappy.

I did not believe the preacher's statements regarding the Devil appearing in his hotel room. I strongly believe that this man was lying and worse, he was lying over spiritual matters. He was using this devil conjuration simply to bring in more money for his practice. If he is not lying then he should be able to make this devil appear again. I would gladly go with him to see if he was telling the truth. I would like to interview this devil if it really exists. But all of this is moot. I do not believe one bit that the preacher is telling the truth. His story is all made up and for obvious reasons. When a man or a woman has to lie when they are discussing religion/spirituality, then they lose their credibility in my view. These people's society does not chastise them to any preventive degree, however. They obviously are not fearful that in the spirit world they will pay dearly for their lies. Their society has not taught them to be seriously concerned about lying in this life.

If the Devil exists, then why is it no one, absolutely no one can ever come up with one? Possibly, when one is into hallucinogens or drugs they may experience such an entity but this example I would not consider as a credible experience. If people state that they have seen a devil or talked to a devil then why is it that they cannot reproduce it when called upon? If an eagle comes to an Indian ceremony and hovers over it, usually that phenomenon will happen again. If a prediction is made by a sincere and devout holy man and from a powerful ceremony, usually that holy man will go on and do another ceremony or many just as powerful and with similar strong predictions. When Bill Eagle Feather's ceremony found the six bodies under snow and ice within a few days after his Yuwipi was held at the University of South Dakota that was spiritual connection. The ceremony was in the interest of good or harmony—to find the missing bodies for the bereaved parents. Bill Eagle Feather performed other ceremonies that called on the spirit world to help people. He was able to be repetitive, like Nature can be repetitive.

To believe in a devil or a so called 'bad force,' indicates to me that this Great Creator is not harmonic or has some kind of "bad" tendencies. Simply hold and observe a bouquet of flowers and you should be able to understand. Yes, a bouquet of intricately designed, refreshing and pleasant flowers! Who, What designed those flowers? Thousands of varied designs, thousands of pleasant smelling scents each creation emanates. Seriously contemplate what other refreshing scenes exist for us daily, too numerous to adequately portray. The Ultimate Designer provides such abundant evidence that I simply refuse to believe It would allow conversely; what to me is actually Man's design and imagination which eventually found its way into Man's religious books.

Will not Creator deem such holding as offensive and distracting from It's primary intent that Man needs to become wholly Harmonic to better insure one's entry into the Spirit World? I certainly do not intend to jeopardize my chances regarding a respecting entry and proven track record as the standard for judgment.

Commonality: The Judaic and some of the migrated Plains Tribes.

It is noticeable that I have not included Judaism as an Organized Religion with commentary. Therefore I will briefly mention that of all religions, the Spiritual Indigenous, in my opinion, have the most commonality wherein with Judaism, to Wit:

1. They believe in One God. (Admittedly, a minority do not believe in any.) "Thou shalt not have other God's before thee." First Commandment.

2. Most do not Proselytize nor attempt to utilize fear tactics to convert.

3. Most do not superstitiously believe a Devil, Satan, Lucifer or such related Evil Spirits exist or that the Higher Power would allow such within Its Creation.

4. They definitely, not unlike the Indigenous, have suffered severely at the hands of Dominant, Organized Religion.

5. The Jewish Woman, like the Sioux Woman is equal to the Jewish Male. Superstitious, man based, man oriented restrictions are not unfairly placed upon her. PIC of Chained Arab woman. May have to improvise Pic to qualify it.

6. Like the North American Indigenous, rarely have they had cruel, non-humanitarian, non-elected dictators gaining leadership.

7. Both Tribes have received Spiritual Warnings for survival from the Higher Power: Moses on Mt. Sinai and Black Elk's prediction of the Blue Man of Corruption, Greed and dangerous harm to The Planet- the Earth Spirit.

8. Not unlike the Sioux: They have suffered severely but yet remained tribal and kept their Spirituality intact.

9. Neither tribally based people have or allow a hierarchal, governing, controlling chain of command ending with a self-perpetuating titular head.

10. The Philosophy of Judaism and most Northern American Indigenous is a 'Live and Let Live' philosophy.

I do have to offer a disclaimer regarding the Palestinians, however. One of my sons has traveled throughout the Mid-east and speaks Arabic. Unfortunately, he tells me that the Palestinians are one of the most liberal in the Mid-east in regard to Western concepts of their female allowances compared to far more extreme subjugation other countries unfairly require and impose.

The U S Government placed us on our reservations after our valiant conflicts. They were quite wary of we Sioux and Cheyenne as we had fought them quite successfully for three decades before finally being subdued. We killed the Cavalry mostly eight to one which historians are loathe to admit but the Winchester which we had (and the Army did not have) made a huge difference along with our more superb and better trained horses as mentioned earlier. Better leaders in our opinion also. We were placed on reservations but eventually were free to leave or return at will as we became more acclimatized or assimilated into White society. Entering the military as early as WWI speeded our assimilating transition and on into WWII, Korea and Vietnam. Higher education also raised our off reservation freedom. Now there is such inter marriage that soon, eventually there will be very few full bloods among us. Unfortunately, such hatred existing in the Mid-east prevents peaceful co-mingling due to Religion.

The reservation system for us Sioux is restrictive to non-Indians in regard to land purchase, ownership or development however. They are not allowed to buy or purchase our Indian land holdings. This is what I believe Israel needs to practice and employ among the Palestinians and vice versa. I cannot sell my land to a non-tribally enrolled prospective buyer nor Will it to any relative even unless they are tribally registered or enrolled. Hence non-tribal citizens cannot develop or own said land.**

Hitler, al Baghdadi

What of men like Hitler, Stalin, Hussein, Tojo and now ISIS Bakr al Baghdadi? Were or are these men evil? I think that they were allowed into power by other men similar to them. The Nazi party brought Hitler into power and the German people, all Christians, except for the Jews, cheered and condoned his inflammatory and nationalistic speeches. He appealed to their egos, their false sense of Aryan superiority, to their fear of unemployment while stirring blame and prejudice against the Jews. This was an entire nation of Christians that allowed themselves to be influenced and were fortunate that the Allied Powers eventually allowed them to put their country back together again. General Hideki Tojo ruled Japan's military through the combined blessing of historic Samurai-ism and Emperor Hirohito's religious -'Devine Descent from Heaven'. Christians must be reminded that WW II caused far more death and destruction than ISIS has committed and at least five centuries of the Great Inquisition. ISIS however, needs to be eradicated the same as Nazi-ism was and with a definite finalizing, all out, undeterred force. A 'Boots on the Ground' decision is the only effective method to eradicate repeated maiming and death before the terrorists receive far more dangerous weapons than small arms and conventional explosives. The politicians in recent power have proved that they are incapable of ending terrorism.

Final Solution

WW II Germany and Japan were terroristic worldwide. It took two atomic bombs to change the Samurai mindset of the country almost overnight. A leader, President Truman decisively ended a long war. Germany's unconditional surrender partition into East and West dissolved 'the Sieg Heil of the Master Race after the 'No-hold-Back, No –Safe-Havens' all-out military effort. Is it going to take such a catastrophe against the Free Nations to finally awaken the resolve of Western Europe and our nation to finally utilize sheer, effective, ending action? Those politicians who fail to act before an entire city or several are totally destroyed will have that city's blood on their memories after being thrown out of office. Such is not mere fantasy what every fanatic terrorist who is capable of being so religiously bent that he can blow himself up today has as his primary goal if he had the means to do so. Worse, such weapons exist and will be available sooner or later unless the terroristic cancer is totally eliminated.

A new report from the Rand Corporation, stated that al Baghdadi's ISIS has lost most of the territory it once controlled.[87] Seth Jones, the lead author on the report and director of the International Security and Defense Policy Center at Rand, said in a statement that Islamic State's territorial losses indicate that it is evolving from an insurgent group to a clandestine organization that directs and inspires wide-ranging terrorist attacks which are mounted without any direct orders from ISIS leaders. The report outlined the territorial losses ISIS has suffered since 2014: ISIS has lost 57% of its territory and 73% of the people once under its control. At its peak in 2014, ISIS controlled nearly 30,000 square miles of territory containing a population of about 11 million. Rand's report suggested polling data indicates "declining support across the Muslim world for the Islamic State and its ideology." The group still has enough supporters, though, to be considered a serious threat to countries in the Middle East and around the world.

---

[87] Pamela Engel, "New report finds ISIS' caliphate 'is on a path to collapse'," *AOL News*, April 4, 2017, https://www.aol.com/article/news/2017/04/22/new-report-finds-isis-caliphate-is-on-a-path-to-collapse/22051067/

CHAPTER 18
UNDERSTANDING SPIRITUALITY AND CEREMONY

I love a people who keep the commandments
Without ever having read them or heard them preached
from the pulpit
-George Catlin, Artist who lived with the Plains tribes,
Explorer, Author. 1796-1872

Ceremonies for understanding Creator's Code

Ceremonies can help individuals to grow in their life's quest. Many ceremonies are universal. I hope the universal ceremonies can be rescued from some erroneously designed form of ownership in order that all creeds and tribes may rightfully enjoy the blessing of our common ceremonies.

I believe ceremony was the Indian's tool to hone one's intuitive abilities. They enable you to be assured of your perspectives toward truth. After all, one is seeking the highest Truth- Creator! Why would I take mere man's words over all what is daily available from all knowledgeable Creator?

Sun Dance

A Sun Dance certainly hones one's intuitive abilities but yet I am not so gullible or zealously moved to expect many non-tribal folk to participate in or begin such although an increasing number are so doing. We are not praying to the sun as many ignorant historians/anthropologists tend to portray us. We are simply beseeching to our Higher Power concept just as Christians and Moslems attempt to communicate essentially in Church or Mosque. We could easily chide White Man and foolishly ask- "Why do you go inside to pray to Great Spirit who is all around you outside?"... but we are too polite to do so.

This final chapter is for the reader to increase their knowledge about a people who had far less terrorism among them. Their leaders were far more superior to be preventive of such. It is unquestionably worthwhile to learn as much about them and apply facets of their society to one's own lifestyle to move on toward a more harmonious role for the planet. If Creator is All Knowledge then we should attempt to learn as much as we can from the exemplary societies which cultivated a sounder, satisfying and more harmonious lifestyle. What harmoniously worked for other societies, the Celtics for example, should be and needs to be explored. Riane Eisler, *The Chalice and the Blade* (San Francisco, Harper Collins, 1987), tells us of a Bronze Age Society that lived for centuries. Millennia actually, in relative freedom and harmony wherein the females played active leadership roles. Later, the Celtic Age held similar gender respectful lifestyle in their humanitarian society that ruled much of Europe until a devious religious hierarchy arose to obliterate it.

Ceremony- the Sun Dance

A sun dance 'pledger' is one who participates directly under the guidance of the Sun Dance Intercessor (leader), usually your tribal Holy Man or respected Medicine person. People gather and they pray also, along with the sun dancer. This was usually an annual event to thank Creator for all that was allowed to the people for their livelihood and shelter. I have participated directly as a pledger, as mentioned several times in this work and definitely will verify that your spirit becomes deeply honed intuitively with the supernatural. The human body along with your memory bank- your mind, is moved intrinsically toward mystic intuition. Ceremony seems to be the catalyst. The staccato throb of drums and singers matched to the pulse beat of your heart beat stirs the sun dancer into an often spiritual exodus from this world. It is simply the way Creator designed us and most certainly all pledgers who have endured those four intense days of ceremony most often under a hot summer sun and fasting totally, no water and no food unless you are a Diabetic; Well… yes, they (one's fellow pledgers) will most likely agree with what I am having to say regarding becoming 'honed spiritually'.

Lone Cloud Sun Dance

While Senator Bernie Sanders was campaigning for presidency, a lone bird came down and landed fearlessly beside him. Quite possibly, such would indicate to Natural Way folks that the candidate's character, at least, was a bit more humanitarian/environmental. Traditional Indigenous would hold that this was a blessing sign from the Spirit World.

Similarly from Nature, I have witnessed a lone cloud appearing distantly on the horizon while I was in the midst of a Sun dance. It was a no-wind day and no other clouds were in the clear blue sky. We would be pierced within a few hours. That lone cloud slowly moved toward us as we took our turns waiting to be pierced through the skin of our chest and would remain standing, attached to the upper portion of the sun dance tree by our sun dance rope. See drawing. We would be giving our pain in atonement to Creator for answering affirmatively for a special request we had called out to Ultimate Maker. A safe return from war, (Vietnam, the Middle East) or an incurable' disease that became cured or maybe a simple appreciation to Great Spirit for a special healing allowance for one of our children have been reasons. Now we would give back. That lone cloud appeared right above us to end the ceremony as we broke free from a thong binding the rope to our chest; the football sized cloud raining lightly upon us and our surrounding crowd of supporters. Dis-believe if you must but many observable miracles happen in nature-based ceremonies. When you reach the Spirit World you can be verified.

No one owns Vision Quest

All of our ceremonies are simply an attempt to call upon, honor, acknowledge, and/or show appreciation to the Great Mystery. In one ceremony (Chapter 16) we actually experience communication with Creator's helpers- Spirits or Wahnagi (wah nah zhhe). Yes, Ceremony! I can understand why the Indigenous of the past maintained their solid, unbending choice to never question Creator's major reason for why and how Two-legged should travel upon his Earth journey. To travel harmoniously is that journey.

'Evil Spirits?'

We Traditional Sioux do not acknowledge or believe in bad spirits despite the missionaries' constant insistence that somehow we need to have them. Our Creator concept does not allow such. Creator's realm, this earthly abode we presently are in and the spiritual one beyond, is completely positive- our view which its total Creation definitely exhibits. Where in God's Nature do you find White Man's so termed 'Evil'? Creator is All Truth and All Knowledge is it not? Untruth (imaginary Evil Spirits) is not within Creator's allowance, its Beyond World, is our reasoning. We have the opportunity to 'See' into that Beyond World and so far we never encounter the Wahshichu's Devil! Man's 'Evil Spirits' are Man's allowance, his invented creation —our view. Are hurricanes, a tornado, earth quakes, a spewing volcano, a Great White shark encircling your boat, or a marauding man eating Bengal some sort of 'Evil'? Earth quakes/volcanoes are results of Creator's absolute, scientific laws within It's realm of Physics as are extreme meteorological winds. A tiger or shark stalking you as a candidate for its food chain is not 'Evil' per se.

There is nothing 'Evil' regarding an animal needing or stalking for its needed food.

Vision Quest is a ceremony that was practiced by many tribes down through time and not just the Native Americans. Vision Questing or spending an isolated time out in Nature is not owned by any Indian tribe although some may think they do. The Christians claim their Jesus did fast and pray out in the wilderness. Moses, I understand, went out alone to a mountain to commune with his concept of the Higher Power. I did the same on Bear Butte Mountain to fulfill my instructions from Chief Fools Crow through Chief Eagle Feather. "Go up on the mountain and fast and pray before the next sun dance." These were my instructions.

I had a rather startling quest. A rattlesnake actually snapped a portion of my peace pipe off, on a dark stormy night, just below the bowl where the pipe maker had carved an ax blade. The top portion of the pipe was a bowl for peace and the ax was for war. I blocked the snake's hissing strike with my pipe when it struck. I had been a combat warrior but now was no longer such, the ax portion was snapped flush.

When I told my experience to Fools Crow he raised nary an eyebrow and calmly sent me to Chief Eagle Feather in a nearby reservation with the simple words, *"Wah ste aloh!"* (It is good!) I was a bit perplexed but assumed he considered me as more of Chief Eagle Feather's student and politely did not want to interfere.

Chief Eagle Feather was slightly more informative once I described my vision. "You had a good vision quest, Nephew. You were on the path of war flying that big war machine. Now you are on a different warrior's path. You have to fight for the return of our Old Way." He waved back toward where the year's annual event was about to begin within a couple of weeks. "Now you get your things ready for the Sun Dance." I concluded that you should not expect a holy person to give you a detailed explanation of your quest (if there is any). Your own observations are what are most important. Did not Jesus, as I asked earlier, supposedly go out in the desert and do the same?

Sweat Lodge (Inipi)

Sweat Lodge is becoming a popular ceremony and not only participated within by Native Indigenous. Many non-Indians join with Indigenous or conduct the ceremony themselves. I have probably conducted several hundred such 'lodges' from Australia to Sweden, Holland, Germany, U.K and our own U.S.A. of course. By far, many times the eager participants were mostly non-Indigenous. The ceremony consists of a blanket or tarp covered lodge. In the 'Free Days' my tribe used once abundant Buffalo hides for covering a sapling framed supportive structure usually enabling 10 to 20 participants to sit cross legged within. A fire is built to heat stones approximately the size of a cantaloupe. A foot and a half diametric pit, approximately, and as deep is dug in the center of the dirt lodge floor for heated rocks. After a prayerful beseeching opening to Great Spirit, the participants crawl into the covered structure and sit in a circle around the pit. A small drum is used to call out an opening song not unlike what church service people attend, usually to some musical instrument. A bucket of water awaits with a dipper or hollowed horn for throwing water over the hot stones. Steam arises to eventually bring out the participant's sweat as in a Sauna. Actually, Sweat Lodge is a spiritual sauna. Individual prayers are issued to the stimulating atmosphere that is so much more nature based than sitting through an hour's church service. This is a frequent comment made by first time, awed participants. Bear in mind, most North American Indigenous, at least of East Coastal area origin, have no 'Evil Spirits' within our religious/spiritual concepts.

Blank Condemnation

In the interest of abating Terrorism, the 'My Way Only- Right or Wrong' attitude is basically responsible for the overzealous narrow minded down through time. Such terrorism feeds on dangerous jihadist/crusading, demanding religious triumphalism which we should have learned by now. Blank condemnation without direct observation is commonly not accurately conducive toward a needed harmonic world of all faiths and not just one. Please attempt needed open mindedness rather than errant chastisement. Quite possibly you will possibly hone and earn a more fruitful life in that Spirit World beyond if you do. Nature is harmonic; is it not? That indicates to me that Creator desires that we should reflect the same.

Track Record

Participation in Vision Quest, Sweat Lodge and Sun Dance recently affected my grandnephew. I saw a profound integration of newfound confidence and pride when I conversed with him after he finished his Vision Quest and Sun Dance under the tutelage of a Sioux medicine man. His father, my Nephew had no problems with alcohol but decided to pledge the sun dance in Thanksgiving for his son's sudden change for the better after his first sun dance. "I simply wanted to thank Creator for my son's successful turnaround." My nephew went on to do ten annual sun dances and would bring his construction equipment down to the Oglala reservation pre-ceremony to help dig latrines and set-up the shade bower for viewers and pledge supporters. I have another nephew who lost his driver's license due to alcohol. As a four year pledger, which is customary for the addicted, he has not touched alcohol for years because of his many Sun Dances and related ceremonies. One is not limited to four years, however.

All these young men are now much better prepared for life. The ordinary quarrels and pettiness of daily living have little meaning to them; they have higher goals. This transformation has definitely honed their intuitive abilities. My nephews were not sitting and listening in some academic Indian Studies classroom; usually from a Christian Indian (the Indian Studies Directors) who have never participated or understands our Way. My relatives were out upon Mother Earth in all three ceremonies, Sweat Lodge, Vision Quest and Sun Dance. Physically they were immersed in a totally different medium than what Dominant Society experiences especially when it comes to addiction programs. Most counselors I have talked to admit that the ceremonial approach is far more successful. The Veterans Administration, at least in the Mid-west and western states, allows sweat lodge facilities to be built on VA grounds. Many prisons, including the Pennington County jail in Rapid City, have sweat lodges for their prisoners suffering from alcoholism and drug abuse. Again, if it works, do not attempt 'Fixing.'

I stood in the arena during the breaking time, holding my nephew's pipe. The drum beat was mesmerizing, powerful, haunting. The dancers, mostly young men, went in to touch the tree four times, as I had done decades before. Under that vast western sky, many memories returned, of the old sun dances past. Detractors can condemn and criticize our ceremony but it works! Do not attempt to fix what is not broken.

On my grand nephew's third year, toward the fulfillment of his four year pledge, I was called upon to be one of the pipe acceptors near the ending of the ceremony. The sun dancers bring forth their pipes to the acceptors. My mind went back to decades before when three acceptors, accepted our pipes and only eight of us were pledgers. One was a woman. I remember her name. Mary Louise Defender. It is an arduous, tough sun dance near Kyle, where Chief Fools Crow, now deceased once lived. We call it the Marine Corps/Airborne of all the sun dances. It is very demanding of the one hundred and more pledgers but so deeply powerful.

I am so fortunate to view such beautiful four day ceremonies and witness pride and confidence when I see the strong young sun dancers with the medicine people. Yes, I am deeply proud that I stood up for the Way, way back then under the tutelage of Fools Crow and his close ally, Chief Eagle Feather, when so very few showed their colors. Our Way will definitely live, is the message I receive.

There are many who are influenced by the Natural Way and their numbers grow each day. The environmental dilemma is making people extremely concerned about their future and the future of the generations unborn. The inability of organized religion to address these serious environmental matters with their denying, ignoring written words has been a decisive factor in pushing more people toward natural revelation. The apathetic attitude towards the world population explosion, the continual fighting between religious factions, and lack of leadership opportunities for women, are illustrative of many disappointments that are frustrating organized church members. Our country's entire population witnesses the pathetic presidential candidates every four years. Not one, except Senator John McCain, is a combat veteran or volunteered for the active military services. Climate Change, Planetary Heating, record setting weather abnormality is becoming too evident to deny despite Church denial. Of course Terrorism is showing worldwide the futility of fighting repeatedly over what is sheer mystery. People are seeking a closer connection to their Creator while they travel their life's journey. They want to feel and understand a relationship that is much deeper and broader than mere church kinship, blood kinship or bloodied kinship.

Environmental-minded people who exited or never had strong religious ties are considering the Natural Way as a spiritual means to connect to an admitted Great Mystery power. I think that the majority of those who are seeking to walk this path are finding satisfaction with what they are discovering. I do not know how many followers there are because it would be too difficult to count them. Only a rare few ever leave once they discover how powerful Nature based revelation can hone one's spiritual abilities. They are not registered or listed like church membership rolls are. Every dawn the numbers increase significantly. Just go to your bookstores and see the many topics that are addressed in this area, whereas but a few decades ago little information was available.

Membership

Many Europeans are highly respectful of indigenous thought and ceremony, especially the Germans. No membership list exists for them either and I hope that such a record is never devised. For thousands of years, Natural Way people performed exemplary earth stewardship without becoming organized. They avoided electing some sort of titular head who would be eventually ordained in grandiose costume and accoutrements with vast imaginative powers; bestowed by Man, of course.

Spiritual Clues

My spirituality is easy to relate to. I can taste, touch and feel my spirituality every day. Each separate subjected direction has an effect and I easily relate to what the Six Powers represent. It is easier to relate to your planet when you presume that the Earth and Sky are your Mother and Father and each Creator made direction bears each season's differing affect upon your planet. Winter so different from summer. The whole universe is an expression of Wakan Tanka; the Great Spirit, at least to Traditional Indigenous and now our growing non-Indian allies.

I have to hunt, make shelter, protect, give away and provide. While I am about such tasks my mind is immersed in a particular skill or calling and my spirituality is not in intense focus. What is at hand is my occupational and providing focus. If one must live one cannot be consistently pulling at a rosary or kneeling on a prayer rug. Once, in time of war, I had a warrior focus. At times that focus had to be very intense. In the height of combat you must be extremely focused, otherwise you do not survive. Overall, I try to participate in life's functions with respect and acknowledgement because all of your life is a measurement. If I take a four legged or catch a finned, I tell it that I am taking it to provide and I thank it. Many finned I put back into the water and let them go. I can still laugh, play and make mistakes, many mistakes like all humans do. I hope that I never get so caught up with my occupation or travels that I lose the ability to admit that I still make mistakes, commit errors and do a "dumb thing" every so often. When there is time to focus on contemplation, however, then my spirituality comes into a stronger centralization. Introspection is a powerful word to me.

How do I honor or praise Creator?

I attempt to recognize all which Great Ultimate provides for us. Recognition, acknowledgement, being thankful is more important to me than mumbling prayer. How it has designed us and our surroundings so that we can blend in with harmony and positive thought or action I try to contemplate. For example: I realize that I can taste. All foods have differing flavors therefore Great Provider gifts us such pleasing variety. I can see in color. Life would go on if we saw only in black and white as some scientists claim dogs see. Likewise a few people are stricken with the disability of losing taste. Life goes on for them as well. How bounteous that Creator allows us such a myriad of taste - a peach, plum, orange, or banana. Creator made every one of us with differing features (except for Twins). Yet Twins do not have the same exact memories, no one has in the entire planet for all have had differing experiences that go on implanted with new experiences day into day. If we happen to be cut, the wound heals and only the scar remains. A broken or sprained arm becomes immobile. Creator allows pain to remind us not to use that appendage until it heals. A healed appendage no longer emits pain and evolves to normal usage. When one encounters extreme pain, one usually faints or 'passes out'. Such a considerate or kind blessing Creator allows for us. I dislocated a shoulder one icy day. On the way being driven to the hospital emergency admittance I fainted and woke up with my shoulder being numb allowing for a successful and less painful setting. Creator allows pain killing drugs and anesthetics for our major operations and recuperation. The list could almost be endless what Creator allows for two-legged to have for added comfort while we trail down life's journey. None of my recognition or discovery gleaned from direct observation is in your Bible or Koran. No Church service, as an attending youth, did I ever hear such mentioned. Will Creator someday become so disgusted with such non-recognition or lack of appreciation that Natural catastrophe such as Climate Change and Planetary Heating will drastically punish human? If we are "Made in God's image," as most religionists proclaim do we not insist that at least our mates and our children dutifully recognize and acknowledge our efforts to live together? How do we feel when we are errantly, or wrongfully ignored?

Science warns we are heading in that direction. If the Yellowstone Caldera ever blows, American agriculture east of Wyoming will be destroyed by volcanic ash. A bit of appreciation should be sent to Creator every day and not just once a week, if any. Humans love to be appreciated and/or recognized for accomplishments or tasks performed. Creator has placed that want into us, does it not? Maybe IT is telling us that It doesn't mind some recognition as well. Most folks I have met are completely unconscious when it comes to emitting appreciation not only to attentive humans but to the Ultimate Provider as well. Go to your church services next week. See how often, Creator alone, as the Maker, is mentioned or recognized. They may mouth rote phrases but during my lifetime only a very few explain explicitly the many examples that verify It's Benevolence.

If a government has a moral leadership and respects and follows proper Earth stewardship- most often that country is able to feed its citizens adequately. Creator provides benevolently yet where leadership is non-harmonic with Nature and squanders its resources, those citizens starve and often perish. Worse, if it hides behind Religion and Man prophecy and does nothing to accept Direct Observation/Nature's Revelation until it becomes too late to apply effective remedy....Well, that is what is happening now. Such is not Creator's fault. It is Man's.

A couple of reasons why I am reluctant to follow blindly what missionaries try to tell me regarding conversion; I have often wondered why their highly touted Bible says nothing, at least not directly in plain common sense vernacular; Where are the Environmental prophecies that one would expect to shine forth in their Bible regarding Climate Change, Planetary Heating, obvious Over Population danger and Water Pollution/Shortage to name the major dilemmas? Too much water in the case of the oceans rising. If their Jesus is also immortal and Creator's son then I would suppose he would also possess all Knowledge like we Sioux suppose Creator to possess. Why is or was Jesus so mute regarding the so termed 'Four Horses of the Apocalypse? Their Jesus is profoundly silent in light of such major disaster forewarning versus so many minor issues brought forth by J C in comparison. Does such silence indicate that we Earthlings shouldn't harbor any environmental worry? The evangelical Churches primarily do deny considerably these major issues although the present Pope does not deny except for the over-population peril. I have nothing against J C as a mortal and the good example he supposedly set by his adherents and constant refrains for harmonic Truths which is well verified by his supportive peers but am I some sort of 'sinful' to ask common sense questions for the sake of truthful veracity or to encourage the world population to attempt living Creator's harmony? Creator through its Nature example has encouraged me to seek out 'all Truths' while on this journey. I sense commendation from such an encouraging, displayed presentation of dubious Truth from Creator's endless exhibits rather than punishing chastisement.

My tribal friend, Wampanoag elder, Medicine Story tells about the Original Instructions that were handed down to his tribe. He remarked that most people who have an ancient oral tradition speak of such Original Instructions as having been issued from the Creator. Through these Original Instructions, the ancestral people related to their present life. His lineage is from an eastern tribe. There exists a commonality of belief with both of our tribes.

*   *   *   *

Medicine Story

"It is this concept of Original Instructions that most profoundly distinguishes native spiritual belief from all man-made religions of the world. The Original Instructions are not ideas. They are reality. They are actually Natural Law, the way Things Are—the operational manual for a working Creation. They cannot totally be explained in words. They must be experienced. Native People refer to the Original Instructions often in speech and prayer, but rarely attempt to say exactly what they are. They are not like the Ten Commandments carved in stone by a stern authority figure. We have no scriptures, no sacred books to be studied and argued over. The Original Instructions are not of the mind. They are of the spirit, the essence of Creation. Other creatures follow them instinctively. They are communicated to humankind through the heart, through feelings of beauty and love. We observe Nature, we tune in to the spirits and feel the creator's law all around us, silent, mysterious and immutable.

"The people of this continent at one time tried to live their lives according to these Original Instructions. They did not always succeed. They were human beings and were not perfect, but growing and learning like the rest of us. But their lives were structured around these Original Instructions: individual consciousness, family life, social organizations, educational and political and spiritual ways were all in harmony. Despite the frightening tales of the invaders, most of the over five hundred nations of this continent were among the most pacific people that ever inhabited the earth. Here in the Northeast our people created federations of peace that were in place when Alexander was trying to enslave Asia for the Greeks. The Houdinosonie to the west of us created the first United Nations in the world and a peace that has lasted among them for a thousand years. But the Great Law of Peace was not written down. It was kept in the hearts of the People of the Longhouse, so that the spirit, which was attuned to the spirit of Creation, would never be lost. [88]

In Harmony with themselves.

"The first people were in harmony with themselves and all Creation because theirs was not written law. There were no Ten Commandments to be broken, no statutes for police to enforce and lawyers to find loopholes in. An ancient Chinese sage once said, "Where there is no law, there will be no criminals." Human laws create criminals, because they create opposition—they are based on fear and not love. The more laws, the lower the level of trust, and human community functions best on trust. Natural Law enforces itself, there are no loopholes in it. Four hundred years ago on this continent there was no need for a legal profession, and there was no such thing as a criminal profession. [89]

"No one lived by hurting others. The Original Instructions are to be found in no book for the scholars to dispute. They are in our hearts, all the time. We all know what is right. You know what is right. You know when you are doing wrong. And when people point out to someone that he has made a mistake and hurt someone, if they are not condemning but helpful, that person will do anything he can to repay the hurt he has caused in order to feel good about himself again.

"There is no cruelty in the wilderness, in Nature, without human beings. Animals are never cruel. They do not act out of spite or revenge. They do not carry anger or fear beyond the appropriate moment. Only human beings think and understand with their minds that they must die. But with this understanding comes the knowledge of the Original Instructions. For we are the only beings on this earth that can feel and know Beauty in our hearts. When through our acts we create ugliness and imbalance and bad feelings we know this is not the Way of Creation. When we create Beauty and Joy and Love we feel good. Our hearts tell us we are in harmony and in good balance.[90]

*   *   *   *

Medicine Story gives us more deep wisdom that is so appropriate to our journey which we travel on this planet. He tells us that people who

---

[88] Manitonquat (Medicine Story), *Return to Creation*, (Bear Tribe Publishing, Spokane, Washington, 1991), p. 45
[89] Ibid p. 47-48
[90] Ibid p. 48

live very close to the earth and the natural order of things are very simple and very real. "I believe that they are the most happy on this earth." He tells us that the original people of this land embrace the essential spiritual and mysterious nature of the universe. Things are as they are. Whatever is, certainly is.

"Even though the Original Instructions are not written out in some book or scroll of the law, we can perceive them at work through the observation of Nature and by the experience of the people over the continuum of time, transmitted to each generation by tribal lore, ceremony, song and story. This is how we are one in a circle of time with our ancestors and with the unborn generations to come.

"Thus the Original Instructions suggest to us not only the reality, the "is-ness," of all experience and all things, but also their relatedness. All is one circle. We feel a kinship with everything. Animals, plants, stones, mountains, rainbows and stars are all to be addressed as relatives. Even those things which appear strange or frightening in lore or experience have some history, if we can discern it, which connects them in some unknown way to the circle. They have a necessary place.

"This is why we think and live in a realm of circles. We see circles in all of Nature. We gather together in a circle, we think of our communities as circles, of the races of humankind as a circle. The physical structure of the cosmos, from the smallest particle to the very walls of the universe, is a circle. And all these circles are part of one Great Circle of Existence."[91]

Can one convert to this religion, and do members of the Natural Way witness or try to convert others? There is absolutely no attempt to convert others to this spirituality. How would one bring about this conversion? Why would one want to attempt to erase another's accumulated knowledge upon their Disk of Life? What would we do? Pour wild rice or corn pollen over your heads?

Boarding Schools

I think about my brothers and sisters all being taken to boarding school in the fall except for my sister Delores. We would not see them for a long time. A main emphasis at those schools was to convert and stamp out the Indian religion, our natural spirituality. How unnatural (Going against God's Harmony) to separate little children at the age of

---

[91] Ibid p. 53

five and six from their parents to foster assimilation and conversion. Tragic results; Three generations at least, no doubt four or more were denied vital higher academic knowledge to advance onward into the White Man's world. Like giving me a gun to hunt and survive but no bullets. Instead they gave us a worthless Jesus for job hunting to attempt to assimilate or attempt to cultivate a providing occupation. None of my brothers or sisters could qualify for the White Man's higher learning institutions. The White Man saw to it that we could not develop equivalent leaders within his rules, his laws, his acceptance. Yes. Instead he gave us Jesus. Jesus for all his supposed powers we were never specially graced as they promised; Jesus, like Joel Osteen, never came to deliver all those fantasized promises he was supposed to bring. Maybe it was not his fault but those who used his name to make false promises. Their zeal never gave a thought as to the damage they would be doing.

I think of the two little harmless dark specks sneaking into the back of that big cathedral because of the word—conversion. We were afraid and in fear that we would lose our souls as a result of what we were told. We were also in fear because we were meat eaters. We were so poor that often the only food in the house was deer meat or wild cotton tail rabbits which my brothers had provided. Breakfast, dinner and supper, we ate this deer meat or rabbits or the chickens we raised. Besides, we preferred it over many of the white man's staples. We were taught to be in fear if we ate this meat on a Friday, and yet it was all that we had besides some potatoes or maybe corn. Would God actually put two little innocent Indian children in a burning hell simply because we did not attend a white man's ceremony or ate food according to our own customs and what was only available? The Confessionals, I could go on and on. Spirit does not indicate to me that It would do such a thing. Later in life I came to reason how utterly foolish this child imposed charade had been composed and dropped upon us. Yes, and their purgatory too which they now never talk about.

There must have been a bunch of sacrosanct, memory sick, patriarchal old men, attempting to extend their personal power, who came up with these ideas; scaring little kids and actually the whole world with these goofy ideas that never considered the depth of Nature's revelations. Many intelligent people now laugh at and make fun of these bizarre pronouncements. Even their own flock makes fun of these 'imprimatur-ed' rulings. (Imprimatur means sanctioned by the 'infallible' Pope.) Strange written rulings and proclamations actually existed and were not mere suggestions of some fanatical zealot. They were carefully scrutinized, studied and forwarded on to higher authorities who were supposedly more learned. They even gave out compensation in purgatory, "100 days plenary indulgence from the suffering of purgatory for attending a church event." This promise was printed on pamphlets calling attention to certain events (novenas) if you attended them. Purgatory is some human-devised place where your spirit is supposed to go and suffer for an untold amount of time.

I want no part of a system that repels direct observation and daily providing knowledge gathering from what a Higher Power so openly displays for us to learn from. Worse, one that blatantly ignores the All Maker, the Creator in their daily or at least weekly prayers. I have rejected this attempt at conversion. I hope that people will never spawn these kind of man-made fears in the Natural Way. Think all things over before you make proclamations. If you have a vision or a dream, keep it to yourself for a while and think it over. Learn from Black Elk. He had a powerful vision yet kept it to himself for a long period of time. How does it affect the tribe, Mother Earth and the Generations Unborn? Will it move me toward, direct knowledge from the Creator? Will it promote the Harmony that Creator's Harmonic creation- Nature so openly displays and which is so directly observable? These are highly important questions to ask yourself when you find yourself being fed religious information.

Human's Beyond

Yes- what report will one give to Creator whom I suspect will ask (and already have the answer), "What did you do to promote the Harmony I placed all around you? What did you do to make example for others? What did you do with your offspring?" The olde time Indian I strongly suspect was immersed with preparing their selves for that Beyond World. Yes, they somehow were deeply penetrated (subconsciously?) with the ever present guiding thought of pleasing this Mystery Maker; It's desire to have him (The North American Indigenous) constantly conscious of such an honorable and responsible quest. They made the most profound discovery ever! Terrorism, Dictatorship, Environmental Chaos, a high degree of basic Unhappiness, Selfishness, and brutal Crimes could dramatically be reduced! The spiritually based leader most often does not convey Terrorism to the degree that the numerous religiously posing ones project. Simply look at history.

How will you arrive at such a profound acceptance, overwhelming, lifelong, enduring, pursuit? Most of us won't from what I see daily on most internet pages. The vast majority of two-legged are blankly, numbly driving up and down the Interstate consumed with material gain and nary a thought of an afterlife.

As sterling proof, remember, it was the early Indigenous who came down to their own shores and kept a totally opposite valued, at odds religiously conceptualized people successfully through their first winter and on into Spring to teach them to plant and fertilize new crops. Contrary wise such charity would not have been exhibited had these Indigenous sailed up the Rhine or Thames to establish a colonizing campsite. Whoa! .... and to profess One God only as a fathomless Mystery! Obviously these Indigenous had risen to such a Harmonic lifestyle here when the Wahshichu first arrived and which the European's inhibiting, empathy less, blocking ego is never loath to admit.

This life was a mere preparation for that higher and hopefully endless one Beyond and damn well did Creator get it across to them. Surrounding Nature, (featureless of castles and cross topped structures of control and thence later bricks and stone roadways to God minus oblivion), provided obvious spiritually enhanced Ethics, Morals, Honor; all honed through Direct Observation of God's observable and teaching Creation. Selfless leaders evolved to govern an appreciating truly democratic people. This 'Nature respecting way acquired and perpetuated by early Indigenous has now blossomed forth into many of the colonizing progeny who realize the environmental danger confronting the planet. Standing Rock Sioux tribe's confrontation with the White Man's dangerous greed is an example of all those awakened people bravely working together not for materialism but for the future generation's God given right to inherit a clean watered Mother Earth. Nature's Spirituality, which early White Man at Plymouth Rock could never see or admit less: inherit or apply, has survived.

Do you feel your religion (Spirituality) is superior over all others and why is this religion right for you?

It is dangerous to state that your religion is superior to all others although I am reluctant to follow a folly filled, life's excursion trusting solely in Man's advisory guidance for my Spiritual journey vs what Creator can show me daily. Especially so, since abhorring gullibility, I have to weigh in Man's abysmal non-harmonic, non-humanistic Track Record and where it has led us today. False superiority, religious triumphalism is how too many wars have started and are still being fought. Why antagonize another over what is Mystery? Why should I foolishly insist that you should attend a Sun Dance to save your soul? Why should I make a Mecca out of a particular mountain when you live in Florida and have no mountains! I might be adamant that I believe in one Creator but I cannot insist that you should. Why? Because by now one should assume that I also recognize that Mystery, the Great Mystery cannot be clearly defined nor is it limited to only one attempted description. Could it be the Six Powers of Black Elk's Vision? Who knows? Meanwhile I am satisfied with stating simply and comfortably- It is a Creator, Maker or what have you.

To tell of happenings that you would not like to have repeated, may antagonize others but if you are doing this in the interest of truthful prevention of dis-harmony, then you should be commended. The Jewish people do not want the Holocaust or the blatant crowd ignition of racist two-legged behind it to return. They tell their story, even movies, *Schindlers List* or *Ben Hur* for example, and have every right to if we believe that human decency should honor all beings. We Indians have a right to tell our story do we not? We tell it so that the atrocities put upon us do not reoccur. We tell of the Boarding Schools and Wounded Knee so Dominant Society will understand why we were set back several generations. Their emphasizing of their religion over needed academic preparation has done serious damage to the Sioux. Do not accuse us of 'Being angry' if we simply, like the Jews, seek to tell preventive Truth. I tell of Canton Insane Asylum and Boarding school atrocity and academic omission and am banned from the my state's annual author's book fair by the state of South Dakota Humanities Commission of all agencies if you can believe such yet Creator or the Spirits and of course readers still propel me along as a leader in annual book sales over other South Dakota living authors Indian or non-Indian enough so that I can make a coveted, appreciated living at it. A living that many would enjoy due mainly for the freedom it provides. I refuse to alter, diffuse, subjugate, or obsequiously bow down to their constitutional; violating, religious demanding triumphalism that banned our own innocent and more fruitful Nature based spirituality.

Standing Rock Sioux Reservation – Corporate Terror

Many good non-Indians flocked by the thousands to Standing Rock reservation to fight back in a non-armed manner against the DAPL (Dakota Access Pipe Line) which will eventually pollute pure water as all oil pipelines manage to do. Canadian based DAPL was guarded by the North Dakota law enforcement agencies and sprayed water upon the peaceful demonstrators in freezing weather. Corporate greed and dangerous pollution is also Terroristic when it deprives human of their water supply not to mention crossing across sacred burial grounds. In DAPL's case, the pipeline is not needed at present. There is a glut of oil on the world Energy Market. Why take the chance to destroy the length of South Dakota's Missouri River prime Wall Eye fishing as well, let alone other sport species game fishing? If there exists no logistical need for such a danger filled intrusion, why risk such a drastic danger filled venture?

I have been so fortunate to have a surrounding creation which gave me the clear mountain stream where I could swim as a child and the miles of room where I could walk and grow. Sioux traditions developed a kind mother and father who raised me in a happy home despite the surrounding prejudice and false stereotypes that we had to live within emanating from a surrounding reservation border town. I honor the millions of people who lived this nature-respecting lifestyle down through time, down through generation upon generation; each being contributing to the accumulating knowledge within those native people who were here when the first colonizing Europeans came to North American shores. The honor, the bravery, generosity and above all, the truthfulness of those Sioux warriors and women out on the Great Plains was shaped by their ancestors as well. The great gift to humanity—democracy from the Iroquois- was honed by those ancient and evolving ancestors who discovered that key of harmony within all of nature's knowledge. They held firmly to Creator's principles- All Truth, All Knowledge, All Harmonic and definitely- It was a sheer Mystery! If they held to Truth and Knowledge, surely, Harmony would follow. Nature is very democratic and equal. It is not difficult for me to understand why this gift could come from a natural, Nature Based system. Two legged American, however, takes it for granted and knows not who, what people should be given credit for its discovery and implementation. Their ego and false sense of superiority prevents their admittance. As mentioned before, instead they fantasize its formation from slave states- Greece and Rome. TIME Magazine recently claimed such in one of their 2015 Man of the Year article resumes. Yet the immigrants knew nothing about the already implemented, in-practice governmental Democracy Indian tribes were enjoying when they first arrived here.

I must always strive to learn from the underlying theme of these Natural Way based people who actually existed and are not some mere, romantic myth or a fairy tale of magic wands. A pristine environment standing tall with stately trees amid clear flowing streams while further west in this hemisphere's heartland, the Mississippi ran blue, and not muddied, chemically saturated brown. Such is solid proof that they were truly in harmony when the Pilgrims first landed. No detractor can honestly deny this harmonious, environmental fact.

I thank the Great Spirit, Wakan Tanka, that the majority of these native peoples who once trod these lands; I thank you oh Mystery that they did live in the relative freedom of Nature. I am thankful that most of the natural people did experience a complete life out within the comforting yet challenging embrace of the Earth Mother in a time of clean streams and rivers, clear lakes, no endangered species and a land that needed no chemicals to bring forth bounty from planted seeds. Yes and far fewer diseases which increase among us annually, Cancer mainly and also Alzheimer's, Multiple Sclerosis, Parkinson's and Arthritis to name a few. All of these were rare among the early Indigenous. No doubt it was their untainted, non-biotic, non-Monsanto engineered and manipulated foods. They lived this life far longer than counting the first day of the Pilgrims to the day we have now. Yes, far longer, generation upon generation was basically enjoyed. Diabetes, the main life killer of tribal Indigenous now was almost non-existent.

These last few centuries of terrible change are but an eye wink of time in comparison. We are so caught up with our so-called modern lives that there is little realization that family upon family lived out their own lives back in time just as importantly as we consider ours. These families laughed, played, hunted, planted and provided. They took from the daily communion of Father Sky and the Earth Mother. They beseeched, acknowledged, honored and recognized the Higher Power. There was no Monsanto corporation back then. I think that they laughed and played more than we in this modern era. Their bodies and minds were healthier and they were also free from addictions. That in itself could lead one to laugh and play. Above all, in answer to our present dilemma, they give us the confidence to know that a workable way did exist for two legged habitation upon this planet. Can human now build upon such long lived reality with confidence that it will, it can be returned?

I associate strongly with this past but I also realize that I am in a different time span. The whole landscape has even changed. This time span is fraught with serious environmental disaster. The present world situation that I confront has given me a mission, an essential purpose. I can even couple my concept of the beyond world into this mission. That is why I am comfortable with this spirituality or this religion, if you will. It certainly feels right for me.

In all honesty, Dear Reader, I do not expect you to leave your religion for our Spirituality. Father Bill Stolzman never thought he had to. Neither did my Mother. You are too steeped in your Way for substantial change or adaptation. Maybe some can adapt, a few, as is happening due mainly to less control by Organized Religion. Within some countries; some will accept Spirituality and appreciate the information within this work. However for the vast multitudes to come over to Traditional Spirituality would be like the concept of a zealous, proselytizing Christian believing he can convert Islam. It isn't going to happen. Nor will the Catholics ever convert Israel even though they have a prayer stated repeatedly that ends with a calling to convert the Jews. Therefore I can only attempt to emphasize Terrorism and what we can possibly attempt to do positively about it along with challenging the equally significant environmental dangers that also confronts humankind. Both dilemmas can become life or death issues for humanity regardless of which path we have chosen. The two most dangerous issues facing civilization is obviously the ongoing planetary destruction which feeds from a Pope denied Overpopulation. The other - Terrorism.

Modern Communication, Modern Terrorism, Ultimate Eradication, Incapability vs Proven Track Record.

1.   To kill the Blue Man of Black Elk's vision and help save the planet. This means that I must have the courage and bravery to share my knowledge and experiences. Others must realize that this modern communication is the greatest weapon which we have. The Blue Man is not the terrorist per Se. The Blue Man is here in our own land and, of course affiliates with the Blue Men who control other lands. He smoothly operates without blatant terror yet his is a form of subtle, disguised terror for his tragic effect upon the populace is enormous. The controlling 1% in this land is so blatantly obvious that it needs little explanatory information to prove its existent. Sure as Bill Cosby has drugged women for illicit sex, America's destiny is controlled by Organized Religion in linkage

with the 1% of greed and control little different than why the European had to migrate but a few centuries ago. This Blue Man can care less what happens to his after life or the planet as long as they can live in luxury for at least their lifetime upon it.

2.   Modern terrorism cannot be ignored, however. That nemesis, its challenge, can more immediately become solvable than halting Climate Change or Planetary Heating. ISIS and related extremists have nowhere near the power of Nature which is simply reacting according to Creator's scientific reactions to man's foolish greed and ignorance; Man's chosen ability to ignore while Organized Religion denies. Too many pollutants caused mainly by overpopulation results in Planetary Heating and Climate Change. The formula is all fairly simple. Force is also fairly simple. Adequate force is capable and available to eradicate and free us from Terrorism. The realization by man that Creator is definitely a Mystery and no one religion is the only honorable ticket to the Spirit World will have to be accepted by Man before Terrorism will be subdued otherwise Terrorism will remain a smoldering fire waiting to flame back up again. Man has to learn and respect- Mystery or else remain plagued for an eternity. Force will have to be used to expediently remove the dangerously ignorant.

3.   There exists no sane reason to attempt foolish forgiving, political wordage only or Neville Chamberlain gullibility and related wish-list toothless gumming when terroristic leadership has well demonstrated it has become too opiated with extreme hatred and my-Way-only ji-hadist/crusade fomenting excess. Terrorism can be, will be - not should be - eradicated especially when the perpetrators continually attempt their terror. Presently, Nations have the power to abolish them. Once destroyed significantly Nations will have to abolish through preventive laws directly toward lethal weapon procurement. One major, major catastrophe- no doubt atomic based, let loose by or employed by Jihadists or over-zealous religious conversion-ists should provide enough of a catalysis to deliver their finalization. Brute, relentless, unforgiving force needs to be delivered. If leaders cannot find the courage or intelligence to do so then elect new ones. No wasteful, placating discussion is needed for this issue. Electronic stealth, localization and ground force communication are powerful weapons yet out of reach of the terrorists. Enough lessons from Vietnam and now Afghanistan should <u>teach how not to</u> fight terrorism. Wars directed toward the terrorist bases need to be fought from the wisdom of non-politically correct and surely not rank worried military

leaders. Meddling politicians need to be forbidden from combat decision making and journalists limited. Vietnamization of the military leadership – (How we were made to fight in Vietnam (and recently in Afghanistan and President Obama's recent policy/non-policy, if you will) should never be allowed to return. The Trillion dollar war venture against Iraq and not versus worldwide organized terrorism by the Bush/Cheney regime is just as guilty.

4.   Organized Religion has proven that it is not the pathway nor the vehicle to provide the inalienable Human Rights that a harmonic exhibiting, Benevolent Creator hopefully would desire from its rational gifted two legged to someday attain and wherein, controlling dictatorships will find it more difficult to thrive. Since fleeing to the Western Hemisphere, Earth based values have led those two legged to Democracy, indigenous humans greatest non-agrarian gift to fellow human, although the majority of Earth's populace have been led by these migrating non-Indigenous to erroneously mis-believe its true source. Harmony! It is the way Creator governs the Universe! Why should it not desire the same from human? Akin to democracy's freedom, man must learn the necessary undeterred focus to truly discover through his gifted mind the Earth based, spiritual ingredients to become led to this attainment. Organized Religion has had several thousand years, at least, without success. Compared to the proven history of Spirituality mainly via its exemplary, selfless leadership, Organized Religion's record is non-exemplary regarding honorable, compatible ethics, morality, and co-existence with Earth's Flora and Fauna. The further absence/neglect of such co-existence is supremely serious for such foolish neglect will surely prove fatal to humankind. Why were the Sioux leaders absent a harsh, controlling, brutal methodology employed to cruelly rule over their people as present dictators apply and condone. Most modern, dictators of today do not promote or attempt to live the harmonic lifestyle modeled by Indigenous leaders of the past. Chief Joseph, Seattle, Red Cloud and Sitting Bull, to name a few among many were honorable, illustrative examples. The non-indigenous elected leaders carved on Mount Rushmore, as well, thankfully were similar to the Indigenous. Founding Fathers were fresh from the perils of the Great Inquisition yet still active in Europe and Salem witch trials.

    In ending, I wish to restate that these <u>are not</u> necessarily the beliefs of all indigenous people. These are simply my perceptions of the Natural Way and how I was strongly influenced by many of Nature's persuasion, my teachers, and the exemplary living standards upheld by certain indigenous societies.

Environmentally, how has this information affected you, the reader? Terrorism has already killed/maimed thousands but the Environmental dangers have the potential to eradicate millions and the Flora and Fauna as well. We looked at a people who encompassed environmentalism within their spiritual beliefs. They had a spirituality that was very influential in their daily life style yet was not oppressive. It lasted for thousands of years. They, in North America, rarely practiced extreme terrorism, no doubt because of the blessed absence of an organized, man influenced denial and avoidance of Nature's daily, demonstrable teachings. Their values and Nature respecting lifestyle blended serenely in relationship to all other life surrounding them. They walked down to their shores to initially care for both the Roanoke Colony and later to save the Pilgrims through their first winter. In the Caribbean, the Arawak island Indians among other early inhabitants did similar for the European seagoing explorers (Hawaiian and Pacific Islanders). That is proof enough for me how far a nature based Spirituality can advance two-legged toward a harmonic humanity which mirrors the rest of Creator's creation.

North American Indians, primarily the north eastern coastal area tribes strongly influenced by Iroquoian Democracy and those tribes whom migrated inland to avoid the deadly diseases did cultivate a personal respecting fear to not jeopardize their entry and acceptance into that awaiting 'Beyond World'. Harmonic rewarding Codes, Honoring, Discipline and oft exhibited, ceremonial appreciation toward their mystery accepted Higher Power kept them thoroughly within the realm of Harmonic lifestyle while upon their Red Road path of a believed proving trial. Unaltered, non-tailored Truth became their guideline. They managed to cultivate solidly within their conduct towards others and the Flora and Fauna as well, a duty bound moral, ethical code exhibiting far beyond what the European and other immigrating societies displayed if track records are truthfully compared. Can Man return to such a Creator pleasing, true civilization saving Harmonic lifestyle?

Superstition absent Mother Nature (God's creation) will and is now so endeavoring; steadily moving toward this result whether Man cooperates or not. Over-population and resultant Climate Change/Planetary Heating is mathematically unavoidable; exponentially unavoidable, I must reiterate! Superstition bound Man will change! A bit slower than the surviving residents of Hiroshima and Nagasaki but steadily onward Nature is taking its correcting course. Nature will not be dependent upon Man's tailored 'Resurrection' no matter how many adherents clamor and portray. Man will be forced to develop a respecting 'Fear' if he finally must do so to survive. Knowledgeable Scientists will replace the superstition based religious fomenters in a not too distant time to come if Man chooses to live. Over population can be and has to be curtailed. Available land and agricultural fulfilling water has its limits that are fast becoming exhausted. Land does not magically multiply either. Human curtailment is the only reliable answer, not wishful prayer or superstition tailored by the futile control minded religious hierarchy.

Is the Spirit world totally reflected solely within Creator's all-encompassing harmony and devoid of Man influence? I hope so! Will the Harmonic seeking Man who walks his trail of trial positively 'Here' find a calm, serenity filled reward 'There'? Hopefully, you now have an understanding that we are a part of the whole universe, especially this planet. Mitakuye Oyasin. We are related to all things. Ho! Hetch etuh aloh. (It is so, indeed.)

MARIE BUCHFINK DRAWINGS

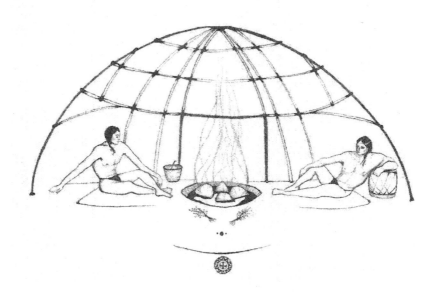

Sweat Lodge

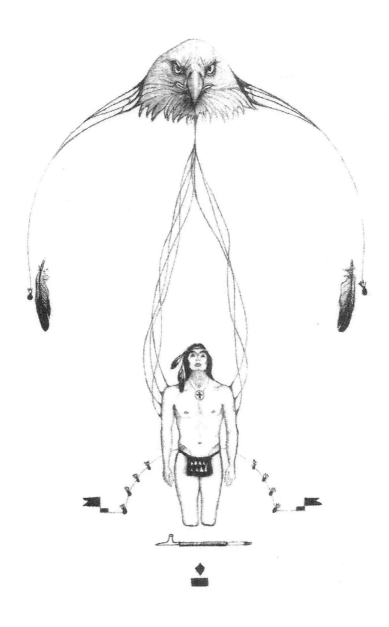

Vision Quest

Sun Dance

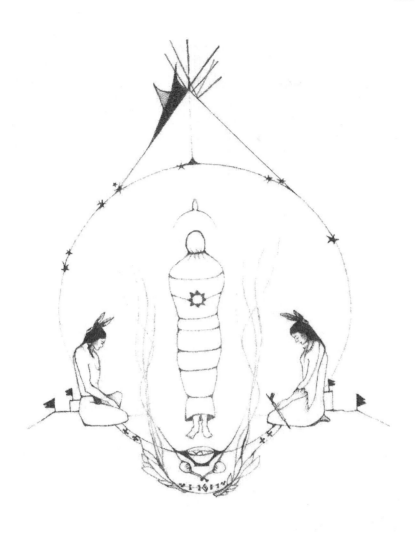

Spirit Calling

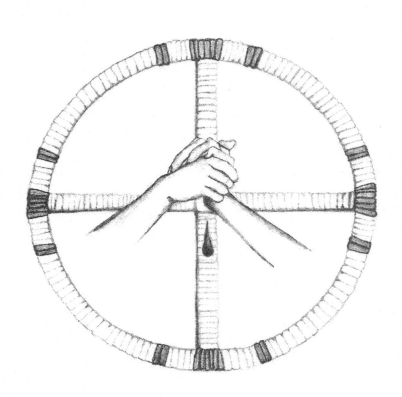

Making of Relative

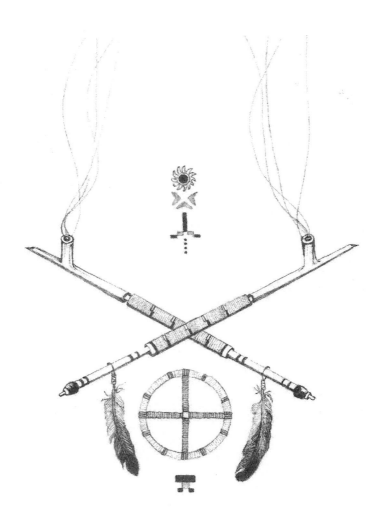

Pipe Ceremony

Animal, Winged Totems

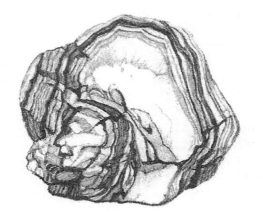

Wotai Spirit Stone

Peace Pipes & Bundles Burned by Cavalry

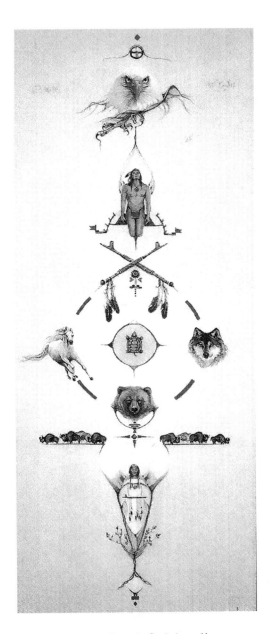

Mother Earth Spirituality

ADDITIONAL PHOTOS

Al Baghdadi

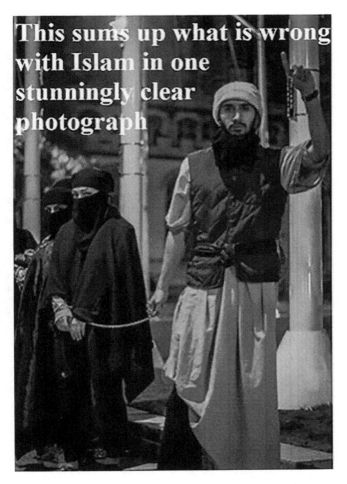

1st and foremost Commandment, "I am the Lord thy God. Thou shalt have no other Gods before me!"

Vietnam War – Ho Chi Minh and General Giap, attempted to arrange a meeting with Secretary of State John Foster Dulles. They simply intended to convey: 'All we wanted was for the French to get out of our country, so we fought them and won. Now we will have to fight you to have our whole country back. We will fight and win.' Dulles, so immersed in his errant, costly supremacist superiority, refused to meet. Over 50,000 American military lives were lost, many more maimed and wounded, mentally and physically. Innocent Vietnamese paid a higher price yet. America names its National Airport after the racist culprit who could have prevented the foolish, unquestionably wrong war. The least America can do for our wasted, lost military is to remove his name and replace it with an honorable one, a Hanoi Hilton POW, my recommendation.

Author - Oglala Sun Dance

Pete Catches, Chief Fools Crow, Chief Eagle Feather

Sweat Lodge

Sun Dance Tree

Asylum for Insane Indians, Canton, SD

OTHER WORKS BY ED MCGAA

Red Cloud: Biography of an Indian Chief

Mother Earth Spirituality: Healing Ourselves and our World

Rainbow Tribe: Ordinary People Journeying on the Red Road

Nature's Way: Native Wisdom for Living in Balance with the Earth

Eagle Vision: Return of the Hoop (Novel).

Native Wisdom: Perceptions of the Natural Way

Crazy Horse and Chief Red Cloud: Warrior Chiefs (Dakota West Books Rapid City, and New Leaf – Lithia Springs, GA).

Creator's Code: Planetary Survival & Beyond

Dakota Pheasant and Iowa too!

Calling to the White Tribe – Moon Books, London, UK

Spirituality for America: Learning Earth Wisdom from the Indigenous (Amazon)

Warrior's Odyssey: Biography (Amazon)

Black Elk Speaks IV- The Hidden Prophecy Revealed. (Amazon)

ABOUT THE AUTHOR

Ed (Eagle Man) McGaa, J.D., is a registered Teton Oglala, born on the Pine Ridge Sioux reservation and is the largest selling, non-fiction, living tribal enrolled Native American author. Following his childhood ambition, he became a Marine Fighter Pilot and flew 110 combat missions in Vietnam. He holds a law degree from the University of South Dakota and is the author of 13 books; including *Mother Earth Spirituality* (Harper Collins Publishers, 50 times reprinted*)*, *Nature's Way*, *Rainbow Tribe* (Harper/Collins), *Native Wisdom* (Council Oak Books) and 3 Amazon/Kindle books. His *Crazy Horse and Chief Red Cloud* is the best seller in the Dakotas. *Black Elk Speaks IV* reveals the Blue Man of Corruption, Greed and Environmental Disaster. The planetary destructive Blue Man is the heart of the Great Warning from Creator. Understandably, Climate Change and Planetary Heating was unknown back in the early thirties, when the original Black Elk Speaks was first published therefore the innocent author and Black Elk are exonerated for not knowing or understanding the major issue/warning within the Great Vision. Yet, oddly, such vital warning is not commented upon in the latter, modern era versions after their decease. Such is Dominant Society's too often, purposeful attempts to foolishly not accept from others. Therefore, as a member of Black Elk's tribe I had to include in detail the 'Blue Man Warning' within BES IV.

CONTRIBUTIONS

Military Religious Freedom Foundation (MRFF).

Mail checks to
Military Religious Freedom Foundation
ATTN: Support MRFF
13170-B Central Avenue, SE Suite 255
Albuquerque, NM 87123
EIN: 20-3967302

MAKE A DONATION TO MRFF ONLINE:
militaryreligiousfreedom.org/support-mrff/

Newsweek, May 22, 2017, breaking top lead story homepage features MRFF's fight in a lead investigation, Trumpian Radical Christianity in the U. S. Military, by award winning investigative journalist, Nina Burleigh.

RECOMMENDED READING

Books

The consequences of the modern, non-tribal evolving world severely limits the often required Nature space for certain Indigenous based ceremony. Understandably, it is difficult for some to leave one's faith, for another entirely. Therefore, the following two books are highly recommended.

The Pipe and Christ – Wm Stoltzman, former Jesuit.
Dakota West Books
Rapid City SD 57101

Deeper Thoughts in the Presence of God - Makenneth Stoffer
The most practical, pragmatic and rewarding Spiritual Writing I can recommend. Available at Amazon. Makenneth can be reached at makennethst@gmail.com, for future workshops and speaking on *Deeper Thoughts in the Presence of God.*

Ed McGaa's ability to convey the emotional traumas our nation has inflicted on its own indigenous family is very significant to our spiritual growth at this time. I feel Ed's awareness of the Lakota path brings us much closer to the historical truth we deserve to know. At times you may feel the heaviness in his heart for the way things have been, but you can also feel his love and deep concern for the planet and our spiritual path as human beings. Ed has deeply inspired my insight into our spiritual connection with nature and our planetary home. Our social interactions, our love for this planet, and our connection to the Creator are the most important issues of our time. Thank you Eagle Man for your insights, wisdom, and opening our hearts and minds with your writing, to these important issues.

Makenneth Stoffer

Rev. Donna Carey McGaa (Song Bird)
Heart in Harmony, llc.
Workshops - International Speaker
Empowering Wellness with Mother Earth Wisdom and Spirituality
Holistic Science-based Cancer Consultation
Licensed Heal Your Life Teacher
Sacred Sound Vocalist and Sound Practitioner

For Consulting and Workshops with Ed and Donna McGaa
Email: donna.heartinharmony@gmail.com

Made in the USA
San Bernardino, CA
08 June 2017